THE

PSALMS

TRANSLATED AND EXPLAINED

BY

J. A. ALEXANDER

PROFESSOR IN THE THEOLOGICAL SEMINARY AT PRINCETON

VOLUME III

NEW YORK

CHARLES SCRIBNER 145 NASSAU STREET

1852

C. W. BENEDICT,
Stereotyper,
201 William st.

THE PSALMS.

PSALM CI.

After propounding as his theme the mercy and justice of the Lord, v. 1, the Psalmist announces his determination to be blameless in his own walk, vs. 2—4, and so to exercise his power over others as to favour the godly and drive out the wicked, vs. 5—8.

1. *By David. A Psalm. Mercy and judgment will I sing; to thee, Jehovah, will I play* (or *make music.*) As such a declaration of a present purpose in the Psalms is always followed by its execution, the older interpreters suppose *mercy and judgment* to be those which David meant to practise, as he states more fully in the remainder of the psalm. But besides that he says nothing in what follows of his *mercy*, there is no usage of the Psalms more settled than that *mercy and justice* are combined to denote divine not human attributes, and that *to sing and make music to Jehovah* never means to praise something else in an address to him, but always to sing praises to himself. See above, Ps. ix. 12 (11.) xiii. 6 (5.) xviii. 50 (49.) xxx. 5 (4.) 13 (12.) xxxiii. 2. lxviii. 5 (4.) lxxi. 22, 23, in all which cases the form of expression seems to be derived from Judg. v. 3. But the psalm before us contains no such celebration of God's mercy and justice

beyond this first verse. The best solution of this fact appears to be the one proposed by Hengstenberg, according to which the execution of the purpose here avowed is contained in Ps. ciii, which then, together with the one before us, and of course the intervening one, compose a *trilogy* or series of three psalms, all by David, each complete in itself, and yet designed to be connected with the others and interpreted by them. Supposing this to be the case, we must regard them all as psalms of David, whose name is prefixed to the third and the one before us, in which he lays down a rule, as it were, for his own government, and that of his successors, in the regal office. The impression made by these inspired instructions on the first of those successors may account for the remarkable coincidences of expression between this psalm and the Book of Proverbs.

2. *I will act wisely in a perfect way. When wilt thou come to me? I will walk in the integrity of my heart within my house.* As to the first verb, see above, on Ps. ii. 10. xiv. 2. Its form here is one expressing fixed determination. *A perfect way*, as in Ps. xviii. 31, 33 (30, 32.) This and other favourite expressions of the same kind, Ps. xviii. 24, 26 (23, 25.) xv. 2, are founded upon Gen. xvii. 1. *When wilt thou come to me*, and bless me, in fulfilment of thy promise, Ex. xx. 21. This interrogative ejaculation implies a sense of his dependence on divine aid for the execution of his purpose. *Integrity* (*integritas*, completeness) *of my heart* is an expression borrowed from Gen. xx. 5, 6. See above, on Ps. lxxviii. 72, and compare 1 Kings iii. 14. Prov. xx. 7. *Way* and *walk* are familiar figures for habitual conduct. *Within*, literally, *in the midst* (or *inside*) *of my house*, i. e. at home, in private life, as distinguished from the house of God and his official conduct there, to which he afterwards adverts.

3. *I will not set before my eyes a word of Belial; the doing of apostasies I hate, it shall not cleave to me.* The positive terms of

the preceding verse are now exchanged for negatives. Having said what he will do, he now says what he will not do. See a similar transition, but in the inverse order, Ps. i. 1, 2. *Set before my eyes*, as a model to be copied, or as an object of approving contemplation. *A word of Belial*, as in Ps. xli. 9 (8), except that *word*, which there most probably relates to slander or false accusation, may here denote a proposition, and the whole phrase a worthless (i. e. wicked) plan or purpose. *Apostasies*, departures, deviations from the right course. See the verbal root as used in Ps. xl. 5 (4), and a cognate verb in Num. v. 12, 19. Some make the word here used a participle or verbal noun, as in the English Bible, *the work of them that turn aside*. But its form and the analogy of Hos. v. 2 entitle the other construction to the preference. *It shall not cleave to me*, I will not be concerned or implicated in it; or more emphatically still, it shall not cleave to me as a reproach or stigma. In favour of the former sense is the analogy of Deut. xiii. 18 (17), from which the expression seems to have been borrowed.

4. *A crooked heart shall depart from me; evil I will not know. Crooked*, froward, or perverse, as in Ps. xviii. 27 (26.) Compare Prov. xi. 20. xvii. 20. The whole phrase might be understood to mean a person having such a heart, and the whole clause that the Psalmist would have no intercourse with such. The parallel term *evil* would then mean *a wicked person*, as translated in the English Bible. On the ground, however, that the person of the sinner seems to be reserved for the latter part of the psalm, the best interpreters take *evil* in the abstract sense of moral evil, wickedness, as in Ps. xxxiv. 17, lii. 5 (3.) The first clause will then naturally mean, my own heart shall not be perverse or froward.

5. (One) *slandering in secret his fellow—him I will destroy: (one) lofty of eyes and wide of heart—him I will not bear.*

Having declared what his own course of life should be, he now describes the conduct which he should require in his confidential servants. Here again the statement is both negative and positive, but in this case beginning with the former. See above, on v. 3. It is not an improbable conjecture that in specifying slander, David had reference to his sufferings from that cause in the days of Saul. See above, on Ps. xviii. 1. lii. 4—7 (2—5), and compare Ps. xv. 3. The verb translated *slandering* occurs, in any of its forms, only here and Prov. xxx. 10. *Wide of heart* means neither magnanimous nor greedy, but proud, self-confident, as appears from Prov. xxviii. 25. Both figurative phrases here used are combined again in Prov. xxi. 4. The last verb in the sentence usually means *to be able*, but is here used absolutely, as in Isai. i. 13.

6. *My eyes (are) on the faithful of the land, to dwell with me.* (One*) walking in a perfect way—he shall serve me. On the faithful*, literally, *in* or *with* them. See above, on Ps. xxxiv. 16, 17 (15, 16), and compare Ps. xxxii. 8 (7.) *My eyes are on them* is equivalent to saying, I will seek them out to dwell with me and serve me. The word translated *faithful* is properly a passive participle meaning *trusted*, relied upon, confided in. Another passive participle from the same root is commonly supposed to be used in the same sense, Ps. xii. 2 (1.) xxxi. 24 (23.) In the first words of the last clause there is manifest allusion to the form of expression in v. 2 above. This clause is to be understood exclusively, such a person and no other. *Shall serve me*, be employed by me, clothed with responsible and honourable offices.

7. *Not in the inside of my house shall dwell* (one) *practising fraud, telling lies; not settled shall he be before my eyes.* Here again the form of expression corresponds to that in the first part of the psalm. Compare *in the midst of my house* with v. 2, and *before my eyes* with v. 3. *Shall not dwell*, or still more strongly,

shall not (even) *sit*, which is the primary meaning of the Hebrew verb. The corresponding verb in the last clause means to be established, permanently settled, as opposed to a mere temporary, transient presence. As if he had said: though they should even gain admission to my house, they shall not take up their abode there.

8. *In the morning will I destroy all the wicked of the land*, (so as) *to cut off from the city of Jehovah all workers of iniquity.* The first phrase literally means *at the mornings*, and may be intended to suggest the twofold idea of early and constantly, in the morning and every morning. See above, on Ps. lxxiii. 14, and compare Jer. xxi. 12. The last clause serves to show, or to remind the reader, that this rigour was not simply prudential or political, but religious. It had reference not merely to Jerusalem as a city, but as the city of Jehovah, his earthly residence, the centre of the theocracy, the temporary seat of the true religion. See above, on Ps. xlvi. 5 (4) xlviii. 2 (1.) lxxxvii. 3. Under the peculiar institutions of the old economy, the safety of the theocratic state required peculiar vigilance and rigour, in exercising even those powers which are common to all governments.

PSALM CII.

1. *A Prayer. By a Sufferer, when he is troubled, and before Jehovah pours out his complaint.* The psalm is called a *prayer* because petition constitutes its substance. See above, on Ps. xc. 1. The translation *for the sufferer* (or *afflicted*) would also be

grammatical, and perfectly consistent with the real design of the composition. But phrases of this kind, in the titles of the psalms, so constantly indicate the author or performer, and when only one occurs the former, that a departure from this usage here is highly improbable, and the assumption of it altogether arbitrary. At the same time, the indefinite expression, *a sufferer*, or *an afflicted person*, seems to be intentionally used for the purpose of giving the psalm an unrestricted application, though the primary reference is no doubt to the suffering kings of Israel, in whom the sufferings of the people were concentrated and represented. The other terms of the inscription all occur in psalms of David; *troubled* (or *overwhelmed*) in Ps. lxi. 3 (2); *complaint* (or *moaning*) in Ps. lv. 3 (2.) lxiv. 2 (1); and *pouring out the soul* in Ps. lxii. 9 (8.) This agrees with the general Davidic character of the composition, and favours Hengstenberg's hypothesis, not otherwise demonstrable, nor even very probable, that this psalm forms the connecting link between the pious resolutions of Ps. 101 and the joyful acknowledgments of Ps. 103, and was composed in prophetic foresight of the straits to which the theocratical state should be reduced, and in which the sufferings of David, here immediately described, should, as it were, be realized anew. The psalm may be divided into two parts, in the first of which the tone of lamentation or complaint predominates, vs. 2—12 (1—11), while in the second it is tempered and controlled by the contemplation of God's attributes, and confident anticipation of his favour, vs. 13—29 (12—28.)

2 (1.) *Jehovah, hear my prayer, and let my cry* (for help) *unto thee come.* With this verse compare Ps. iv. 2 (1.) xvii. 1. xviii. 7 (6.) liv. 4 (2.) There is no more reason for regarding these resemblances as imitations by a later writer in the case before us than in any of the others. And if not such, they may serve to show, that David only asks, for the future or for others, that favour which he has himself sought and experienced already.

3 (2.) *Hide not thy face from me; in the day* (there is) *distress to me, incline to me thine ear; in the day I call, make haste* (and) *answer me.* Compare Ps. x. 1. xiii. 1. xvii. 6. xviii. 7 (6.) xxvii. 9. xxxi. 3 (2.) lvi. 10 (9.) lxvi. 14 (13.) lxxi. 2. We find here accumulated nearly all the phrases used by David to express the same ideas elsewhere. This is not unnatural if we suppose him to have been preparing a form of complaint and supplication for the use of his successors in their worst distresses.

4 (3.) *For wasted in smoke are my days, and my bones like a burning are kindled.* With the first clause compare Ps. xxxvii. 20. The bones are mentioned as the seat of strength. See above, on Ps. vi. 3 (2.) xxxi. 11 (10.) xxxv. 10. xlii. 11 (10.) This description, although strictly applicable to the case of individual sufferers, may also be applied to the decline of the theocratic monarchy and the approach of its catastrophe.

5 (4.) *Smitten like grass and withered is my heart, for I have forgotten to eat my bread.* The first verb is used to describe the effect of the sun on plants, Ps. cxxi. 6. Isai. xlix. 10. (Compare Jon. iv. 7.) The heart is mentioned as the seat of life. The common version of the last clause (*so that I forget*) is ungrammatical. The failure of the strength is rather described as immediately occasioned by the want of food (1 Sam. xxviii. 20), and this by loss of appetite from extreme distress. See below, on Ps. cvii. 18, and compare 1 Sam. i. 7. xx. 34. 1 Kings xxi. 4. *Forgotten to eat*, literally, *forgotten from eating*, so as not to eat, a common idiomatic use of the preposition *from* in Hebrew.

6 (5.) *From the voice of my groaning, my bone cleaves to my flesh.* The word *voice* implies an audible and loud expression of distress. The first clause means, in consequence of the agony which makes me groan. *My bone* may signify each of my bones, or be used collectively for the whole skeleton or framework of the

1*

body. The only natural explanation of this clause is that it describes emaciation, as a consequence and symptom of extreme distress. See above, on Ps. xxii. 15, 18 (14, 17.)

7 (6.) *I resemble a pelican of the wilderness ; I am become like an owl* (haunting) *ruins.* The simple idea conveyed by these figures is that of extreme loneliness and desolation. Beyond the fact that they inhabit solitudes, the natural history of the birds mentioned is of no exegetical importance.

8 (7.) *I have watched, and have been like a sparrow dwelling alone upon a house-top.* The first words suggest the idea of a solitary vigil. As to the word translated *sparrow*, see above, on Ps. lxxxiv. 4 (3.) The word *dwelling* is supplied in the translation of the last clause, in order to retain the form of the original expression, which is that of an active participle. Some suppose the idea to be that of a bird, deprived of its mate or of its young.

9 (8.) *All the day my enemies have taunted me ; my infuriated* (foes) *swear by me.* The verb in the first clause suggests the ideas of contempt and hatred, calumny and insult. See above, on Ps. xlii. 11 (10.) The first word of the last clause is a passive participle, *my enraged* (or *maddened*) *ones*, those who are mad (i. e. insane with enmity) against me. The last phrase does not mean *swear at me*, i. e. vent their rage by oaths and curses, nor *are sworn against me*, neither of which is justified by Hebrew usage ; but *swear by me*, i. e. use me as a formula of execration, imprecating upon others misery like mine. Compare Isai. lxv. 15. Jer. xxix. 22. The preterite forms imply a long previous continuance of this furious persecution, as *all the day* does its constant, unremitted raging.

10 (9.) *For ashes like bread have I eaten, and my drink with weeping have mixed.* The ashes, in which he sat, or with which

he was covered, as a sign of mourning, became mingled with his food, and his tears fell into his *drink*. This last word is, in Hebrew, of the plural number, *drinks* or *beverages*, analogous to *victuals* as a simple synonyme of *food*. As an opposite example of the same idiomatic difference, the word translated *ashes* is a singular in Hebrew. The whole verse is a strong poetical description of constant and extreme distress.

11 (10.) *Because of thine indignation and thy wrath; for thou hast taken me up and cast me away.* The first clause describes his suffering as the fruit of God's displeasure. See above, on Ps. xc. 7. The antithesis presented in the common version of the last clause (*lifted me up and cast me down*) does not seem to be the sense of the original, in which there is probably allusion to the figure of a storm or whirlwind catching things up and blowing them away. The Prayer Book version of the first verb (*taken me up*) is more exact.

12 (11.) *My days (are) like a shadow inclined, and I (myself) like the grass wither.* An *inclined shadow* is an unusual and obscure expression, but seems to mean a shadow verging towards its disappearance, ready to vanish away. The double or reflexive pronoun (*I myself*) in the translation of the last clause is necessary to convey the full force of the Hebrew pronoun, which is seldom expressed, except when it is meant to be emphatic. *I wither*, am withering, or about to wither.

13 (12.) *And thou, Jehovah, to eternity shalt sit, and thy memory* (shall endure) *to generation and generation.* Here again the pronoun is emphatic, and exhibits a strong contrast between God's eternity and human frailty. While I wither like the grass, thou endurest forever, and not only so, but reignest, sittest on the throne. See above, on Ps. ix. 8 (7.) xxix. 10. lv. 20 (19.) The word *memory* seems here to be employed for the sake of the anti-

thesis which it implies. While I perish and am utterly forgotten, thy existence and thy memory shall last forever. It may, however, have the same sense as in Ps. xxx. 5 (4), namely, the divine perfection, associated in our memory with the name of God. Thou shalt not only reign forever, but be worthy, as an infinitely perfect being, so to do.

14 (13.) *Thou wilt arise, wilt have mercy upon Zion, when* (it is) *time to favour her, when the set time is come.* The pronoun is again emphatic. Thou, the God thus glorious and immutable, wilt certainly arise from this apparent inaction, and have mercy or compassion on thy people, when the time fixed in thy eternal purpose is arrived. The sense of *when*, thus given to the Hebrew particle (כִּי), although less usual, is sometimes absolutely necessary, and is therefore admissible in this case, where it suits the sense much better than the ordinary sense of *for*. Or the one may be resolved into the other, by explaining the whole thus: thou wilt certainly arise and have compassion upon Zion, at the proper time, FOR there is a time fixed at which thou dost design to favour her. For the meaning of the word translated *set time*, see above, on Ps. lxxv. 3 (2.)

15 (14.) *When thy servants love her stones, and her dust regard with favour.* Both verbs in Hebrew mean to favour, or more strongly, to delight in, to take pleasure in. See above, Ps. lxii. 5 (4.) lxxxv. 2 (1.) *Stones* and *dust* are here put for ruins or rubbish, as in Neh. iii. 34 (iv. 2.) iv. 4 (10.) The verse may be understood as a condition or a premonition of her restoration, that before it takes place, God will fill his servants with affectionate concern for her desolate condition. The same sense may be obtained without departing from the usual sense of the particle. Thou wilt have mercy upon Zion, FOR thy servants already look with interest and strong desire on her ruins, a sure sign of the approaching restoration.

16 (15.) *And nations shall fear the name of Jehovah, and all kings of the earth thy glory.* The impression of awe, unavoidably produced by these exhibitions of Jehovah's attributes, shall not be limited to Israel but extend to other nations, and even kings shall vie with each other in their reverential admiration of his regal honours. Compare the similar expressions of Isaiah (lix. 19.)

17 (16.) *Because Jehovah has built Zion; he has been seen in his glory.* These are not *praeterita prophetica*, describing future events as past; nor are they to be taken as mere presents, but as denoting a relative past, dependent on the futures of the verse preceding. The nations and their kings are to fear because Jehovah has built (i. e. will then have built) Zion. Still another construction may seem possible, viz. 'when Jehovah has built Zion, he shall be seen in his glory.' But in this case, Hebrew usage would require the last verb, if not both, to have the future form.

18 (17.) *He has turned unto the prayer of the destitute, and has not despised their prayer.* This verse continues to assign the reason why the nations and their kings will be struck with awe, viz. because this great and glorious God has turned round, as it were, and listened to the prayer of the destitute and granted their petition. The word translated *destitute* occurs only here and in Jer. xvii. 6; but from its etymological affinities and its intensive form, appears to mean stark naked, and then figuratively, stripped of every thing, impoverished, entirely destitute.

19 (18.) *This shall be written for an after generation, and a people* (yet to be) *created shall praise Jah.* This fulfilment of God's promise and illustration of his attributes is left on record for the learning or instruction of posterity. Compare 1 Cor. x. 11. *An after generation*, as in Ps. xlviii. 14 (13.) lxxviii. 4. Equivalent in meaning, but abridged in form, is the expression in the passage

upon which these are founded, Ps. xxii. 31 (30.) See also Ps. lxxi. 18. *Created* may have the force of a gerundive, as the passive particle often has in Hebrew ; or it may mean (*then*) *created* (*but not now.*) See above, on Ps. xxii. 32 (31.) As the verb (ברא) *create* is applied only to divine acts, its use here seems to indicate that what is meant is not merely a future generation, a race yet to come into existence, but a *people* in the strict sense, an organized body to be formed hereafter by sovereign authority and almighty power. *Shall praise Jah*, recognize Jehovah as possessing and as being all that is denoted by his name.

20 (19.) *For he has leaned from the high-place of his holiness ; Jehovah from heaven to earth has looked.* The first word may also be translated *that*, and the verse be understood as an amplification of the pronoun *this* at the beginning of v. 19 (18.) This is what shall be written for a future generation ; this is what they shall praise Jah for ; viz. that he has looked, etc. To avoid the repetition of the English verb, as well as to add life to the description, the Hebrew verb is here represented by what seems to be its primary meaning. See above on Ps. xiv. 2. lxxxv. 12 (11), and compare Deut. xxvi. 15.

21 (20.) *To hear the groaning of the prisoner, to loose the sons of mortality.* The construction is continued from the foregoing verse, and the design of God's thus looking down is stated. The word translated *groaning* is almost peculiar to the psalms of David, and according to its etymology properly denotes suffocation. To *loose*, literally to *open*, sometimes applied to the opening of a dress for the purpose of removing it, as in Ps. xxx. 12 (11) ; then to the loosening of chains, as in Ps. cxvi. 16 ; then to the deliverance of the prisoner himself. *Sons of mortality* or *death*, i. e. those doomed to die. See above, on Ps. lxxix. 11.

22 (21.) *To recount in Zion the name of Jehovah and his praise*

in Jerusalem. This, according to the laws of Hebrew syntax, does not necessarily denote an act of God himself, as the similar construction in the preceding verse does, but may have a vaguer sense equivalent to saying, *that his name may be declared in Zion.* To recount God's name is to recount the mighty deeds which constitute it, and the celebration of which constitutes his praise. Zion is still represented as the great scene of Jehovah's triumphs, not however as the capital of Israel or Judah merely, but as the radiating centre of religious light and influence to all the earth.

23 (22.) *In the gathering of peoples together, and kingdoms to serve Jehovah.* This verse is necessary to complete and qualify the sense of that before it. God has looked down from heaven to deliver his people and receive their praise, not in their secluded, insulated state, but in their glorious reunion with the converted nations. The first verb is a passive infinitive in Hebrew, *in their being gathered.* The preposition *in* relates both to the time and to the act of convocation. *To serve Jehovah*, not only as a King, but as a God, to be both his subject and his worshipper. Compare Ps. ii. 11.

24 (23.) *He has humbled in the way his strength; he has shortened my days.* The Psalmist here resumes the tone of complaint, but only for a moment, and as an introduction to what follows. *Humbled*, weakened, or afflicted. *In* or *by the way* of his providential guidance, as distinguished from the glorious end to which it led. *His strength* and *my days* seem clearly to refer to the same person. To avoid this harsh enallage, the masoretic critics changed a single letter, and for (כחוֹ) *his strength* read (כֹּחִי) *my strength*, which, though adopted in most versions, is an obvious evasion of a supposed difficulty. With the last clause compare Ps. lxxxix. 46 (45.) See also Ps. lv. 24 (23.)

25 (24.) *I will say, Oh my God, take me not up in the half*

of my days; through generation of generations (are) *thy years. Take up*, cause to ascend, i. e. as some suppose, like smoke, which is very forced and far-fetched. Others make it simply mean to take away, which gives a good sense, but is not sufficiently sustained by usage. Better than either is the supposition that death or removal out of life is here described by a figure corresponding to the actual departure of Enoch and Elijah. See Gen. v. 24. 2 Kings ii. 1, 3, 5, 10, 11. *In the half* (or *midst*) *of my days;* see above, on Ps. lv. 24 (23), and compare Isai. xxxviii. 10. *Generation of generations*, i. e. all generations, as in Ps. lxxii. 5. Isai. li. 8. He prays that God, whose years are endless, would not, as it were, grudge the few days granted to his creatures. See above, on Ps. xxxix. 6 (5.)

26 (25.) *At first thou the earth didst found, and the work of thy hands* (are) *the heavens.* The phrase at the beginning means originally *to the face*, and then *before*, as an adverb both of time and place; but this would be ambiguous here, since it might be understood as a conjunction, *before thou didst found the earth*, expressing the same idea as in Ps. xc. 2. It here means long ago, of old, in the beginning. With the last clause compare Ps. viii. 4 (3.) xix. 2 (1.) xxxiii. 6. God's creative power is here added to his eternity, in order to enhance the contrast between his infinity and man's littleness, as a reason for compassion to the latter.

27 (26.) *They shall perish and thou shalt stand, and all of them like a garment shall wear out, like a dress shalt thou change them and they shall change.* The contrast is brought out as pointedly as possible in Hebrew, by the insertion of the pronouns *they* and *thou*, neither of which is grammatically necessary to the expression of the meaning. *Stand*, stand fast, endure, remain, continue. *All of them*, without exception, even the noblest of God's works, shall at least lose their present form, and in that sense perish, a

sense which may be still more readily put upon the parallel verb *pass away* or *change*. The twofold usage of the English verb, as active and neuter, or transitive and intransitive, makes it an appropriate representative of the primitive and derivative forms of the Hebrew verb (חלף). The corresponding verb, in the second member of the sentence, means not only to *wax old*, but, as the necessary consequence, to *wear out*. See above on Ps. xxxii. 3, and compare Ps. xlix. 15 (14.)

28 (27.) *And Thou (art) He—and thy years shall not be finished.* The construction of the first clause is disputed. Some read it, *Thou thyself and thy years shall not end.* Others, *Thou art the same*, giving הוא the same sense with the Greek ὁ αὐτός, which is actually used here to translate it in the Septuagint. In favour of the version first above given, is its agreement with the usage of the Hebrew words, with the analogy of Deut. xxxii. 39 and Isai. xliii. 10, and with the context here. The meaning then is, Thou art the Unchangeable One just described. Or, it is Thou, and nothing else, that shall thus endure. *Be finished*, spent, consumed, as the Hebrew word invariably means. What is elsewhere literally said of the violent destruction of human life is here transferred to the lapse of time.

29 (28.) *The sons of thy servants shall abide, and their seed before thee shall be established.* This might also be translated as a prayer, *let the sons of thy servants continue*, which is really included even in the prediction. *Before thee*, as in Gen. xvii. 1. Ps. lxxxix. 37 (36.) *Be established*, as in Ps. lxxxix. 38 (37.) ci. 7. With this conclusion of the whole psalm compare Ps. lxix 36, 37 (35, 36.) xc. 16, 17.

PSALM CIII.

The Psalmist calls upon himself to praise God for personal favours already experienced, vs. 1–5. From these he rises, in the body of the psalm, to the contemplation of God's attributes, in themselves considered, and as manifested in his dealings with his people, vs. 6–19. He concludes as he began, with an exhortation to bless God, no longer addressed merely to himself, but to all creatures, vs. 20–22. According to the exegetical hypothesis already mentioned, this is the song of *mercy and judgment* promised in Ps. ci. 1. The arguments in favour of this theory have been already stated. The principal objection to it, and that by no means a conclusive one, is the want of unison and even concord, as to tone and spirit, between the psalm before us and the two preceding it. Be this as it may, the psalm before us is a complete and finished composition, being one of the most simple and yet regular in structure that the book contains. This has contributed, with other obvious peculiarities, to make it a favourite vehicle of thankful praise among the pious of all ages.

1. *By David. Bless, oh my soul, Jehovah, and all within me* (bless) *his holy name!* The attempts which have been made by modern critics to discredit the inscription in the first clause chiefly consist in representing the many imitations and allusions to this noble composition in the later scriptures as a cento of citations from those scriptures by the writer of the psalm itself, a preposterous inversion of the laws of evidence to which the neological

critics are especially addicted, and by which any thing and every thing can be disproved or proved at pleasure. *Bless*, when applied to God, means to praise, but with a strong implication of devout affection. By calling on his soul to do this, he acknowledges his own obligation, not only to praise God, but to praise him cordially, *with all the heart*, according to the solemn requisition of the Law (Deut. vi. 5), to which there is perhaps a reference in all such cases. See above, on Ps. iii. 3 (2.) The parallel expression, *all within me*, is the plural form of one repeatedly used elsewhere and denoting the *inside* of any thing, and more especially of man, his mind or heart, as distinguished from his mere professions or external acts. See above, on Ps. v. 10 (9.) xlix. 12 (11.) The literal translation of the form here used is *my insides* or *inner parts*, the strong and comprehensive meaning of the plural being further enhanced by the addition of *all*, as if to preclude exception and reserve, and comprehend within the scope of the address all the powers and affections. *His name of holiness* (or *holy name*), i. e. the revelation of his infinite perfections. See above, on Ps. v. 12 (11.) xxii. 4 (3.)

2. *Bless, oh my soul, Jehovah, and forget not all his dealings.* The positive exhortation is repeated as a kind of foil to the negative one following, in which there seems to be allusion to the frequent admonition in the Law to Israel, not to forget the Lord who brought him up out of the land of Egypt. See Deut. vi. 12. viii. 11, 14. The last word in the verse before us is the passive participle of a verb which means to *treat*, and commonly to *treat well*. See above on Ps. vii. 5 (4.) The idea here conveyed is that of *treatment*, determined by the context to be kind and gracious treatment. The latitude of meaning and the plural form are both represented in the English word *dealings*, which, though susceptible of either application, can, in this connection, only have a good one.

3. *Forgiving all thy guilt, healing all thy sicknesses.* The participles are to be grammatically construed with *Jehovah* as the object of the praise required, and assign a reason for the requisition, furnished by the personal experience of the soul itself. The original expression is still more definite, each participle having the article prefixed, *the (one) forgiving, the (one) healing.* See a similar construction carried out still further in Ps. xviii. 33–35 (32–34), 48–51 (47–50.) The last word in the verse is an unusual one borrowed from Deut. xxix. 21, where *sicknesses* are joined with *plagues* or *strokes*, to signify calamities considered as penal inflictions. The same idea is expressed in other words, Ex. xvi. 26. The relation of the clauses, in the verse before us, may be that of cause and effect. Forgiving all thy guilt and thereby removing all the misery occasioned by it.

4. *Redeeming from the grave thy life, crowning thee (with) mercy and compassions.* The combination of the article and participle is the same as in v. 3, *the (one) redeeming, the (one) crowning.* The continuation of the sentence in this form keeps the attention fixed upon the reasons for which, or the characters in which, the Lord is to be praised. As if he had said, Bless him as the one forgiving thee and healing thee, redeeming thee and crowning thee. *Redeeming* means delivering, but with a strong implication of cost and risk. For the twofold sense of (שַׁחַת) the word translated *grave*, see above, on Ps. xvi. 10, and compare Ps. xxx. 10 (9.) The peculiar form of the possessive pronoun, in this verse and the one before it, has been represented as a proof of later date, but really belongs to the dialect of poetry, from which, in all languages, certain expressions are continually passing into that of common life, so that what in one age is poetical is in the next colloquial, and seems therefore to belong to the later period and to show the recent date of any composition in which it occurs. The familiar use of such words as *oftentimes, perchance*, etc. in our own day may thus be used hereafter to prove

the writings of our older poets spurious. The figure of *crowning*, which occurs above in Ps. lxv. 12 (11), suggests the ideas of dignity and beauty, while the absence of merit in the object, and the sovereign freeness of the gift, are indicated by making the crown itself a crown of *mercy and compassions.* The last word in Hebrew is expressive of the warmest and tenderest affections. See above, on Ps. xviii. 2 (1.) xxv. 6. xl. 12 (11.)

5. *Filling with good thy soul—(then) is renewed, like the eagle, thy youth.* The peculiar construction of the two preceding verses is continued through the first clause of the one before us, and then suddenly abandoned. *Filling, the (one) filling*, in the sense of satisfying or abundantly supplying, but without the accessory notion of satiety. See above, on Ps lxxxi. 17 (16.) xci. 16. *With good*, literally *the good*, by way of eminence, the chief good or the real good. *Thy soul* is not a literal translation of the Hebrew term, which, in every other case where it occurs, means *ornament* or *decoration.* See for example Ps. xxxii. 9 (8.) The translations *mouth*, *life*, etc. are gratuitous conjectures from the context. The best explanation is that furnished by the analogous word (כָּבוֹד) *honour*, *glory*, which is sometimes applied to the soul as the nobler part of man. See above, on Ps. xvi. 9. This explanation is confirmed by the frequent combination of the noun *soul* and the verb to *satisfy*. See above, Ps. lxiii. 6 (5), and below, Ps. cvii. 9, and compare Isai. lviii. 11. It is also sanctioned by the ancient versions; for although the Targum makes it mean *old age*, a palpable conjecture, the Septuagint and Vulgate have *desire* (ἐπιθυμίαν, *desiderium*), a frequent sense of (נֶפֶשׁ) *soul* in Hebrew, and Jerome translates it literally, *ornamentum.* The word *then* is introduced into the translation of the second clause, in order to retain the Hebrew collocation, which is not without its emphasis. *Is renewed*, or retaining the reflexive form of the original, *renews itself*. The supposed allusion in this clause to a fabulous or real renovation of the eagle in its old age,

rests upon a misconception of the language, as the only point of comparison with the eagle is its strength and vigour, as in 2 Sam. i. 23. Isai. xl. 31, and the whole verse may be paraphrased as follows. 'So completely does his bounty feed thy strength, that even in old age thou growest young again, and soarest like an eagle.'

6. *Doing righteousnesses* (is) *Jehovah, and judgments for all oppressed.* Thus far the reasons urged for praising God were personal, i. e. derived from individual experience. With these, from the very constitution of our nature, all our grateful exercises must begin. But if genuine they do not stop there, as the Psalmist, at this point, ascends from private causes of thanksgiving to more general views of God's administration, as a basis for the universal call with which the psalm concludes. The connection here may thus be stated. 'Such have been the Lord's compassions to myself, but these are only samples of his goodness. He is not only merciful to me, but to all who are oppressed, and to deliver whom he executes his judgments.' There is no contrast here intended between mercy and justice, with respect to different objects of the Lord's compassion. The meaning is, that man's injustice is redressed by God's mercy. The redemption of his people is often represented as coincident wtth the condign punishment of their oppressors. Compare my note on Isai. i. 27. *Doing*, i. e. *practising* in general, and *executing* in particular cases. The participle (*doing*) signifies habitual and constant action ; the plural form (*righteousnesses*) completeness and variety, adapted to all possible emergencies. *Judgments*, as usual, denotes judicial acts, as distinguished from mere attributes or principles.

7. *He makes known his ways to Moses, to the children of Israel his* (mighty) *deeds.* The general statement of the fact in the preceding verse is now followed by the great historical example furnished in Jehovah's dealings with his people. This serves,

not only to illustrate what was said before, but to show that it was not a mere vague declaration of what God will do to all men, but a definite assertion of his purpose and his practice with respect to his own people. *All the oppressed*, to whom he grants or promises deliverance, are not mankind in general, without distinction or exception, but his own people when in that condition. The first clause contains an obvious allusion to the prayer of Moses, as recorded by himself, Ex. xxxiii. 13, from which passage it appears, that the ways of God, which he desired to know, were his modes of dealing with his people, or the course of his dispensations towards them. See above, on Ps. xxv. 4. lxvii. 3 (2.) The knowledge thus imparted was experimental or afforded by experience. The parallelism between *Moses* and the *Children of Israel* shows that the latter were represented by the former. The last Hebrew word is one constantly applied to God's exploits or mighty deeds in behalf of Israel. See above, on Ps. ix. 12 (11.) lxxviii. 11.

8. *Compassionate and gracious (is) Jehovah, slow to anger, and rich in mercy.* See above, on Ps. lxxvii. 10 (9.) lxxviii. 38. lxxxvi. 15, in all which cases, as in this, the terms of the description are borrowed from Ex. xxxiv. 6. There is here an evident progression in the thought. Not only is God good to me, but to all his people in distress; not only did he prove this to Moses and to Israel by saving them from Pharoah and their other enemies, but by bearing with their own offences. The previous context might have seemed to concede innocence, if not merit, to God's people, as the object of his kind regard; but they are here exhibited as sinners, needing his forbearance and forgiveness.

9. *Not to perpetuity will he strive, and not to eternity retain* (his anger.) This of course implies that he is sometimes angry, even with his people, and sometimes strives in opposition to their strivings against him. But as he is always in the right, and they

are always in the wrong, it is a signal proof of the divine compassion, that he does not strive and is not wroth forever. The first clause is closely copied by Isaiah (lvii. 16.) The second is itself derived from Lev. xix. 18, where we find a verb meaning to *retain* or *reserve* used absolutely in the sense of harbouring a grudge or cherishing a secret spite. This remarkable form of expression is copied in the case before us and in Nah. i. 2. Jer. iii. 5, 12. The original passage is a prohibition, in obeying which the Lord, as it were, here sets his people an example. Compare Matt. v. 48. 1 Cor. xi. 1. Eph. v. 1.

10. *Not according to our sins has he done to us, and not according to onr iniquities has he dealt with us.* That the people stood in need of the divine forbearance, is now still more distinctly intimated. The last verb is the one of which the participle occurs in v. 2, and might here be rendered, with still closer adherence to the strict sense of the Hebrew preposition, *has he bestowed upon us.* See the same construction in the Hebrew of Ps. xiii. 6. cxvi. 7. cxlii. 8 (7.) The past tense has reference to the previous history of Israel as a nation, but involves the statement of a general truth. At the end of the verse, we may suppose it to be tacitly added: as he might have done, not only in strict justice, but in execution of his express threatening, Lev. xxvi. 21.

11, *For as the heavens are high above the earth, mighty is his mercy above those that fear him.* The Hebrew preposition is the same in both clauses, and cannot be varied in translation without weakening the sentence. In the last clause it suggests the ideas of descent from above, superior power, and protection, in addition to that of mere relation or direction, which is all that is conveyed by the translation *to* or *towards.* The force of the original is likewise impaired by substituting *great* for *strong* or *mighty.* The idea meant to be conveyed is not that of mere extent but of efficiency. The literal meaning of the first words is, *like the height of the heavens*, or *like their being high*. *His fearers*, or *those fearing him*, is a common description of the righteous or God's people, who are more particularly characterized in v. 18.

12. *As far as the east is from the west, he hath put far from us our transgressions.* The form of expression at the beginning is the same as in v. 11, *like the distance of the east*, or *like its being far*. The Hebrew words for *east* and *west*, according to their etymology, denote the place of sunrise and the place of evening. *Put far from us*, as no longer having anything to do with us, a figure which suggests the idea both of pardon and renewal, justification and sanctification.

13. *As a father has compassion on (his) children, Jehovah has compassion on his fearers.* The compound phrase, *has compassion*, is here substituted for the simple verb *pity*, in order to retain the preposition *on*, which follows it in Hebrew, and also because the plural form *compassions* was necessarily employed in v. 4 to translate the cognate noun. The Hebrew verb is peculiarly appropriate in speaking of parental love. See above, on Ps. xviii. 2 (1.) The preterite forms represent the fact alleged as one already known and well attested by experience.

14. *For he knows our frame, mindful that dust (are) we.* The fragility of man is here again assigned as a ground of the divine compassion. See above, on Ps. lxxviii. 39. lxxxix. 48 (47.) *Frame*, formation, constitution, or as we say familiarly in English, *our make, our build*. The Hebrew noun is derived from the verb used in Ps. xciv. 9, and may therefore be intended to suggest the same idea that is there expressed. He who formed us knows of course how we are formed. The same noun is applied to the moral constitution, Gen. vi. 5, viii. 21, Deut. xxxi. 21. The word

translated *mindful* is, in form, a passive participle, (זָכוּר) meaning *remembered*, but equivalent in use to the active, *remembering*, or the verbal adjective *mindful*, just as the like form (בָּטֻחַ) *trusted* is equivalent to *trusting*, Ps. cxii. 7, the English *rejoiced* to *rejoicing*, etc. *We are dust*, i. e. made of it, and tending to it. Compare Gen. ii. 7, iii. 19, Ps. xc. 3.

15. (As for) *man, his days* (*are*) *like the grass; like the blossom of the field, so he blossoms.* As the preceding verse expresses the fragility of man by referring to his origin and end, so this verse does the same by a familiar but beautiful comparison, borrowed from Ps. xc. 6, and repeated in Isai. xl. 6—8. Job xiv. 2. The very name here given to the race is one denoting frailty and infirmity. See above, on Ps. viii. 5 (4.)

16. *For a breath passes over him and he is not, and no more shall his place know him.* The pronouns may, with equal grammatical correctness, be referred to the grass and rendered *it, its.* The primary meaning of the first noun (*breath*) is, in this connection, stronger than the secondary (*wind.*) The wind may be a whirlwind; but to say that a mere breath is sufficient to destroy one is the strongest possible expression of fragility. That the wind is called the breath of God, as the thunder is his voice, is a striking and poetical but needless supposition. *He is not* or *no more*, there is none of him, no such thing or person. See above, on Ps. xxxvii. 10. With the first clause compare Isai. xl. 7; with the second, Job vii. 10. The last verb means to *recognize* or know again, as in Ps. cxlii. 5 (4), and the whole clause, that death makes men strangers to the objects with which they have been most familiar.

17. *And the mercy of Jehovah* (*is*) *from eternity even to eternity upon those fearing him, and his righteousness to children's children.* Having carried the description of man's frailty to the

furthest point, the Psalmist suddenly contrasts with it God's everlasting mercy. The use of the simple copulative *and*, in such a marked antithesis, where *but* might to us seem indispensable, is one of the most striking and familiar Hebrew idioms. *Upon those fearing him* suggests the idea of a gift from above. *To children's children* simply means given (or belonging) to them. Unless we make the last clause a threatening of hereditary vengeance to the wicked, *his righteousness* can only mean his rectitude, including his veracity and faithfulness in exercising covenanted mercy. *Children's children*, literally, *sons of sons*.

18. *To the keepers of his covenant, and to the rememberers of his laws, to do them.* This is the necessary qualification of a promise which might otherwise have seemed too absolute. Even to the descendants of those fearing him the promise availed nothing, unless they themselves were faithful to his covenant and obedient to his law. The last words (*to do them*) show that the remem brance of the law required was not merely intellectual but practi cal and tending to obedience.

19. *Jehovah in the heavens has fixed his throne, and his kingdom over all rules.* Not only is he infinitely merciful and faithful, but a universal and almighty sovereign, no less able than willing to fulfil his promises and execute his purposes of mercy. The word translated *fixed*, like its English representative, suggests the two ideas of preparing and establishing. The same combination with *throne* occurs above, Ps. ix. 8 (7.) See also Ps. xi. 4. xlvii. 9 (8.) *Over all;* the original expression is still stronger, *over the whole*, the universe, τὸ πᾶν. The same phrase is applied to the entire human race, Ps. xiv. 3. The past tense of the last verb represents this unlimited dominion as already established or revealed. The future would have made its ulterior continuance the prominent idea.

20. *Bless Jehovah, ye his angels, mighty in strength, doing his word,* (so as) *to listen to the voice of his word.* Having finished his assertion of God's claims to universal praise, the Psalmist resumes the tone of exhortation with which he began. His appeal, however, is no longer to his own soul, but to the hosts of heaven, the noblest of God's creatures, the highest order of finite intelligences. *Mighty in strength*, more exactly, *mighty (ones) of strength*, or, as the first word is applied as a substantive to warriors or conquerors, *heroes of strength* or *mighty heroes.* See above, on Ps. xxiv. 8. lxxviii. 25. The construction in the last clause is obscure. The infinitive may here have the force of a gerund, *audiendo, auscultando*, by listening to the voice of his word, or, as in Ps. lxxviii. 18, it may denote the extent or the effect of their obedience, *so as to hearken*, or *so that they hearken*, i. e. listen for the faintest intimation of his will. The expression *hearken to his voice*, as thus applied, is a Mosaic one. See Deut. xxvi. 17. xxx. 20.

21. *Bless Jehovah, ye his hosts, his ministers, the doers of his will.* As the word *hosts* is applied both to the angels and the heavenly bodies (see above, on Ps. xxiv. 10), some interpreters, in order to relieve this verse of a tautology, suppose it to relate to the heavenly hosts in one sense, as the preceding verse does in another. In the same way they account for the change of expression in the last clause. Only intelligent creatures can be literally said to listen for God's word and to obey it; but even the inanimate creation may be said, without a metaphor, to execute his will. This last phrase occurs also in Ps. xl. 9 (8.)

22. *Bless ye Jehovah, all his works, in all places of his realm; bless thou, oh my soul, Jehovah!* The angels and heavenly bodies, with men and every other creature, are now summed up in the comprehensive phrase, *all his works*, i. e. all that he has made, all creatures, and invited to bless God, which invitation the

Psalmist then addresses once more to himself, and thus, by a beautiful transition, brings us back to the point from which we started.

PSALM CIV.

We have here another of those psalms, in which the hopes of God's people are excited and their faith strengthened by a view of the authority and providential care which he exercises over the creation. The sum of the whole psalm is contained in the first verse, and its application indicated in the last. Here, as in Ps. viii, xix, xxix, lxv, the description of God's glory, as exhibited in nature, is entirely subservient to a moral and religious purpose, and the psalm is therefore fully entitled to a place in the collection, and adapted to the permanent use of the church. The ar rangement of the psalm is founded on the history of the creation, but with such variations as were suited to the writer's purpose. After a general statement of this purpose, v. 1, the Psalmist traces the creative and providential agency of God in the works of the first and second day, vs. 2—5, then in that of the third, vs. 6—18, then in that of the fourth, vs. 19—23, then in that of the fifth, vs. 24—26, with an allusion to the rest of the seventh day in v. 31. The psalm closes with a summary statement of the dependence of all living creatures upon God's care and bounty, vs. 27—32, a resolution to glorify him accordingly, vs. 33—34, and a pregnant inference, that they who are under such protection have nothing to fear from human enemies, v. 35. According to Hengstenberg, this and the two next psalms compose a trilogy, added to the Davidic one immediately preceding (Ps. ci—ciii) about the time of the Babylonish exile. This hypothesis, he thinks, accounts for the occurrence of Davidic psalms in this part of the Psalter, which would otherwise have found their place among the Psalms of David in the first division of the book. But having been made the basis or the nucleus of later compositions, they were naturally placed with these in their proper chronological position.

1. *Bless, oh my soul, Jehovah! Oh Jehovah, my God, thou art great exceedingly; honour and majesty hast thou put on.* The resemblance of the first clause to Ps. ciii. 1 shows the designed connection of the two psalms. The remainder of the verse is a kind of response to this invocation, and contains, as it were, the words in which his soul does actually bless God. At the same time it exhibits in advance the sum and substance of the whole composition, the design of which is to describe the glories of creation and providence as the royal robe of the divine sovereign. Compare Ps. xlv. 4 (3.) xciii. 1. xcvi. 6. Job xl. 10. Isai. li. 9.

2. *Wearing light like a robe, spreading heaven like a curtain.* In carrying out the idea summarily stated in the first verse, he begins where the cosmogony in Genesis begins, with the light and the firmament, not the act of their creation, but their use, as the Creator's robe and curtain. It follows of course that *light* and *heaven* must be taken in their popular and ordinary sense, and not as denoting the heaven of heavens and the light inaccessible in which he is elsewhere represented as dwelling. The definite forms of the original, *the robe, the curtain*, as contrasted with the vaguer forms, *light, heaven*, may be intended to suggest the idea of the robe and curtain known and used in common life, which man puts on and stretches out with perfect ease, but not more easily than God puts on the light and stretches out the sky. Compare Gen i. 6. Isai. xl. 22. Job. ix. 8.

3. *Framing with water his halls; making clouds his conveyance; moving on wings of the wind.* The first word means laying beams or rafters. The next phrase may either mean *in* or *with water.* The first is more obvious, the last more striking, as it represents a solid building, made of a liquid or fluid material. In the other case the waters meant are those above the firmament. See Gen. i. 6, 7. Ps. xviii. 12 (11), where the clouds and the wings of the wind are also mentioned in the same connection. The word translated *halls* denotes the highest room of an oriental house, which is frequently the largest. Hence the frequent mention, in the New Testament, of the ὑπερῷον as a place of assembly. *Making*, literally, setting, placing. *Chariot* is too specific a translation of the Hebrew word, which means anything on which a person rides. The preposterous figure of *walking on wings* belongs entirely to the versions, ancient and modern. The Hebrew word, though often so applied, is a generic one, denoting all progressive movement, and nearly equivalent to our word *going*, which is not so agreeable, however, in this place, to English usage, as the more general and poetical term *moving*. See above, on Ps. xviii. 11 (10.)

4. *Making his angels winds, his ministers flaming fire.* According to the simplest and most obvious construction of this verse, it can only mean that God makes his angels or ministering spirits swift and ardent in his service. But such a statement would be wholly out of place in a psalm, the rest of which relates exclusively to the material creation. The best interpreters are therefore of opinion that *angels* and *ministers* are predicates not subjects, or in other words, that the idea meant to be conveyed is, that he makes the winds his messengers or angels, and the flaming fire his minister or servant. This agrees exactly with the previous declaration that he makes the clouds his chariot or conveyance, and moves upon the wings of the wind. It may seem, however, to be inconsistent with the use made of the passage in

Heb. 1. 7, as a proof that the angels are inferior to the Son of God. But how could this inferiority be proved by the fact that the angels are spirits, or even wind and fire? The latter cannot be literally true, and if metaphorical, can only mean that they are swift and ardent in God's service, which they might be and yet equal to the Son in nature, who, considered as a messenger or agent of the Father, exhibits precisely the same qualities. The truth is that the passage, as thus understood, is perfectly irrelevant and useless to the argument, and therefore that this mode of explaining it is not entitled to the preference, whatever difficulties may attend the other. Let it be observed, too, that the Septuagint version, which is quoted in Heb. i. 7, is an exact transcript of the Hebrew, both as to the sense and collocation of the words, so that if the original admits of a different construction, it may be extended to the version likewise. The most satisfactory conclusion is, that the words are not quoted as an argument or proof of the inferiority of angels, but merely as a striking yet familiar form of words in which to clothe the writer's own idea, which is this, that angels are mere messengers and ministers, and as such may be classed with the material agencies which God employs in execution of his purpose. The wind and the lightning are God's angels and his ministers, and are expressly so described in the Old Testament; but they are never called his sons, much less addressed directly as the sovereign, eternal, righteous, ever-blessed God. Nor are the ministering spirits, who share with these material agencies the character of messengers and servants, ever so described or so addressed. By thus supplying the suppressed links of the chain of argument, the verse before us, in the only sense of which the context really admits, will be found not only as appropriate as the other to the purpose for which it is quoted in the New Testament, but incomparably more so.

5. *He founded the earth on its bases; it shall not be moved for-*

ever and ever. The idea of *bases* is rather suggested by the context, and especially the verb *founded*, than expressed by the Hebrew noun itself, which properly means *places*, or more specifically, fixed and settled places. See above, on Ps. lxxxix. 15 (14.) xcvii. 2, and with the whole verse compare Ps. lxxviii. 69. lxxxix. 12 (11.) cii. 26 (25.)

6. *(With) the deep, like a garment, thou didst cover it; above the mountains stand the waters.* Next in importance to the separation of the land and water in the beginning (Gen. i. 9, 10), was the temporary confounding of the two in the universal deluge (Gen. vii. 19, 20), which the Psalmist therefore here connects with the creation, as equally demonstrative of almighty power, and also for the purpose of founding on this seeming violation of the promise in the last clause of v. 5, a still more solemn repetition of it. The grammatical objection that the pronoun in the phrase *didst cover it* is masculine, and cannot therefore refer to *earth* which is feminine, is easily removed by a reference to the general license of the Hebrew syntax with respect to genders, and the idiomatic tendency to use the masculine, not as a distinctive but as a generic form, in cases where the subject is sufficiently indicated by the context. There are moreover several clear examples of the masculine construction of this very noun (אֶרֶץ) besides those in which *earth* or *land* is put for its inhabitants. See e. g. Gen. xiii. 6. Isai. ix. 18. The allusion in the last clause to Gen. vii. 19, 20, is too plain to be mis taken.

7. *At thy rebuke they flee, at the voice of thy thunder they hasten away.* The same power that produced the deluge put an end to it. The verbs agree with *waters* in v. 6. The divine command that they should cease or disappear is poetically spoken of as a *rebuke*. See above, on Ps. xviii. 16 (15.) lxxvi. 7 (6), and compare Isai. l. 2. The Hebrew particle means *from*, denoting both

the time and cause of the effect described. The last verb is a passive meaning strictly to be panic-struck, or to flee in consequence of being panic-struck. See above, on Ps. xxxi. 23 (22.) xlviii. 6 (5.) The *voice of thy thunder* may be literally understood to mean the sound of thunder, or, according to a well-known Hebrew idiom, thy voice of thunder, or thy thundering voice.

8. *They go up mountains, they go down valleys, to this place thou hast founded for them.* The first clause is a beautiful description of the fluctuations which attend the subsidence of swollen waters, not only in the case of Noah's flood (Gen. viii. 4—5) to which the words relate in the first instance, but in all other cases, where the same rule still holds good, so that the verse, by an insensible transition, founds the statement of a general truth on that of a particular event. The use of the demonstrative (*this*) is highly idiomatic. The original construction is, *to a place, this (which) thou hast founded for them.* This form of expression is equivalent to pointing with the hand, and therefore adds not a little to the graphic vividness of the description.

9. *A bound thou didst set, they shall not pass over, they shall not return to cover the earth.* This grand exception to the law which governs the relations between land and water is the only one to be permitted or expected. The limits broken were renewed with an assurance that henceforth they should be inviolable. See Gen. ix. 15. Besides the immediate reference to the flood, the verse contains the statement of a general fact in the economy of nature, and thus furnishes a natural transition to the similar statements of the next verse.

10. *Sending springs into the valleys; between hills they go.* The participial construction, interrupted by the parenthetical account of the flood, is here resumed, the participle, like the others,

agreeing directly with Jehovah understood, as *the (one) sending*, which is the precise form of the original. See above, on Ps. ciii. 3—6. *Springs* or *fountains*, not in the restricted sense, but comprehending both the source and stream, as in Joel iv. 18 (iii. 18.) The word translated *valleys* is restricted in usage to such as have streams flowing through them. The last word is the one translated *walketh* by the English Bible in v. 3 above, but here *run*, although *walk* is given in the margin, as a more precise and literal translation, while Jerome inserts it in his text, *ut inter medios montes ambulent.*

11. *They water every beast of the field;* (at them) *wild asses quench their thirst.* The subject of the first verb is still the *waters.* The verb itself means to *water*, in the sense of giving drink to animals, though sometimes metaphorically applied to irrigation. See Gen. ii. 10. The form of the parallelism in this verse is peculiar, although not uncommon in Hebrew poetry, the last clause containing a specification of the general statement in the first. What is first said of animals, or wild ones in the general, is then said of the wild ass in particular. *Quench*, literally, *break*, i. e. subdue, assuage. A derivative noun is applied in Hebrew to corn or grain, as that which *breaks* or assuages hunger, although most interpreters and lexicographers suppose a reference to the literal breaking or grinding of the corn itself.

12. *Above them the birds of heaven dwell, from between the branches they give voice.* The poetical character of the composition is in nothing more obvious than in these minute strokes of exquisite painting, superadded to the more essential parts of the description. At the same time, these are not to be regarded as mere lavish or gratuitous embellishments, since the Psalmist's purpose is to celebrate God's wonderful and bountiful provision for his living creatures, and the running brooks would fail to answer one of their most valuable ends, if there were no birds to *give*

voice or sing among the branches of the overhanging trees. The word translated *birds* is a collective answering to the old English *fowl*, not as used in the version of this psalm, where it is plural, but in that of Gen. i. 20, 22, 26, 28. That passage furnishes an explanation of the phrase *fowl* (or *birds) of heaven*, in the fuller description (Gen i. 20), *fowl that may fly above the earth in the open firmament of heaven*, i. e. through the air, across the face of the expanse or visible heaven.

13. *Watering mountains from his upper rooms—from the fruit of thy works is the earth filled.* He still returns to God as the author of these merciful provisions, and represents him, by a beautiful figure, as pouring this abundant supply of water from his *upper rooms*, the same word that was rendered *halls* in v. 3; but here the connection seems to require that its precise etymological import should be prominent. *The fruit of thy works*, the result or product of thy creative energy. *Filled*, not in the sense of being occupied, which would require a different Hebrew verb, but in that of being abundantly supplied or saturated. See above, on Ps. ciii. 5. The sudden apostrophe to God himself enhances the poetical effect.

14. *Causing grass to grow for the cattle and herb for the culture of man*, (so as) *to bring forth bread from the earth.* In this verse there is a transition from God's care of the inferior animals to his care of man. The word translated *herb* denotes any green plant or vegetable, and is here applied to such as constitute or furnish human food. The common version of the next words, *for the service of man*, can only mean for his benefit or use, a sense not belonging to the Hebrew word, which, as well as its verbal root, is applied to man's servitude or bondage as a tiller of the ground (Gen. iii. 17—19), and has here the sense of husbandry or cultivation, as in Ex. i. 14. Lev. xxv. 39, it has that of com-

pulsory or servile labour. The infinitive in the last clause indicates the object for which labour is imposed on man.

15. *And wine gladdens the heart of man*—(so as) *to make his face shine more than oil—and bread the heart of man sustains.* The general expression at the end of v. 14 is now rendered more specific by distinctly mentioning the great staples of production and subsistence in the Holy Land. The only doubt is whether two or three are mentioned. The text of the English Bible makes *oil* a distinct item in the catalogue, *and oil to make his face to shine.* But this is an impossible construction of the Hebrew, in which the infinitive (*to make shine*) bears the same relation to what goes before as the infinitive (*to bring forth*) in the verse preceding, and is therefore expressive not of a distinct cause and effect, but of a consequence resulting from the one just mentioned. The true construction is given in the margin of the English Bible, *to make his face shine with oil*, or *more than oil.* To the first of these alternative translations it may be objected that wine cannot make men's faces shine with oil, unless there is allusion to the festive unctions of the ancients, which however were restricted to the head. The other, therefore, seems to be the true sense, in which oil is merely mentioned as a shining substance. The description of food as sustaining the heart is very ancient. See Gen. xviii. 5. Judg. xix. 8.

16. *Full are the trees of Jehovah; the cedars of Lebanon which he planted.* Full, i. e. abundantly supplied, saturated as in v. 13. The English versions supply *sap;* but the idea suggested by the context is the more general one of moisture, irrigation. The mutual relation of the clauses is the same as in v. 11. What is first said of trees, or of the noblest trees, in general, is then said of the cedars in particular. The *trees of Jehovah*, like the *cedars of God* in Ps. lxxx. 11 (10), are those which he has planted (Num. xxiv. 6), those which, by their loftiness or fruitfulness or

beauty, bear the strongest impress of their Maker's hand. The *cedars of Lebanon* are often mentioned as the noblest and most famous of their kind. See above, on Ps. xxix. 5. xcii. 13 (12.)

17. *Where the (small) birds nestle; (as to) the stork, the cypresses (are) her house.* He again recurs to the provision made for birds, which is here connected with the trees, as it is in v. 12. The word translated *birds* is not the one there used, but the same with that in Ps. lxxxiv. 4 (3.) cii. 7, where it is commonly translated *sparrow*, though supposed to be a general term for small birds, so called from their chirping, twittering noise. Here it may represent the smaller and the stork the larger class of birds. The Hebrew name of the stork means *merciful* or *pious*, and is supposed to have reference to the natural kindness of that bird, both to its parents and its young. *Nestle* or *build their nests.* The choice between the old translation, *fir-trees*, and the new one, *cypresses*, is exegetically unimportant.

18. *Mountains, the high (ones), are for the wild-goats—rocks (are) a refuge for the conies.* The idea seems to be, that even the wildest situations, and the most inaccessible to man, afford shelter and subsistence to some form of life, and are therefore proofs of the divine benevolence and wisdom. Of the names of animals here mentioned, the first occurs also in the book of Job (xxxix. 1); the second in the lists of unclean beasts, Lev. xi. 5. Deut. xiv. 7; and both in the writings of Solomon, Prov. v. 19. xxx. 26. Of the second, various explanations have been given, but none of them more probable than that derived from the rabbinical tradition. Nor is the question of the slightest exegetical importance, since the only peculiarities involved are those suggested by the text itself, to wit, that the animals intended must be such as inhabit rocks and mountains. Some supply *a refuge* in the first clause from the second; but a better sense is yielded by the simpler construction, *they belong to* (or *are intended for*) *the wild*

goats, which agrees exactly with the drift of the whole psalm to show that all parts of the inanimate creation contribute something to the comfort of the living sentient creature.

19. *He made the moon for seasons; the sun knows his setting.* Even the heavenly bodies have a reference to man's advantage. The moon is a measure of time, and the sun defines the period of active labor. The word translated *seasons* is the plural of the one translated *set time* in Ps. lxxv. 3 (2.) cii. 14, and the same that means *assemblies* in Ps. lxxiv. 4, 8. It is here put for all divisions of time, including the succession of day and night, to which there is perhaps a special reference, as in the other clause, where the meaning seems to be, that the sun knows when and where to set, and does not make the day, with its attendant toils, perpetual. This is a strong poetical description of an obvious and familiar fact, and no more presupposes a particular theory or system of astronomy than the similar language of uninspired poets among ourselves.

20. *Thou makest darkness and it is night; in it begins to move every beast of the forest.* The first verb in Hebrew means to *set* or *place*, but is used precisely as a word of the same meaning is in v. 3. Its abbreviated form does not indicate an optative meaning, but is substituted for the full form by poetic license. *It is night*, or night is, night begins to be. The same inceptive meaning is expressed in the translation of the third verb, which denotes animal motion, but is specially applied to that of reptiles. The idea of a secret, stealthy motion, as suggested by the common version (*do creep forth*), can hardly be intended, as the context shows the main idea of the passage to be this, that as the day affords a time for active motion to mankind and to domestic animals, the night affords a like time for the wilder beasts, or *beasts of the forest*, an expression which occurs above, in Ps. l. 10

21. *The young lions roaring for the prey, and to seek from God their food.* By translating the participle and infinitive both as presents, the common version makes this a distinct proposition. But in Hebrew it forms part of the preceding sentence, and contains a specification of the general statement there made. When night comes on, all the beasts of the forest are aroused, and among the rest the lion, roaring for his prey, (is roused) to seek his food from God. This last expression implies no such purpose on the lion's part, but merely that he seeks what can only be bestowed by an almighty being, which idea is suggested by the name of God here used.

22. *The sun rises—they are gathered—and in their dens lie down.* The first clause may also be translated, *let the sun rise, they are gathered*, or paraphrased in more accordance with our idiom, *when the sun rises they are gathered;* but neither of these constructions is so striking and poetical as the exact version first above given. *Gathered*, i. e. called in from their wanderings and dispersions. The word translated *dens* means *abodes* or *homes*, and is a cognate form to that in Ps. xc. 1; but the form here used is specially applied to the lairs or resting places of wild beasts, not only here but in Am. iii. 4. The last verb is also one appropriated to the lying down of animals. See above, on Ps. xxiii. 2. The construction is a pregnant one: *they lie down to* (or *into*) *their dens*, i. e. go into them and lie down.

23. *Forth goes man to his work, and to his labour until evening.* This verse presents the day-scene corresponding to the night-scene of the two preceding verses. When night comes on, the beasts of the forest are in motion; when the sun appears, they gather to their lairs, and man comes forth to labour *until evening*, when the scene is shifted as before. Leaving out of view all higher claims to admiration and respect, the poetical merit of

this whole description is of the highest order. The word translated *labour* is the same that was translated *culture* in v. 14.

24. *How manifold are thy works, Jehovah; all of them in wisdom hast thou wrought; full is the earth of thy riches.* The first verb in Hebrew strictly means *are many*, but as the context has respect to the variety, and not to the mere number, of God's works, the sense is well conveyed by the term used in the English versions (*manifold.*) *Works* and *wrought* represent a cognate verb and noun in Hebrew, a combination which adds point and animation to the sentence. The last word in the verse is derived from a verb which means to acquire, either by creation or by purchase. While the noun, therefore, strictly denotes acquisitions or possessions, its etymological affinities would instantly suggest to every Hebrew reader the idea of creation, as the ultimate source of these possessions, a modification of the thought which cannot be conveyed by any mere translation.

25. *Here is the sea, great and wide on all hands; there are moving things, and without number, small animals with great.* The exclamation or reflection in the preceding verse affords a transition to the survey of other parts of the creation, not included in the catalogue before recited, yet no less striking in themselves, and as proofs or illustrations of the Maker's wisdom. *Such is the sea*, or *here for instance is the sea*, are the phrases which would probably be used in our idiom, to introduce the first example The same thing was probably intended by the Hebrew phrase, *this (is) the sea*, as if the speaker at the same time pointed to it. See above, on v. 8. *Wide of both hands* is another idiomatic phrase used also by Moses (Gen. xxxiv. 21) and Isaiah (xxxiii. 21.) It obviously means stretching out in all directions. The sense of *hand*, as thus used, is the same as in the English phrase *on all hands*, and is probably derived from the use of the right and left hand to distinguish position or direction. *Moving things*

is here used to translate a single Hebrew word (רֶמֶשׂ), the cognate noun of the verb employed in v. 20 to denote animal motion. It is applied to marine animals, as here, in Gen. i. 9. Ps. lxix. 35 (34.) The use of the word *beasts*, in the common version of the last clause, is not consistent with its modern usage, which restricts it to terrestial quadrupeds.

26. *There the ships go—Leviathan—this (that) thou hast formed to play therein.* While the ships connect the sea with man's activity and interests, Leviathan, the standing representative of aquatic monsters, may be here put for the population of the sea itself. *To play therein*, as in his native element. Compare Job xl. 20. The idiomatic use of *this* is like that in v. 25. The word translated *go*, in the common version of the first clause, is the same that was rendered *walk* in v. 3, and *run* in v. 10.

27. *All of them on thee rely, to give their food in its season.* The *all of them* obviously relates to all the living creatures previously mentioned, and not to any one or more exclusively, the proposition being no less true of men than brutes, or of brutes than men. *On thee rely* is not an exact translation of the Hebrew, which indeed does not admit of one, because it combines a verb and preposition which cannot be combined in English. The form of the original is, *to thee wait*, *expect*, or *hope*, the verb expressing confidence, the particle the act of looking towards the object thus confided in. The description of the animals as thus expecting their supplies from God, is merely the poetical costume in which the Psalmist clothes the fact, that they are really, although unconsciously, dependent on him. In precisely the same manner, other poets represent the earth, in time of drought, as parched with thirst and longing for the rain, which expressions no sane man would either charge with falsehood, or consider as implying a belief in the conscious personality of

Earth. Compare my note on Isai. xlii. 4. *In its season*, i. e. when they need it.

28. *Thou givest to them, they gather; thou openest thy hand, they are filled (with) food.* The point of the significant antithesis is this, that God as easily bestows as they receive. He has only to give, they have only to gather. He has but to open his hand, and they are instantly provided, even to satiety. *Filled*, satisfied, abundantly supplied, as in v. 13. The verb rendered *gather* means to pick up or collect from the ground. It is used in the history of the manna (Ex. xvi. 1, 5, 16), to which there is obvious allusion. The act of gathering from the ground seems to presuppose a previous throwing down from heaven The common version, *that* (meaning *what*) *thou givest them they gather*, weakens the sentence, if it does not render it unmeaning

29. *Thou hidest thy face, they are confounded; thou withdrawest their breath, they expire, and to their dust return.* The hiding of God's face is the opposite of looking with a favourable aspect. See above, on Ps. xiii. 2 (1.) It here means the suspension or withdrawing of the various benefits before described. *They are troubled* is, in every case, a feeble version of one of the strongest words in the language, which has been already more than once explained. Even *confounded*, though much stronger, does not perfectly convey the idea, which is that of being agitated, terror-stricken, or convulsed. See above, on Ps. ii. 5. lxxviii. 33. xc. 7. *Their breath*, the vital principle imparted by the Spirit of God (Gen. ii. 7), who is the God of the spirits of all flesh, i. e. the author of all life whatever. See Num. xvi. 22. xxvii. 16, and compare Heb. xii. 9. The verb *expire* is used in the account of the destruction of all living creatures by the flood, Gen. vii. 21, 22, to which there is no doubt allusion, as there is in the next clause to Gen. iii. 19. Compare Ps. xc 3 ciii. 14. Ecc. xii. 7

Their dust, their own, their native dust, to which they belong, and from which they sprang.

30. *Thou sendest thy breath, they are created, and thou renewest the face of the earth.* The absolute power of God over the life of his creatures is expressed by representing him as annihilating and creating the whole race at pleasure, by a breath. With equal correctness we might read *thy spirit*, but *thy breath* is more poetical, and therefore better suited to the context as the primary meaning, though the spirit be really intended. *They are created* refers the effect more directly to God's power than *they live* or *they revive* would do. In the last clause there is evident allusion to the renovation of the earth desolated by the flood, and the joyous change of its face or aspect when re-peopled.

31. *Let the glory of Jehovah be forever; let Jehovah rejoice in his works.* The optative form of the first verb here determines the meaning of the other. It would also be grammatical, though much less natural in this connection, to regard the abbreviated form of the first verb as a mere poetic license, and explain both as futures proper. *The glory of Jehovah shall be to eternity; Jehovah shall rejoice in his works.* The grammatical question is of less importance, because one of these senses really implies the other. The wish is not for something doubtful but infallibly certain, and the prediction is in strict accordance with the wish of him who utters it. In this verse some interpreters suppose an allusion to God's satisfaction in his own work of creation when he rested from it on the seventh day. See Gen. ii. 1, 2.

32. *He that looks at the earth and it quakes, touches the hills and they smoke.* There is something in the form of this verse similar to that of v. 28. God has only to look at the earth to make it quake. He has only to touch the mountains and they smoke. His controlling and terrifying acts are as prompt and easy as his

acts of grace. There seems to be a reference to the words of Moses in describing the effects of the theophany at Sinai, when its summit smoked, and its very roots or bases were on fire. See Ex. xix. 18. Deut. xxxii. 22. To those familiar with the constant use of mountains as a symbol of great monarchies, this verse would necessarily suggest the thought, that God's power over states is no less absolute than that which he exercises over individuals, or over the inanimate creation.

33. *I will sing to Jehovah while I live, I will make music to my God while I still (exist.)* This is the Psalmist's conclusion from the view which he has taken, with respect to his own interest and duty. If the Lord be such a God to all his creatures, then I can do no better than expend the remainder of my life in praising him. The two verbs are those continually joined to denote vocal and instrumental praise. The closing words of each clause, and especially the second, have a highly idiomatic character. The phrase translated *while I live* means literally *in my life* or *lives.* The corresponding one can scarcely be translated, as it is composed of the preposition *in*, the adverb *yet* or *still*, and the pronoun of the first person, *in my yet*, i. e. *in my (being) yet*, while I still am, or continue to exist.

34. *Sweet shall be of him my meditation; I will rejoice in Jehovah.* The ancient versions and the Prayer Book, with some of the best interpreters, put an optative sense upon the first clause, *may my thought (or speech) be acceptable to him.* In favour of this interpretation is the fact that a synonymous verb, followed by the same preposition (עַל), means to be pleasing to a person, in Ps. xvi. 6. In favour of the other is the want of anything to indicate a wish, and the parallelism of the second clause, which relates to the expression of his own feelings towards Jehovah, not to the dispositions of Jehovah towards himself. Thus understood, the whole verse completes the Psalmist's practical conclusion from

the view which he has taken of God's power, wisdom, and goodness, namely, that the knowledge and possession of this God is happiness.

35. *Consumed are sinners from the earth, and* (as for) *wicked men, they are no more. Bless, oh my soul, Jehovah. Hallelujah!* This verse has no perceptible connexion, either with the verse immediately before it, or with the general drift of the whole psalm, except upon the supposition, that the whole psalm was intended to derive, from the view of God's authoritative care over his works, an encouraging assurance that his people must be safe; that he who feeds and shelters the inferior animals, and makes provision for the physical necessities of men in general, cannot fail to provide for the security and happiness of those whom he has set apart for himself, or to free them from the malice of those sinners who are equally the enemies of God and of his people. The psalm, like the one before it, closes with the same words which began it. The last word, *Hallelujah (praise ye Jah)*, occurs here for the first time, and is supposed by some to form no part of the original composition, but to have been added for the purpose of adapting it to some public service at a later date.

PSALM CV.

This, like the Seventy-Eighth, is a historical psalm, recounting God's ancient dealings with his people, especially in Egypt. The practical design of the commemoration is not to bring the people to repentance, as in the case referred to, but to excite their hopes of an analogous deliverance. According to a theory already mentioned, this is the second member of a trilogy, added to one of older date (Ps. ci—ciii) during the time of the captivity. It differs from the psalm before it in deriving from history the same consolation which is there derived from nature. After the introduction, vs. 1—7, the arrangement is simply chronological, beginning with the promise to Abraham, and ending with the conquest of Canaan, vs. 8—44. The first fifteen verses of this psalm are found in 1 Chron. xvi, combined with Ps. xcvi and three verses of Ps. cvi. See above, on Ps. xcvi. 1.

1. *Give thanks unto Jehovah, call upon his name, make known among the nations his exploits.* The original meaning of the second phrase is, *call (him) by his name*, i. e. give him the descriptive title most expressive of his divine perfections; or more specifically, call him by his name Jehovah, i. e. ascribe to him the attributes which it denotes, to wit, eternity and self-existence, together with that covenant relation to his people, which though not denoted by the name was constantly associated with it, and therefore necessarily suggested by it. The meaning of the next phrase is obscured, if not entirely concealed, in the common version, *among the people.* The plural form and sense of the original expression are essential to the writer's purpose, which is to glorify the God of Israel among all nations. See above, on Ps. xviii. 50 (49.) lvii. 10 (9.) For the meaning of the last word, see above, on Ps. ciii. 7.

2. *Sing to him, play to him, muse on all his wondrous deeds.* The exhortation seems to be addressed to the Gentiles, who are called upon to join in the praises and to share the blessings of the chosen people. For the meaning of the last verb, see above, on Ps. civ. 34.

3. *Glory in his holy name! Glad shall be the heart of those who seek Jehovah.* Congratulate yourselves that you possess a right

and interest in the favour of so glorious a Being. The last clause presents as an inducement, that to seek the favour of this God is a source, and by implication the only source, of joy and happiness. Compare Ps. xxxiv. 3 (2.) xl. 17 (16.) lxix. 7 (6.)

4. *Seek Jehovah and his strength, seek his face evermore.* The Hebrew verbs, although synonymous, are not identical. *And his strength*, the protection secured by his almighty power. Seek him, not as a finite being, but as the omnipotent Jehovah, the source, as well as the possessor, of all strength. *Seek his face*, not merely his presence, but his countenance, his favourable look or aspect. With the several expressions of this verse compare Ps. ix. 11 (10.) x. 4. xiv. 2. xxiv. 6. xxxiv. 5 (4.) lxi. 4 (3.) lxii. 8 (7.) lxiii. 3 (2.) lxviii. 35 (34) xcvi. 7.

5. *Remember his wondrous deeds which he did, his miracles and the judgments of his mouth.* They are exhorted not to forget them, as Israel is charged with doing, Ps. lxxviii. 11. *Miracles*, prodigies or wonders, proofs of divine power. There is no need of identifying these with the *judgments of his mouth*, which include his laws and the sentences pronounced upon his enemies. The latter is probably the prominent idea as best suited to this context.

6. *Ye seed of Abraham his servant, ye sons of Jacob, his chosen (ones.)* Descendants of the patriarchs, and therefore heirs of the patriarchal promises. The common version of the last phrase (*his chosen*), though exact, conveys a wrong idea, as it seems to make *chosen* an epithet of *Jacob*, which would also seem to be required by the parallelism ; but the Hebrew word is plural and describes the object of address as the church or chosen people. Compare Isai. lxv. 9. Abraham is called the Servant of God, in an emphatic sense, as being his chosen instrument and confidential

agent. See above, on Ps. xviii. 1, and compare Ps. xc. 1. The parallel passage (1 Chr. xvi. 13) has *Israel his servant.*

7. *He is Jehovah our God; in all the earth (are) his judgments.* His covenant relations are with us the seed of Abraham; but the proofs of his existence and vindicatory justice are common to all nations. This whole introduction seems intended to dispose both Jews and Gentiles to the praise of God.

8. *He remembered forever his covenant, the word he commanded for a thousand generations.* There is here a kind of antithetical allusion to the exhortation in v. 5. They should remember what he did, since he remembers what he promised. What he has done involves a pledge of what he will do. He has remembered (and will remember) his covenant to eternity. *The word* is the word of promise. He is said to have commanded it, partly because his promise is conditional and annexed to his commandment, and for that reason called a covenant; partly because all that God says must of necessity be said with authority, so that even his promises partake of the nature of commands. The last phrase, *a thousand generations*, is Mosaic. See Deut. vii. 9, and compare Ex. xx. 6.

9. *Which he ratified with Abraham, and his oath to Isaac.* The sentence is continued from the foregoing verse. *Ratified*, literally *cut;* see above, on Ps. l. 5. *His oath* (which he sware) *to Isaac*, or, *his oath for* (the benefit of) *Isaac.* The distinction, if any be intended, is that the covenant was formally made only with Abraham, and merely sanctioned or confirmed by oath to his successors. See Gen. xv. 18. xxvi. 3. xxviii. 13. *His oath* is governed by *remembered* in v. 8. Compare Ps. lxxxix. 28, 34 (27, 33.)

10. *And confirmed it to Jacob for a statute, to Israel (for)*

an everlasting covenant. Confirmed it, literally, made (or let) it stand, instead of suffering it to expire with the person to whom it was originally given. *A statute*, in the wide sense of a permanent arrangement, a perpetual constitution, or, as it is called in the last clause, *a compact of eternity*, an everlasting covenant. See Gen. xxviii. 13. xxxv. 12.

11. *Saying, To thee will I give the land of Canaan, as the portion of your heritage.* The subject or substance of the promise is now more distinctly stated. The word translated *portion* primarily means a *line*, especially a *measuring line*, and then what is measured by it, to wit, a piece of land, a lot of ground. This was not to be given to the patriarchs in person, but to their descendants, as the portion of their heritage or their hereditary portion. The plural *your* may refer, however, to the patriarchs themselves, as the promise was repeated to Abraham, Isaac, and Jacob.

12. *When as yet they could be numbered—very few, and strangers in it.* The first clause involves an antithetical allusion to the promise, afterwards fulfilled, that they should be innumerable as the stars, or as the sand upon the shore, Gen. xxii. 17. The form of the original is highly idiomatic, *in their being men of number, like a little*, or like littleness itself. See above, on Ps. lxxiii. 2, and compare Isai. i. 9. *Strangers*, sojourners, living on the lands of others, at their will, or by their sufferance. See above, on Ps. xxxix. 13 (12.) *In it*, the land of Canaan, mentioned in the preceding verse. The whole verse qualifies the previous account of the patriarchal covenant, which was not made with Israel when already a great nation, but with their ancestors when few in number and without a settled home. The parallel passage (1 Chron. xvi. 19) has *when ye were.* See Gen. xxxiv. 30, and compare Deut. xxxiii. 6. Isai. x. 19.

13. *And they went about from nation to nation, from kingdom to another people.* This may be regarded as in contrast with v. 12, *and (yet) they went about*, notwithstanding their small number and their being strangers. Or vs. 12, 13, may be the protasis of the sentence, and v. 14 its apodosis. 'When they were few and strangers, and went from nation to nation, he let no man, etc.' This verse describes the characteristic feature in the condition of the chosen people, during the patriarchal period of their history, namely, their migratory intercourse with various nations. These are mentioned in the first clause as distinct races, in the last as distinct states or bodies politic. Where we might have expected *from kingdom to kingdom*, the ear is somewhat disappointed by the phrase *from kingdom to another people*, which may have been intended to distinguish the Egyptian and other monarchies from the more democratical or patriarchal institutions of the Arabians and other nations. *They went about* seems to be the force of the reflexive or frequentative verb, as distinguished from that of the primitive, *they went*. See above, on Ps. xxvi. 3. xxxv. 14. ci. 2, and compare Gen. v. 22. xvii. 1. xxiv. 6, 9, 40. xlviii. 15.

14. *He suffered no man to oppress them, and reproved, for their sake, kings.* The precise sense of the first clause is, he suffered not man (or men in general) to oppress them. The protection of the patriarchs is certainly one of the most striking facts in sacred history. The kings mentioned in the last clause are the kings of Egypt and Gerar (Gen. xii. 17. xx. 3), not without reference perhaps to those mentioned in Gen. xiv. 1.

15. *Touch not mine anointed (ones), and to my prophets do no harm.* These are the words of God himself, and are designated as such, in the English Bible, by supplying the word *saying*, which is expressed in the analogous case, v. 11. *Touch not*, as in Gen. xxvi. 11, 29. In the Old Testament, unction is the symbol of spiritual gifts, and especially of those imparted to the

great theocratical offices. See above, on Ps. ii. 2. From the case of Elisha (1 Kings xix. 16) it would seem that prophets were anointed when inducted into office. The patriarchs are here called *prophets* in the proper sense of the term, as denoting men inspired of God, and admitted to confidential intercourse with him. The allusion here is to Gen. xx. 7, where God says to Abimelech of Abraham, "Restore the man his wife, for he is a prophet, and he will pray for thee, and thou shalt live."

16. *And he called (for) a famine on the land; every staff of bread he brake.* The psalmist now passes from the Patriarchal to the Egyptian period of the history, by stating the occasion of Israel's migration into Egypt. The meaning of the first clause seems to be, that he summoned famine, as his instrument or servant, to come down upon the land, as sent from above, that is to say, from himself. The meaning of the last clause is, that the people were deprived of every customary means and source of subsistence. The figure of a staff or stay is a Mosaic one. See Lev. xxvi. 26, and compare Isai. iii. 1. It is near akin to the description of food as staying or sustaining the heart. See above, on Ps. civ. 15. The historical reference in the verse before us is to Gen. xli. 54.

17. *He sent before them a man; sold for a slave was Joseph.* The same providential purpose is assigned to Joseph's bondage by himself, Gen. xlv. 5. With the last clause compare Gen. xxxvii. 36. Some interpreters, assuming, as we have already seen, that this psalm was composed in the time of the captivity, suppose a parallel, in this verse, between Joseph and Daniel, both of whom, in addition to their personal qualities, were sent into captivity before the body of their brethren; both gained the royal favour and were exalted to high station in the land of their captivity; and both employed the influence thus gained for the advantage of their countrymen. To the Jews in exile, such a

parallel must have been not only interesting, in a historical or poetical point of view, but consolatory and encouraging as *a token for good*, a sign that God was about to renew the exodus from Egypt in an exodus from Babylon.

18. *They hurt, with the fetter, his feet; into iron came his soul.* That Joseph was actually chained or fettered, is included in the true sense of the word *bound*, applied to him in the history. See Gen. xl. 3, and compare Gen. xxxix. 20, 22. *They*, the Egyptians, or his gaolers; or the verb may be indefinitely construed, as if it had been said, *his feet were hurt.* The verb means elsewhere to humble or mortify, but is here used in its strict sense of afflicting, causing to suffer. The Prayer Book version of the last clause, *the iron entered into his soul*, is ungrammatical, the word for *iron* being masculine, while that for *soul* is, like the verb, feminine. The general sense is given in the text of the English Bible, and the exact form in the margin. The mention of the soul, as in many other cases, is of course not meant to be exclusive of the body, but to suggest the idea of intimate and heartfelt suffering. See above, on Ps. iii. 3 (2.) xi. 1, etc.

19. *Until the time that his word came* (to pass), *the saying of Jehovah tried him.* The last verb properly denotes the assaying of metals, but is figuratively applied to moral trial and purgation. See above, on Ps. xii. 7 (6.) xvii. 3. xviii. 31 (30.) xxvi. 2. The most probable meaning of the verse is, that during the two years which intervened between his explanation of the prisoners' dreams and the favourable issue to which it ultimately led, his faith in the divine promise, both to himself and to his people, was severely but favourably tried. Compare the history in Gen. xl, xli.

20. *The king sent and loosed him—the ruler of nations, and set him free.* Both verbs strictly apply to the removal of his fetters, the first meaning properly to knock off (Isai. lviii. 6), the other to

open for the purpose of removing. See above, on Ps. xxx 12 (11.) The king of Egypt is called a *ruler of peoples*, either in reference to the tribes or nomes of Egypt itself, or because there were other nations tributary to him.

21. *He made him lord of his house and ruler of all his wealth.* The literal meaning of the first clause is, *he placed him lord to his house.* See Gen. xli. 40, 41, 43. xlv. 8. For the meaning of the last word in the sentence, see above, on Ps. civ. 24. It is one of the points of resemblance which are thought to identify the two psalms as the work of the same author.

22. *To bind his chiefs at his pleasure, and his elders to make wise.* The words translated *chiefs* and *elders* are those commonly applied to the heads of tribes and families, the hereditary magistrates under the patriarchal system. The application of the second word to Egypt is found also in the history, Gen. l. 7. *At his pleasure*, literally, *with his soul*, which some explain as a bold metaphor, describing Joseph's mind or soul as the cord or chain with which he bound the Egyptians, i. e. forced them to perform his will. But see Ps. xvii. 9. xxvii. 12. xli. 3 (2.)

23. *And* (so) *Israel entered Egypt, and Jacob sojourned in the land of Ham.* This was the main event, to which those just recited were preparatory. *Israel* and *Jacob* are the names both of the individual patriarch and of his descendants as a nation. In this case both the applications are admissible, or rather requisite, in order to exhaust the writer's meaning. The patriarch himself came into Egypt, but his sons literally came with him, and all his descendants figuratively in him. *The land of Ham*, from whom *Mizraim* was descended. See above, on Ps. lxxviii. 51.

24. *And he increased his people greatly, and made them stronger than their enemies. Increased*, literally, rendered fruitful. The

same verb is used in the promise to Abraham and Jacob (Gen. xvii. 6. xxviii. 2), and in the history of Israel in Egypt, Ex. i. 7. The word here used for enemies is one implying persecution and oppression. The singular pronouns in the Hebrew, *made him stronger than his enemies*, are in strict grammatical agreement with the collective noun *people*.

25. *He turned their heart to hate his people, to deal craftily with his servants.* The first clause asserts God's sovereign control even of the free acts of his sinful creatures, a truth repeatedly affirmed in the history which this psalm recapitulates. See Ex. iv. 21. vii. 3, and compare 1 Sam. xxvi. 9. 2 Sam. xvi. 10. xxiv. 1. The last verb occurs only in the history of Joseph, Gen. xxxvii. 18. The corresponding term in Exodus (i. 10) is *let us deal wisely*, or more exactly, *let us make ourselves wise*, as the verb in this case may be rendered, *let us make ourselves subtle* or *crafty*, both being reflexive forms. The historical allusion is of course to the murderous policy, which preceded the violent oppression of the Hebrews.

26. *He sent Moses his servant* (and) *Aaron whom he chose.* The meaning is not *Moses* (who was) *his servant*, or (because he was) *his servant*, but (to be) *his servant*, his instrument in the great work of delivering his people. See above, on v. 6, and on Ps. xviii. 1. xxxvi. 1. lxxviii. 70.

27. *They placed among them the words of his signs and wonders in the land of Ham.* The first phrase seems to mean nothing more than *set before them* or *exhibited to them*. *Words of signs* is by some understood to mean *matters* (or *affairs*) *of signs*, and to be either a pleonastic phrase for *signs* alone, or an emphatic phrase denoting *all the signs*. See above, on Ps. lxv. 4 (3.) The first is a gratuitous assumption, the last a forced interpretation Better than either is the explanation which gives to *words*

its proper meaning, and supposes stress to be intentionally laid on the divine word of Jehovah, and the prophetic word of Moses and Aaron, in the way of threatening and command, as well as on the physical effects which followed these denunciations. Compare the use of *words* in Ps. vii. 1, and the explanation there given. *Signs*, i. e. tokens of God's presence and activity, and indications of his will. *Wonders*, prodigies, miracles, the same word that occurs above in v. 5.

28. *He sent darkness and made it dark, and they did not resist his words*, or according to the marginal reading, *his word*. This is by some understood to mean the plague of darkness, which immediately preceded the slaughter of the first born, Ex. x. 22. But to this explanation there are two objections; first, that it entirely disturbs the order of the plagues, which is otherwise observed with great exactness, the only deviation being very trivial compared with this; secondly, because it would then be necessary to apply the last clause to Moses and Aaron, or to Israel in general, thereby making it unmeaning, or else to admit a contradiction of the history, which expressly says that the Egyptians did resist the word of God even after the plague of darkness, Ex. x. 27. The only remaining explanation is, that darkness, in the verse before us, as in many other cases, is a figure for calamity in general, and applied not to one plague in particular, but to the whole series, of which a more detailed account is then subjoined.

29. *He turned their waters to blood and killed their fish.* Here begins the more particular enumeration of the plagues of Egypt. Compare Ps. lxxviii. 44, where the inconvenience specified is that they could not drink the water, whereas here it is the loss of their accustomed food. This last word is used as a collective in both languages.

30. *Their land teemed with frogs—in the chambers of their kings.* That even these were not safe from the hateful intruders, is an

aggravating circumstance, particularly mentioned in the original threatening, and implied in the narrative of its execution. See Ex. viii. 3, 9. The first verb means to bring forth in abundance, and is so used in the history of the creation, with particular reference to the genesis of animals, Gen. i. 20.

31. *He said, and the fly came and gnats* (or *lice*) *in all their border.* See above, on Ps. lxxviii. 45, where the gnats or lice are omitted, and the flies precede the frogs. So here, the flies precede the lice, a slight departure from the order of the history. See Ex. viii. 5, 16. *He said*, i. e. he said so, which is tantamount to saying, *he commanded. In all their border*, i. e. every where within it, throughout the land. This expression is borrowed from the history. See Ex. viii. 2 (vii. 27.)

32. *He gave them hail for rain* (and) *flaming fire in their land.* This, which is the common version, represents the sense correctly, but with a deviation from the form of the original, which is highly idiomatic. A bald translation is, *he gave their rains hail, fire of flames in their land.* The terms are chosen for the sake of an allusion to the promise in Lev. xxvi. 4, *I will give your rains in their season.* Instead of these he gave the Egyptians a destructive hail-storm. Compare Ps. lxxviii. 48.

33. *And smote their vine and their fig-tree, and shattered the trees of their border.* Compare Ps. lxxviii. 47, where sycamores are particularly mentioned. The history says nothing of the vines, but speaks of the breaking of the trees, using the same intensive verb as here. See Ex. ix. 25. *Their border*, as before, means their land or territory in its whole extent, just as *the ends of the earth* is put for all its parts. See above, on Ps. ii. 8.

34. *He said, and the arbeh came, and the yelek, and* (that) *without number.* The two Hebrew words, here retained, denote

varieties of the locust, and have no equivalents in English. See above, on Ps. lxxviii. 46, where the first word here stands second, and the place of the other is supplied by *hasil*, another distinctive term of the same kind. *Without number*, literally, *there is no number*. See the same expression, Ps. civ. 25.

35. *And devoured every herb in their land, and devoured the fruit of their ground.* The verb, though varied in the common version, is the same in both clauses of the Hebrew. See above, on Ps. xlviii. 46, and compare the original narrative, Ex. x. 5, 15.

36. *And he smote all the firstborn in their land, the first-fruits of all their strength.* For the meaning of the last clause, see above, on Ps. lxxviii. 51, and compare Ex. xii. 29, 30.

37. *And he brought them out with silver and with gold, and there was not in his tribes a totterer* (or *stumbler.*) The first clause relates to the spoiling of the Egyptians, Ex. xii. 35, 36. The last word denotes a person unfit for military service. Compare Isai. v. 27.

38. *Glad was Egypt at their going forth, for their fear had fallen upon them.* This panic terror, which followed the last plague and facilitated the escape of Israel (Ex. xi. 1. xii. 31—33), accounts for the readiness with which the Egyptians gave whatever was demanded, and completely vindicates the children of Israel from the charge of borrowing what they never meant to pay. The terms used in the history denote the acts of asking and giving, not those of borrowing and lending. The terms of the last clause are derived from Ex. xv. 16. Deut. xi. 25.

39. *He spread a cloud for a covering, and fire to give light by night.* See above, on Ps. lxxviii. 14. The poetical description

of the cloud as covering the host is derived from the statement that "the cloud of Jehovah was over (or above) them by day," Num. x. 34. Compare Num. ix. 16. Neh. ix. 12. Isai. iv. 5, 6.

40. (The people) *asked and he made quails come—and bread of heaven satisfied them.* See above, on Ps. lxxviii. 25—27, and compare Ex. xvi. 4—13. Num. xi. 31. As to the alternation of the singular and plural forms, see above, on v. 24. *Bread* may either be the subject of the verb, as given above, or a qualifying term, *(with) bread.*

41. *He opened a rock and forth gushed waters; they ran in the wastes, a river.* See above, on Ps. lxxviii. 16, 20. The word translated *wastes* means, according to its etymology, dry places.

42. *Because he remembered his holy word with Abraham his servant.* This brings us back to the statement in vs. 8, 9, in proof of which this long array of facts has been presented. Nothing of all this would have taken place if God had been forgetful of his covenant. This covenant is here meant by *his holy word*, which is therefore followed by the preposition *with*, as in Ex. ix. 24, where the covenant is expressly mentioned.

43. *And brought out his people in joy, in triumph his chosen (ones.)* He remembered his promise and in execution of it brought out his people, etc. The parallelism of *people* and *chosen* throws light upon the latter term, as used in v. 6.

44. *And gave to them nations' lands, and peoples labour they inherit.* The prominent idea is not that of *gentiles* or *heathen*, in the religious sense, but that of other nations, and whole nations, to whose place and possessions they succeeded. *Labour* is put for its result or product, as a synonymous Hebrew word is in Ps. lxxviii. 46.

45. *To the end that they might keep his statutes and his laws observe. Hallelujah!* The emphatic phrase at the beginning, corresponding to our phrases, to the end, for the purpose, or in order that, points this out as the qualification or condition of the promise which had been so gloriously verified. The same condition is expressed or implied elsewhere. See above, on Ps. lxxviii. 7, and compare Gen. xviii. 19. Deut. iv. 40. xxvi. 17. *Hallelujah* (*praise ye Jah*) as above, in Ps. civ. 35.

PSALM CVI.

After an introduction, praising the divine goodness, and expressing the hope of a participation in it, vs. 1—5, this psalm contains a solemn confession of the sins of Israel through all the periods of his history; in Egypt, v. 6—12; in the wilderness, v. 13—33; in Canaan, vs. 34—43; and a prayer, founded on encouraging tokens of the Lord's compassion, that he will save his people from the punishment incurred by their unfaithfulness, vs. 44—48. According to Hengstenberg's hypothesis already mentioned, this is the third psalm of the trilogy added to Ps. ci—ciii, in the times of the captivity, and a direct continuation of the series, since the moral condition of God's covenant, propounded at the close of Ps. cv, is here acknowledged to have been violated by his people, who are also represented as actually suffering the punishment of this violation, but encouraged by returning tokens of a favourable change, to hope and pray for the forgiveness of their sins and the removal of the judgments which they have so well deserved. The first verse and the two last form a part of the mixed composition in First Chronicles, which has been already mentioned. See above, on Ps. xcvi. 1. But a still more interesting parallel to this psalm is the prayer or confession in the ninth chapter of Daniel, which resembles it so much in subject, tone, and diction, that although not otherwise demonstrable, it would not be absurd to regard the psalm before us as a lyrical paraphrase of that confession, prepared for permament and public use by Daniel himself or some contemporary writer.

1. *Hallelujah! Give thanks unto Jehovah, for (he is) good, for unto eternity (is) his mercy.* The *Hallelujah (praise ye Jah!)* which concludes the two preceding psalms, stands both at the beginning and the close of this. The exhortation to *give thanks unto Jehovah* is also found at the beginning of Ps. cv. The reason here assigned, *that he is good, and his mercy endures forever*, is expressed in the same words, Ps. c. 5.

2. *Who shall tell the mighty deeds of Jehovah?* (Who) *shall utter all his praise?* The potential meaning (*who can tell?*) is here included in the simple future. *Mighty deeds* answers to a single word in Hebrew meaning *strengths* or *powers*. The expression is borrowed from Deut. iii. 24, where the English Bible has the singular form *might*. The verb translated *utter* is a causative, who shall cause to hear or to be heard? See above, on Ps. xxvi. 7. The interrogation involves a negative assertion, namely, that they cannot be fully expressed or duly celebrated.

3. *Happy the keepers of judgment, the doer of righteousness at every time.* The form of expression at the beginning is the same as in Ps. i. 1. The *keepers of judgment* are those who observe justice as the rule of their conduct, the same idea that is afterwards expressed in other words, *the doer* (or *practiser*) *of righteousness*, not occasionally merely but at all times. The change from the plural to the singular is common, where the latter denotes an ideal individual, the representative of a whole class

The condition here propounded is identical with that in Ps. cv. 45. ciii. 18. Dan. ix. 4.

4. *Remember me, Jehovah, with the favour of thy people; visit me with thy salvation.* The speaker is the Church or chosen people, and therefore prays to be remembered with the kindness due to her as such. *Visit me*, manifest thy favourable presence. See above, on Ps. viii 5 (4.) Such a prayer, uttered by the church itself, implies that the tokens of God's favourable presence had been interrupted or withdrawn.

5. *To witness the welfare of thy chosen* (*ones*), *to rejoice in the joy of thy nation, to glory with thy heritage.* Our idiom requires the subject of the verb to be more distinctly indicated. The meaning evidently is, *that I may witness*, *that I may rejoice*, *that I may glory*. The phrase translated *witness the welfare* literally means *to see in the good*, i. e. to look on, to be a spectator, when thy chosen ones are in possession or enjoyment of good. *Thy nation* is here used instead of the customary phrase *thy people*, perhaps because the meaning is, the nation which is thy chosen people. The general meaning of the whole verse is, that I may once more be recognised and treated as thy people.

6. *We have sinned with our fathers, we have done perversely, we have done wickedly.* The connection with the foregoing context may be made clear by supplying a few intermediate thoughts. 'True, we have no right to expect this, much less to demand it. We have not performed the condition of thy covenant; we have not kept thy statutes or observed thy laws; we have not kept judgment or done righteousness.' The national confession here begun is nearly co-extensive with the psalm itself. The terms of this verse are borrowed, here as well as in Dan. ix. 5, from that great model of ecclesiastical and national devotion furnished by Solomon, in his prayer at the dedication of the temple, 1 Kings

viii. 47. Compare Isai. lix. 12. *With our fathers*, not merely like them, but as sharing their responsibility and guilt. Of the three verbs used in this confession, the first denotes failure to discharge one's obligations, the second wilful perversion or distortion, the third disorderly or turbulent transgression. See above, on Ps. i. 1.

7. *Our fathers in Egypt did not understand thy wondrous works, they did not remember the abundance of thy mercies, and rebelled upon the sea, at the Red Sea.* The general confession in v. 6 is now followed by a more detailed acknowledgment, beginning with the exodus from Egypt. The *wondrous works* of God, the things done wonderfully by him, then and there, for the deliverance of his people, the great body of them did not understand. Even those who referred them to their true source and author, did not fully appreciate the end for which they were performed, or enter into the majestic plan, in executing which they were permitted to be God's co-workers. The truth of this charge is abundantly established by the narrow, grovelling, selfish views and feelings so repeatedly betrayed by the generation which came out of Egypt, showing clearly that they did not *practically understand* God's dealings with them. This is probably the idea meant to be conveyed by the Hebrew verb, which usually means to *act wisely*, but is here modified by governing a noun directly. See above, on Ps. ii. 10. xiv. 2. The two-fold local designation, *on the sea*, *at the Red Sea*, was probably suggested by the parallelism in Ex. xv. 4. The variation of the particle seems merely a poetical embellishment; the difference in meaning is no greater than in our *on* and *at*. The *Sea of Sea-weed* was the name given by the Hebrews and Egyptians to that bay or gulf of the Indian Ocean, which was called the Red Sea by the Greek geographers.

8. *And he saved them for his name's sake, to make known his might.* This is an answer to a tacit objection, namely, that their

conduct had been sanctioned by God's saving them. True, he did save them, because they were necessary to his purpose. He saved them not for their sake but his own, to accomplish his own ends, and exhibit his own power.

9. *And he rebuked the Red Sea and it dried up, and he made them go through the deeps like the desert.* This is merely a specification of the general statement in the preceding verse. The divine intervention here commemorated was the more remarkable because it took place on the very spot where they first rebelled, as mentioned in v. 7. Though they disobeyed him at the Red Sea, he nevertheless dried the Red Sea, i. e. as much of it as was required to furnish them a passage. *Rebuked*, as in Ps. civ. 7. *Like the desert*, as in the desert, i. e. in a level and extensive plain, without obstruction or unevenness. See my note on Isai. lxiii. 13, where the same comparison is used.

10. *And he saved them from the hand of the hater, and redeemed them from the hand of the enemy.* Both epithets are intended to apply to Pharaoh, not only as a personal oppressor of the Israelites, but as the representative of Egypt, all of which now feared and hated the occasion of its multiplied and aggravated sufferings.

11. *And the waters covered their adversaries; not one of them was left.* The Psalmist dwells upon the completeness of the overthrow and destruction experienced by Pharaoh and his host, in order to aggravate the previous and subsequent ingratitude of Israel, as well as to enhance the free grace of Jehovah, and the fidelity with which he executed his engagements, even to the faithless.

12. *And they believe his words, they sing his praise.* Then (and not till then) do they believe. This is not an encomium on their faith, but a confession of their unbelief. It was not till the pro-

mise was fulfilled that they believed it. With the first clause compare Ex. xiv. 31 ; with the second, Ex. xv. 1.

13. *They made haste, they forgot his deeds, they did not wait for his counsel.* Their propensity to evil was so strong, that they are said to have hastened to forget what God had done for them, which means much more than that they soon forgot it. They did not even wait for the promise to be verified by the event. The expression in the first clause is borrowed from Ex. xxxii. 8. The works or deeds of God are not in this case, as in Ps. ciii. 22. civ. 24, the works of nature, but the plagues of Egypt. See Deut. xi. 3, and compare Dan. ix. 4.

14. *And they lusted a lust in the wilderness and tempted God in the desert.* The confession now passes from their sins in Egypt to their sins in the wilderness. The strong expression in the first clause relates to their wanton craving of animal food. See Num. xi. 4, 34. With the last clause compare Ps. lxxviii. 18. The two words for wilderness and desert are the same as those in Ps. lxxviii. 40. See also Ps. lxviii. 8 (7.)

15. *And he gave them their request and sent (them) leanness in their soul.* The last phrase is by some translated *against*, by others *into their soul;* but it is really a qualifying phrase, designed to show that the emaciation or decay which was sent upon them was not bodily but spiritual. See Num. xi. 18, and compare Ps. lxxviii. 10, 18.

16. *And they were envious at Moses in the camp, at Aaron, the Holy One of Jehovah.* This is another of their wilderness sins. See Num. chap. xvi. Aaron is not called the *Saint of the Lord* in reference to his personal holiness, which does not seem to have been eminent, but his *Holy* (or *Consecrated*) *One*, in reference to his sacerdotal dignity.

17. (Then) *opens the earth and swallows Dathan, and covers over the company of Abiram.* This relates to the destruction of those followers of Korah who were not Levites. See Num. xvi. 32, 33, and compare Deut. xi. 6. From the first of these passages some interpreters supply *her mouth* after *opens;* but the absolute use of the verb is perfectly consistent with our idiom.

18. *And a fire devours their company, a flame consumes* (those) *wicked* (men.) This relates to the destruction of Korah himself and his Levitical followers. See Num. xvi. 35. xxvi. 10.

19. *They make a calf in Horeb, and bow down to a molten image.* This was a third sin committed in the wilderness. See Ex. xxxii. 1—6, and compare Ex. xxxiv. 4. The golden calf appears to have been an imperfect and diminutive copy of the bull Apis, worshipped in Egypt.

20. *And exchange their glory for the likeness of an ox eating grass.* This must be read in the closest connection with v. 19, in order to complete it. Their folly consisted in exchanging the true God, whose worship and whose favour was their highest honour, for the mere likeness of an irrational brute. *Eating grass*, not in the act, but in the habit, of so doing. Although the golden calf at Horeb, and the golden calves at Dan and Beer-sheba, were all regarded as representatives of Jehovah himself, their worship was uniformly treated as idolatry, and as a virtual though not a formal or avowed renunciation of his service. Compare Jer. ii. 10—13.

21. *They forgot God that saved them, that did great* (things) *in Egypt.* That saved, that did; literally, saving, doing.

22. *Wonderful* (things) *in the land of Ham, terrible* (things) *on the Red Sea.* Wonderful, literally, (things) made wonderful

or strangely done. Terrible, literally, to be dreaded. Compare Ps. cv. 23, 27.

23. *And he said he would destroy them—unless Moses his elect had stood in the breach before him, to turn back his wrath from destroying.* The first and last verbs are different in Hebrew, but have only one exact equivalent in English. The second clause is not a part of what God said, but a historical statement of what really prevented the execution of his threatening. He said he would destroy them, and he would have done so, had not Moses, etc. Moses is called the Elect or Chosen of Jehovah, as having been selected and set apart to be God's instrument in the great work of deliverance and legislation. The plural is elsewhere applied to the whole nation as the chosen people. See above, v. 5, and Ps. cv. 43. *Stood in the breach* is a military figure, drawn from the desperate defence of a beseiged town or fortress. Compare Jer. xv. i. Ez. xiii. 5. xxii. 30. The historical reference is to Ex. xxxii. 11—14. Deut. ix. 18, 19. *To turn back his wrath* is to prevent its accomplishing its object. See above, on Ps. lxxviii. 38, and compare Num. xxv. 11.

24. *And they rejected the pleasant land, they did not believe his word.* This refers to the refusal of the people to invade the land of Canaan in the first year of their exodus from Egypt, and to their believing the report of the ten spies in preference to God himself. See above, on Ps. lxxviii. 22, 32, and compare Num. xiv. 31. *The land of desire*, the desired or desirable land, is a name also found in Jer. iii. 19.

25. *And they murmured in their tents; they did not hearken to the voice of Jehovah.* The form of expression in the first clause is borrowed from Deut. i. 27; in the second from Num. xiv. 22.

26. *And he lifted his hand to them, to make them fall in the wil-*

derness. The first phrase does not mean, he raised his hand against them, or to strike them, but as the ancient gesture of swearing. See Num. xiv. 28, 30. Deut. i. 34. ii. 14. The last clause contains the oath itself, or what he swore, to wit, that he would make them fall, slay them, in the wilderness. See Num. xiv. 29, 32.

27. *And to make their seed fall in the nations, and to scatter them in the lands.* As the appointed punishment of the older generation was to die in the wilderness, so that of their descendants was to die in dispersion and captivity among the Gentiles. See Lev. xxvi. 33, 38, and compare Deut. xxviii. 32, 36, 64, 68. The recollection of this threatening must have been peculiarly affecting to the Jews in Babylon.

28. *And they joined themselves to Baal Peor, and ate the sacrifices of the dead.* He now adds a sin committed near the end of the long error, and on the very borders of the Promised Land. The first verb is properly passive, *they were joined*, but this of course does not mean by others but themselves, and thus the simple passive comes to have a reflexive meaning. Baal Peor is the name given to Baal, or the supreme God of the Tyrians and Moabites, as he was worshipped, with licentious rites, at Peor, a mountain in the land of Moab. See Num. xxv. 1—3. *The dead*, not dead men, in allusion to necromantic superstitions, but the dumb or lifeless gods whom they worshipped. See below, on Ps. cxv. 4—7, and compare 1 Cor. xii. 2.

29. *And they provoked him by their crimes, and the plague broke out among them.* The first verb means to excite both grief and indignation. Compare the use of the cognate noun in Ps. vi. 8 (7), and of the verb itself in Ps. lxxviii. 58. The word translated *plague*, like its English equivalent, has both a generic and specific meaning; that of a divine stroke or infliction in general,

and that of a pestilential disease in particular. See Num. xxv. 18, 19.

30. *Then stood up Phinehas and judged, and* (so) *was stayed the plague.* He *stood* (or *rose*) *up* from among the rest, presented himself before the people. He *judged* i. e. assumed the office and discharged the duty, from which the regular official judges seemed to shrink. The verb includes the act both of pronouncing and of executing judgment. See the narrative in Num. ch. xxv. The form of expression in the last clause is borrowed from Num. xvii. 13 (xvi. 48.)

31. *And it was reckoned to him for righteousness, to generation and generation, even to eternity.* The form of expression is borrowed from Gen. xv. 6; but what is here meant is evidently not a justifying act by which Phinehas was saved, but a praiseworthy act for which he, a justified or righteous man already, received the divine commendation and a perpetual memorial of his faithfulness. Compare Deut. vi. 25. xxiv. 13. The particular reward promised (Num. xxv. 13), that of a perpetual priesthood, is not here mentioned, but was familiar to the mind of every Hebrew reader.

32. *And they angered* (him) *at the waters of Strife, and it went ill with Moses, on their account.* See above, on Ps. lxxxi. 8 (7) xcv. 8. xcix. 8. The Hebrew word for *strife* is the name given to the place, *Meribah.* The object of the first verb is *Jehovah,* as in v. 29. *It went ill with Moses,* or, more literally, *it was bad for Moses.*

33. *For they resisted his spirit, and he spake unadvisedly with his lips. His spirit* may grammatically signify either that of God or that of Moses. The latest writers are in favour of the first construction, which is not without analogies in other parts of

Scripture (Isai. lxiii. 10. Eph. iv. 30), but the other seems entitled to the preference in this connection, because the first clause then contains the ground or reason of the other. It was because the mind of Moses was excited by their opposition, that he spake unadvisedly with his lips. The last verb is one used in the law to denote a precipitate inconsiderate engagement, Lev. v. 4.

34. *They did not destroy the nations which the Lord said to them.* The confession now passes from the sins of the wilderness to those of Canaan. The neglect to destroy the Canaanites completely was not only a direct violatiom of God's precept, but the source of nearly all the public evils that ensued. There is no need of giving to the last verb a rare and dubious sense (*commanded.)* The meaning of the clause is, *which Jehovah said to them* (must be destroyed.)

35. *And they mixed themselves with the nations and learned their doings.* The reflexive verb at the beginning indicates an active and deliberate amalgamation, as distinguished from a passive and involuntary one. *The nations* of the Canaanites, and those which inhabited surrounding countries. The primary idea is not that of *gentiles* or *heathen*, in the religious sense. *Learned their doings* or *practices*, learned to do as they did. With the first clause compare Jos. xxiii. 12, 13. Judg. iii. 6; with the second, Deut. xviii. 9. xx. 18.

36. *And served their idols, and they were to them for a snare.* The word translated *idols*, by its etymological affinities, suggests the idea of vexations, pains. See above, on Ps. xvi. 4. *A snare*, i. e. a temptation to idolatry. Compare Deut. vii. 16.

37. *And they sacrificed their sons and their daughters to the demons.* This last is the Septuagint version and, if not directly sanctioned, is at least referred to in the New Testament (1 Cor.

x. 20.) That the worship of idols was connected with that of fallen spirits, is neither improbable in itself nor contradictory to Scripture. According to the modern etymologists, the Hebrew word means *lords* or *masters*, and is a poetical equivalent to Baalim, which means the same thing. Compare Deut. xxxii. 17, and the κύριοι of 1 Cor. viii. 5. The word translated *devils* in Lev. 17. 7 is entirely different.

38. *And they shed innocent blood, the blood of their sons and daughters, which they sacrificed to the idols of Canaan; and defiled was the land with bloods.* The first verb means to pour out and here implies a copious or abundant bloodshed, corresponding to the next verb, which is an intensive form of that used in v. 37. *Blood*, in the singular, is used in a physical sense; the plural *bloods* in a moral one, always implying guilt, and especially the guilt of murder. See above, on Ps. v. 7 (6.) xxvi. 9. li. 16 (14.) lv. 24 (23.) The first three members of the sentence have respect to the prohibitions in Deut. xii. 31. xviii. 10. xix. 10. With the last clause compare Num. xxxv. 33.

39. *And they were polluted by their own doings, and went a whoring by their own crimes.* They defiled not only the land of promise but themselves. Or rather, this verse is explanatory of the last clause of v. 38, and shows that the pollution of the land was nothing more nor less than that of its inhabitants. The figure of spiritual whoredom or adultery is often used to signify the violation, by the chosen people, of their covenant with God, which is constantly described as a conjugal relation. See above, on Ps. xlv and compare Ps. lxxiii. 27. This is not stated as an additional offence but as an aggravating circumstance attending the iniquities already mentioned.

40. *And the anger of Jehovah was enkindled at his people, and he abhorred his heritage.* This is the strongest form in which his

detestation of their sins could be expressed, but does not necessarily imply the abrogation of his covenant with them. The feeling described is like that of a parent towards his wicked children, or of husbands and wives, who do not cease to love each other, though grieved and indignant at each other's sins. The word *heritage* adds great point to the sentence. He abhorred the very people whom he had chosen to be his, not merely for a single generation, but for many. See above, on Ps. lxxviii. 59, 62.

41. *And he gave them into the hand of nations, and over them ruled their haters.* The same nations whom they had rebelliously spared, with others of like spirit—the same nations who had led them into sin—were used as instruments of punishment. Compare Lev. xxvi. 17. Judges ii. 14.

42. *And their enemies oppressed them, and they were bowed down under their hand.* They not only governed them, but governed them tyrannically, so that they were not only under coercion and constraint, but humbled and degraded from the rank of an independent state to that of tributaries and bondsmen. With the terms of this verse compare Judg. i. 34. iii. 30. iv. 3. viii. 28.

43. *Many times he frees them, and they resist* (him) *by their counsel, and are brought low by their guilt.* Having given in the preceding verses a brief but lively summary of the Book of Judges, the Psalmist now passes, by an almost insensible transition, to the later periods of the history, and indeed to its catastrophe; for the meaning of the last clause seems to be, that after all their fluctuations, they at length sink or fall into a ruinous condition, as the ultimate fruit of their rebellions. The meaning of the first clause is, that by their self-willed plans and projects they continually come into collision with the will of God, and with that great providential purpose, in promoting which it was

their duty, and would have been their happiness, to co-operate. With the last clause compare Lev. xxvi. 39. Ezek. xxxiii. 10.

44. *And he has looked at their distress when he heard them cry.* The idiomatic form of the original may thus be represented by a bald translation, *and he saw in the distress to them in his hearing their cry.* As this follows the brief statement of their downfall, there is much probability in the opinion, that it relates to the "tokens for good," which were granted to the exiled Jews in Babylon long before their actual restoration. With the first clause compare Ex. ii. 25. iv. 31. Deut. iv. 30. Ps. xviii. 7. cii. 3.

45. *And he has remembered for them his covenant, and repented according to the abundance of his mercy.* For them, i. e. in their favour, for their benefit. It does not qualify *covenant*, but *remembered.* With the first clause compare Lev. xxvi. 42, 45. Ps. cv. 8, 42; with the second, Num. xiv. 19. Ps. v. 8 (7.) lxix. 14 (13.) Neh. xiii. 22. The common version of the last word (*mercies*) rests upon the marginal or masoretic reading; the more ancient text is *mercy.*

46. *And has given them favour before all their captors.* The literal translation of the first clause is, *and has given them for mercies* or *compassions.* This remarkable expression is borrowed from 1 Kings viii. 50 (compare 2 Chr. xxx. 9), not only here but in the history of Daniel and his fellow-captives (Dan. i. 9), which makes it not at all improbable, that what is there recorded is among the indications of returning divine favour here referred to by the Psalmist.

47. *Save us, Jehovah, our God, and gather us from the nations, to give thanks unto thy holy name, to glory in thy praise.* Encouraged by these tokens of returning favour, the church prays that the hopes thus raised may not be disappointed, but abundantly

fulfilled in the restoration of the exiles to their own land, in return for which she indirectly engages to render praise and thanksgiving to Jehovah as her liberator. We are thus brought back to the beginning of the psalm, and the voice of confession is again lost in that of anticipated praise. Instead of *our God*, the parallel passage (1 Chr. xvi. 36) has *God of our Salvation.* The word translated *glory* occurs only in that passage and the one before us. It is synonymous, however, with the one used in Ps. cv. 3, and often elsewhere, both meaning properly to praise one's self. With the second clause compare Ps. xxx. 5 (4.)

48. *Blessed* (be) *Jehovah, God of Israel, from eternity even to eternity. And all the people says Amen. Hallelujah!* Some interpreters regard the psalm as closing with the preceding verse, and the one before us as a doxology added to mark the conclusion of the Fourth Book. But here, as in Ps. lxxii. 19, it is far more probable that this doxology was the occasion of the psalm's being reckoned as the last of a Book, notwithstanding its intimate connection with the one that follows. This probability is strengthened, in the case before us, by the addition of the words, *and all the people says Amen*, which would be unmeaning, unless the doxology formed part of the psalm itself. The additional words are borrowed from Deut. xxvii. 15—26. The parallel passage (1 Chr. xvi. 36) has, *And all the people said Amen and give praise* (or *gave praise*) *to Jehovah*, which last words are represented, in the verse before us, by the *Hallelujah* (*Praise ye Jah!*)

PSALM CVII.

After propounding as his theme the goodness of God in delivering his people, and especially in bringing them back from their dispersions, vs. 1—3, the Psalmist celebrates this great event, under the various figures of safe conduct through a desert and arrival in a populous city, vs. 4—9; emancipation from imprisonment, vs. 10—16; recovery from deadly sickness, vs. 17—22; deliverance from the dangers of the sea, vs. 23—32; then describes, in more direct terms, the fall of the oppressor, the restoration of Israel, and his happy prospects, vs. 33—42; ending, as he began, with an earnest exhortation to remember and commemorate Jehovah's goodness, v. 43. The psalm is so constructed as to admit of being readily applied, either literally or figuratively, to various emergencies; but its primary reference to the return from exile seems to be determined by vs. 2, 3. According to Hengstenberg's hypothesis, this psalm was added to the double trilogy by which it is preceded (Ps. 101—106), immediately after the return from exile, when the holy city was re-peopled, and the first harvest had been gathered, but the rebuilding of the temple had not yet begun. The whole seven then compose one series or system, intended to be used together in the public worship of the ancient church.

1. *Give thanks unto Jehovah, for he* (*is*) *good, for unto eternity* (*is*) *his mercy.* The repetition of the first words of the foregoing psalm, as the beginning of the one before us, strongly favours the

opinion, that the latter was designed to be a kind of supplement or appendix to the former.

2. (So) *say the Redeemed of Jehovah, whom he has redeemed from the hand of distress* (or *of the enemy.*) What they are to say is not the exhortation in the first clause, but the reason for it in the last clause, of the foregoing verse. Let them acknowledge his unceasing mercy, who have just experienced so remarkable a proof of it. The ambiguous word (צר) should probably be taken in the same sense which it elsewhere has throughout this psalm. See below, vs. 6, 13, 19, 28, and compare Ps. cvi. 44. Indeed the two senses may be reconciled by simply supposing the distress to be personified. Compare the unambiguous expression in Ps. cvi. 10. The *Redeemed of the Lord* is a favourite expression of Isaiah (xxxv. 9, 10. lxii. 12. lxiii. 3.)

3. *And from the lands has gathered them, from the east and from the west, from the north and from the sea.* The Babylonish exile is continually spoken of as a dispersion, either because it is considered as including other minor deportations, or because the migration of the great mass of the people into Babylonia was unavoidably accompanied, followed, or preceded, by a less extensive and more scattering migration of many individuals and families to other quarters. On the false assumption of a perfect parallelism as indispensable, some have supposed that *sea* is here put for the *south.* But this is not the only case in which the enumeration of the cardinal points is complete only in number. See Isai. xlix. 12, and compare Isai. xliii. 5, 6. lvi. 8. The mention of the sea instead of the south may perhaps have reference to the prophecy in Deut. xxviii. 68. The verse before us records the answer to the prayer in Ps. cvi. 47, and thus affords another indication, that the writer of the later composition had the earlier in his eye, and wrote with some intention to illustrate or complete it.

4. *They wandered in the wilderness, in a desert way; a city of habitation found they not.* Here begins the first metaphorical account of the Captivity and Restoration, in which the exiles are described as wanderers in a *desert way*, i. e. as some suppose a pathless desert, which sense, however, can scarcely be extracted from the Hebrew words. Others understand the phrase to mean a way, i. e. a course, a region to be traversed, which is desert; but this supposes *way* to be the subject and *desert* the qualifying term, as they would be in English, but in Hebrew the precise sense is a *desert of way*, or a *way-desert*, which some interpreters explain to mean a desert in reference to its ways or paths, thus arriving, by a different course, at the meaning first suggested, namely, that of a pathless wilderness. *City of habitation* may mean a habitable or inhabited city in general, or a city for them to inhabit in particular. The latter is more probable, because the word translated *habitation* is not an abstract but a local noun, meaning the place where men sit or dwell, according to the primary and secondary meaning of the verbal root. See above, on Ps. i. 1. It may here be either governed by *city*, as above, or in apposition with it, *a city, a dwelling-place*, i. e. a city in which they might dwell. There is obvious allusion to Jerusalem, as well as to the great Arabian wilderness, although the contrast of the city and the desert suggests the idea of suffering and relief, by a natural as well as a historical association. See Ez. xxix. 5, and compare Job xii. 24.

5. *Hungry—also thirsty—their soul in them shrouds itself.* This verse continues the description of the wanderers in the desert. To avoid the ambiguity of an exact version, in which *hungry* and *thirsty* might seem to agree with soul, the substantive verb may be supplied in the first clause, (*they are*) *hungry, also thirsty.* The primary sense of the reflexive verb at the end of the sentence seems to be that of covering one's self with darkness, or sinking overwhelmed beneath some great calamity. See above,

on Ps. lxxvii. 4 (3), and compare the cognate forms in Ps. lxi. 3 (2.) lxv. 14 (13.) cii. i. Isai. lvii. 16.

6. *And they cried to Jehovah in their distress ; from their straits he frees them.* Both the nouns, according to their etymology, convey the idea of pressure, compression, painful restraint. *In their distress*, literally, *in the distress to them*, that which they had or suffered. See above, on Ps. cvi. 44, and compare Deut. iv. 30. The change from the past tense to the future seems intended merely to describe the act denoted by the second as more recent.

7. *And he led them in a straight course, to go to a city of habitation.* No exact version can preserve or imitate the paronomasia arising from the etymological affinity of the first verb and noun, analogous to that between the English *walk* and *to walk*, though the Hebrew forms are only similar and not identical. The idea of physical rectitude or straightness necessarily suggests that of moral rectitude or honesty, commonly denoted by the Hebrew word.

8. *Let* (such) *give thanks to Jehovah* (*for*) *his mercy, and his wonderful works to the sons of man.* Some interpreters make this the close of a long sentence, beginning with v. 4, and adopt, in all the intervening verses, a relative construction, as if he had said, let such as wandered in the wilderness, whose soul fainted in them, who cried unto the Lord, whom he led etc. let such give thanks unto his name. But although this is certainly the logical connection of the passage, its involution and complexity of form are as far as possible removed from the simplicity of Hebrew syntax, which prefers a distinct enunciation of particulars to all such artificial combinations. This verse constitutes the burden or chorus of the psalm.

9. *For he has satisfied the craving soul, and the hungry soul*

has filled with good. This is merely the conclusion of the first scene or picture, with a change of figure but a very slight one, as the want of food is one of the most painful and familiar hardships of a journey through a desert, and as such would necessarily occur to every Israelite who knew the story of the error in the wilderness. The first verb has the same sense as in Ps. civ. 13; the last noun the same sense as in Ps. ciii. 4. civ. 28. The unusual word translated *craving* is borrowed from Isai. xxix. 8.

10. *Dwelling in darkness and deathshade, bound in affliction and iron.* Here begins the second picture which exhibits the same sufferers, no longer as wanderers in the desert, but as closely confined prisoners. The *darkness* primarily meant is that of the dungeon, but not without reference to the frequent use of darkness in general as an emblem of misery. See above, on Ps. lxviii. 7 (6.) The idea of darkness is then expressed in a still stronger form by the striking compound *deathshade* or shadow of death, a bold but beautiful description of the most profound obscurity. See above, on Ps. xxiii. 4. The leading words of the two clauses might, in one respect, be more exactly rendered, *inhabitants of darkness, prisoners of affliction.* See above, on Ps. lxxviii. 61. There is no mixture of literal and figurative terms in the last clause, but only the addition of a specific to a general term. The *affliction* particularly meant is that produced by *iron*, i. e. chains or fetters. See above, on Ps. cv. 18, and with the verse before us compare Isai. xlii. 7. xlix. 9. Job xxxvi. 8. Luke xiii. 16.

11. *Because they resisted the words of the Mightiest, and the counsel of the Highest contemned.* This verse introduces what was wanting in the first scene, the fact that these were not innocent sufferers. However cruel or unjust their sufferings at the hands of men, they were but condign punishments as sent by God. This is a point of contact and resemblance with the preceding

psalm, which is not without importance. *Resisted*, rebelled against, a favourite expression in these psalms. See above, on Ps. cv. 28. cvi. 7, 33, 43. *Words* or *sayings*, commonly applied to promises, and even here combining that idea with the sense of command, because the command which they resisted or rebelled against had reference to the plan or *counsel* of the Lord for the deliverance of his people. The word translated *mightiest* is (אֵל) one of the divine names, here represented by an English superlative, in order to preserve the antithesis with *Most High* in the other clause.

12. *And he brought down, with trouble, their heart; they stumbled and there was no helper.* The remedial design and effect of their punishment are beautifully set forth in the first clause. The word translated *trouble* means originally work or labour, then the pain attending it or flowing from it. *Stumbled* may here be put for *fell*, or have the milder sense of tottering or stumbling, as distinguished from a total fall. *No helper*, or *none helping*, except God, as intimated in the next verse; or against God, when he chose to punish them.

13. *And they cried to Jehovah in their distress; out of their straits he saves them.* An exact repetition of v. 6, except that the first verb is exchanged for a cognate one, differing only in a single letter, and the last verb for a synonyme still more familiar. As to the consecution of the tenses, see above, on v. 6.

14. *He brings them out from darkness and deathshade, and their bonds he severs.* The terms used in describing the deliverance are studiously made to correspond with the account of the captivity in v. 10. It is more remarkable, though possibly fortuitous, that the words of the second clause are the same which David puts into the mouth of the revolted nations, Ps. ii. 3. The English word *severs* is here used instead of *breaks*, in order to represent the more uncommon and poetical term used in Hebrew.

15, 16. *Let* (such) *give thanks unto Jehovah* (*for*) *his mercy, and his wonderful works to the sons of man, because he has broken doors of brass, and bars of iron has cut asunder.* The burden in v. 15 is in all respects identical with v. 8, but the supplementary verse differs, according to the prominent figures in the two scenes or pictures. As the idea of famine was selected, in v. 9, from among the hardships of the wilderness, so here the fastenings of the prison are presented in precisely the same manner. In this striking regularity of form, combined with vividness and beauty of conception, there is evidence of art and skill as well as genius. The verb in the first clause of v. 16 is an intensive form of the verb to *break*, and might here be rendered *shattered*, *shivered*, or the like. The corresponding verb in the last clause is a similar intensive of the verb to *cut*. The whole verse is copied from Isai. xlv. 2, where we find the promise, of which this is the fulfilment.

17. *Fools by their course of transgression, and by their crimes, afflict themselves.* Here begins the third scene or picture, at the very opening of which the charge of folly is added to the previous one of guilt. The reflexive meaning of the verb is essential and cannot be diluted into a mere passive, without weakening the whole sentence, the very point of which consists in making them the guilty authors of their own distresses. The word for transgression is the one that originally means revolt from God, apostasy. See above, on Ps. xxxvi. 2 (1.) *Course*, literally, way or path. *By*, literally, *from*, as when we speak of an effect as arising or proceeding from a cause.

18. *All food their soul abhors, and they draw near to the very gates of death.* This verse abruptly brings before us the same persons whom we lately beheld wandering in the desert, and then chained in a dark dungeon, now suffering from disease, such as not only mars their pleasures, but threatens to abbreviate their lives. Compare Ps. cii. 3. Job xxxiii. 20. The expression *very*

gates, in the translation of the last clause, is intended to convey the full force of the Hebrew preposition (עַד) which is stronger than (אֶל) *to*. See above, on Ps. lvii. 11 (10.) With the last clause compare Ps. ix. 14. lxxxviii. 4 (3.) Job. xxxiii. 22. Isai. xxxviii. 9.

19. *And they cry to Jehovah in their distress; out of their straits he saves them.* See above on vs. 6, 13, with the last of which this agrees exactly.

20. *He sends his word and heals them, and makes them escape from their destructions*, i. e. those which threatened them, and from which escape appeared impossible. *He sends his word*, he issues his command, exerts his sovereign power and authority. The last word in the Hebrew occurs only here and once in Lamentations (iv. 20.) The modern interpreters have *pits* or *graves;* but such a derivation from the verbal root is without example or analogy. See above, on Ps. xvi. 10. With the first clause compare Ps. xxx. 3 (2.) xxxiii. 9. Isai. lvii. 18; with the last Ps. ciii. 4.

21, 22. *Let* (such) *give thanks unto Jehovah* (for) *his mercy, and his wonderful works to the sons of man; and let them sacrifice sacrifices of thanksgiving, and recount his deeds with* (*joyful*) *singing*. The freedom from technical and artificial rules of rhetoric or versification, even in those parts of the composition which exhibit most of art and skill, is peculiarly observable in this verse, where, instead of adding to the uniform chorus or refrain some particular image from the scene just closing, as in vs. 9, 16, the Psalmist continues and completes the sentence by repeating the exhortation to give thanks, in another but still figurative form, derived from the musical and sacrificial customs of the temple worship. They must not only utter thanks but offer them in sacrifice. They must not only offer them in sacrifice but sing them. With the first clause compare Ps. l. 14.

23. *Going down the sea in ships, doing business in the many waters.* Here again the scene is shifted, and the exiles pass before us, not as wanderers in the desert, or as captives in the dungeon, or as suffering from sickness, but as mariners engaged in an adventurous voyage. *Descending, going down*, seems to be an idiomatic phrase, borrowed from Isai. xlii. 10, and equivalent to *going out* to sea in English. The expression may have reference to the general elevation of the land above the water (see above, on Ps. xxiv. 2), but is directly opposite to our phrase, *the high seas*, and to the classical usage of *ascending* ships, i. e. embarking, and *descending*, i. e. landing. *Doing business* has its ordinary sense, as applied to trade or traffic. The last words may also be translated *great* or *mighty* waters; but the usage of the Psalms is in favour of the version *many waters*, which moreover forms a beautiful poetical equivalent to *sea* or *ocean*. This image could not fail to suggest, however indirectly, the idea of the world with its commotions, of which the constant emblem is the sea. See above, on Ps. xlvi. 4 (3.) lxv. 8 (7.) lxxxix. 10 (9.) xciii. 3, 4, and compare Matt. viii. 23—26. Mark iv. 36—41. Luke viii. 22—25.

24. THEY *saw the works of Jehovah, and his wonders in the deep.* The pronoun at the beginning is emphatic, (it is) *they* (that) *see* (or *saw*) *the works of the Lord*, as if others could lay claim to no such privilege or honour. Both the senses of the phrase *God's works* are appropriate in this connection, his works of creation and his works of providence. The last word is another poetical equivalent to *sea* or *ocean*. See above, on Ps. lxix. 3 (2.)

25. *And he said—and there arose a stormy wind, and it lifted up his waves.* He now parenthetically specifies some of the divine

works which he had just mentioned in the general. The form of expression at the beginning, as in all like cases, involves an allusion to the history of the creation, where each creative act is preceded by God's saying, *let it be.* So here, the full sense is, *and God said* (let a stormy wind arise) *and a stormy wind arose.* See above, on Ps. xxxiii. 9. *Arose,* literally, stood, stood up, as in Ps. cvi. 30. A *stormy wind,* literally, a wind of storm or tempest. Instead of *his waves* we may read *its waves,* and refer the pronoun to the remoter antecedent (*sea*) in v. 23. *Deep,* in v. 24, is of a different gender. It is equally correct, however, and more natural, to refer it to Jehovah, as the maker of the sea and the ruler of its waves. Compare the expression *thy waves and thy billows* in Ps. xlii. 8. See also Isai. li. 15. Jer. xxxi. 35.

26. *They rise* (*to*) *the heavens ; they sink* (*to*) *the depths ; their soul with evil dissolves itself.* That the verbs in the first clause relate not to the waves but to the mariners, is evident from the last clause. The words *rise* and *sink* are used instead of *ascend, descend,* or *go up, go down,* because the Hebrew verbs have no etymological affinity, nor even a single letter common to their roots. The ellipsis of the preposition *to* is frequent, or rather verbs of motion in Hebrew may be construed directly with a noun, where our idiom requires the intervention of a particle. *Evil* in the last clause may denote their evil state or painful situation, with all the circumstances comprehended in it ; or more specifically, their distress and painful feelings. Compare Gen. xli. 29. The reflexive form of the last verb is not essential to the meaning of the sentence, as in v. 17, and may therefore be explained as an intensive or emphatic passive, *it is melted.* See above, on Ps. xxii. 15 (14.) With the whole verse compare Ps. civ. 8.

27. *They reel and stagger like a drunken* (*man*), *and all their wisdom is confounded.* By *wisdom* we are here to understand

reason, common sense, that which makes men rational and raises them above the brutes. This is plain from the comparison with drunkenness, the only point of which must be the loss of reason. The reeling and staggering may relate to the irregular and violent motion of a vessel in a storm, or, as the last clause does, to the mariners themselves. The last verb literally means *is swallowed up*, or retaining the reflexive form, still more strongly, *swallows itself up*. But see above, on the last word of v. 26.

28. *And they cried to Jehovah in their distress, and out of their straits he brings them forth.* The consecution of the tenses corresponds to the relation of the acts which they denote, as viewed by a spectator. 'Now they have cried to the Lord, and now he is bringing them forth.' The verse differs from vs. 13, 19, in the first verb, which agrees with v. 6, and in the last verb which is unlike both.

29. *He stills the storm to a calm, and silent are their waves.* This is an amplification of the last phrase in v. 28, and shows how it is that *he brings them forth.* The first verb strictly means *he makes it stand*, but in a sense directly opposite to that of a synonymous though different verb in v. 25. *Calm*, literally, silence, stillness. *Their waves*, the waves from which they suffer, by which they are buffeted. Compare *his waves* in v. 25.

30. *And they are glad that they are quiet, and he guides them to their desired haven.* The connection might be rendered clearer by translating with the English Bible, *then are they glad, etc.* The last word in the verse occurs only here, and is by some translated *shore*, by others *goal;* but it is safer to retain the old interpretation, which affords a perfectly good sense, and rests upon the joint authority of the Rabbinical tradition and the Septuagint version.

31, 32. *Let* (such) *give thanks to Jehovah (for) his mercy, and his wonderful works to the sons of man ; and let them exalt him in the congregation of the people, and in the session of the elders praise him.* Here again we have a striking instance of variety combined with uniformity. The burden or chorus, as in v. 22, is followed by a solemn exhortation to connect the required thanksgiving with the forms of public worship. But instead of the temple with its sacrifices and its chants, the reference in this case, it should seem, is to the spiritual worship of the synagogue. The word translated *congregation* is one constantly applied to Israel, as actually gathered at the place of worship. See above, on Ps. xxii. 23 (22.) The word *session* is employed in the translation of the last clause, not for the sake of a verbal coincidence with Presbyterian institutions, a coincidence however which is not to be denied, but because it adequately represents the Hebrew (מוֹשַׁב) in its double acceptation, as denoting both the act and the place of sitting, and especially of sitting together. See above, on v. 4. The *elders*, here as elsewhere, are the heads of tribes and families, the hereditary chiefs and representatives of Israel.

33. *He turns streams into a wilderness, and springs of water to a thirsty place.* As the shifting of the scene is not renewed in the remainder of the psalm, which, on the other hand, if viewed as a distinct and independent portion of the poem, mars its symmetry of structure, it seems best to regard these verses as an episode belonging to the last scene and containing the praises of the people and their elders. The figures in this verse are often used, particularly by Isaiah, to denote an entire revolution, whether physical or moral, social or political. Compare Isai. xliv. 26, 27. l. 2. Jer. l. 38. li. 36. It thus prepares the way for the subsequent rejoicings in the downfall of Babylon and the restoration of the exiled Jews.

34. *A fruitful land to saltness, for the wickedness of those dwelling in it.* The sentence is continued from the foregoing verse, the nouns being governed by the verb *he turns*. The first phrase literally means a *land of fruit*. The next noun may be taken either in the abstract sense of *saltness* or the concrete one of a *saline soil* or *region*, and by implication barren. *For*, literally *from*, as in v. 17 above. Compare the threatening in Isai. xiii. 19, and the great historical type of all such judgments, the destruction of Sodom and Gomorrah.

35. *He turns a desert to a pool of water, and a dry land into springs of water*. This is the reverse of the description in v. 33, to which the terms are studiously conformed. In both cases the first verb literally means *he sets* or *puts*, and the noun translated *springs* means issues or places where the waters issue. Compare Isai. xxxv. 7. xli. 18. xliii. 20.

36. *And has settled there famished* (*men*), *and they have established a city to dwell in*. There is no need of assuming, that the desert thus transformed is Palestine or Canaan. It is better to adhere to the general import of the figures, which is change for the better. *Settled*, literally, caused to dwell. The primary meaning of the last clause is that those once homeless have a home; but there is of course a reference to the repossession and rebuilding of Jerusalem. The last phrase in Hebrew is the same with that translated *city of habitation* in v. 4.

37. *And have sowed fields, and planted vineyards, and made fruits of increase*. The form of all these verbs requires them to be understood, like those of v. 36, as referring to time actually past, from which some have inferred that the date of the psalm itself lay between the first ingathering of the fruits by the returned Jews and the founding of the temple, to which there is here no allusion. The word translated *increase* is applied elsewhere to

the annual productions of the earth. See Lev. xxv. 16. To *make* these is to gain or acquire them by cultivation, as we speak of *making* money, but of *raising* corn. See above, on Ps. lx. 14 (12.)

38. *And he has blessed them, and they have increased greatly, and* (even) *their cattle he does not diminish. Increased*, not in numbers merely, but in wealth, strength, and prosperity. See Deut. xxx. 16. The verb to *diminish* is borrowed from Lev. xxvi. 22. The negation may be understood as a *meiosis*, meaning to increase or multiply. The whole of this description agrees well with the encouraging appearances, by which the Restoration was attended and immediately followed, before the colony experienced reverses or had lost the fresh impression of their recent sufferings and privations, which are mentioned in the next verse.

39. *And they were diminished and brought low, from oppression, suffering, and grief.* The only grammatical construction of the verbs is that which refers them to a former time, i. e. to the condition of the people under Babylonian oppression. The sense is therefore quite mistaken in the English, though correctly given in the ancient versions. The contrast is intended to enhance the joy and thankfulness of the restored exiles. These, now so prosperous, are the very men who lately were in abject misery.

40. *Pouring contempt on princes—and he has made them wander in a waste* (where there is) *no way.* From the exiles he reverts to their Deliverer, and describes him as spurning the most lordly of their persecutors—nay as making them take the place of those whom they oppressed, which idea is conveyed by the figure before used of wanderers in a pathless desert. See above, on v. 4, and compare Job. xii. 21, 24. The word for *waste* or *void* is one of those used in Gen. i. 2, to describe the original condition of the earth.

41. *And has raised the poor from affliction, and made like a flock families.* The first verb suggests the two-fold idea of elevation from a wretched state, and security from future danger. For its ordinary sense, see above, on Ps. xx. 2 (1.) xci. 14. The last clause simply means, he has increased the people who were so reduced in strength and numbers.

42. *The righteous shall see and rejoice, and all iniquity stop her mouth.* The righteous are the true Israel, as in Ps. xxxiii. 1. Num. xxiii. 10. Dan. xi. 17. With the last clause compare Job v. 16. Isai lii. 15.

43. *Who (is) wise and will observe these things, and attentively consider the mercies of Jehovah?* The change of number in the Hebrew does not affect the meaning. *Whoever is* wise will observe these things, and *all who are* wise will consider them. With this conclusion compare Hos. xiv. 10. Isai. xlii. 23. Jer. ix. 11.

PSALM CVIII.

1. *A Song. A Psalm. By David.* This is not an original or independent composition, but a compilation from two other psalms, which have already been explained. The introduction, vs. 2—6 (1—5) is substantially identical with Ps. lvii. 8—12 (7—11) ; the body of the psalm, vs. 7—13 (6—12), with Ps. lx. 7—14 (5—12.) The supposition of erroneous copies, or of later corruptions, is still more improbable in this case than in those of Ps. xviii, liii, lxx. The best solution which has been

proposed is, that David himself combined these passages to be the basis of a trilogy (Ps. cviii—cx), adapted to the use of the church at a period posterior to the date of Ps. lvii. and lx. The comments here will be confined to the variations, as in Ps. liii and lxx.

2 (1.) *Fixed is my heart, oh God, fixed is my heart; I will sing and play—also my glory.* See above, on Ps. lvii. 8 (7.) The words here added, *also my glory*, correspond to the first clause of the next verse in that psalm, *awake my glory!*

3 (2.) *Awake lute and harp! I will awaken the dawn* (or *morning*.) See above, on Ps. lvii. 9 (8.) The only variation is the one already mentioned, the omission here of the words *awake my glory*, for which the last clause of v. 2 (1) is a substitute.

4 (3.) *I will thank thee among the nations, oh Jehovah, I will praise thee among the peoples.* See above, on Ps. lvii. 10 (9.) The only variation is the substitution of the name *Jehovah* for *Adhonai*, a change scarcely perceptible in the English versions.

5 (4.) *For great from above the heavens (is) thy mercy, and unto the clouds thy truth.* See above, on Ps. lvii. 11 (10.) The only variation is the change of (עַד) *unto* into (מֵעַל) *from above*, apparently intended to suggest the idea of God's mercy as descending upon man.

6 (5.) *Be thou high above the heavens, oh God, and above all the earth thy glory.* See above, on Ps. lvii. 12 (11.) The only variation is the introduction of the copulative *and* at the beginning of the second clause.

7 (6.) *In order that thy beloved (ones) may be delivered, save with thy right hand, and hear* (or *answer*) *us.* See above, on

Ps. lx. 7 (5), with which this verse agrees in all points, not excepting the keri or various reading in the last word (*me* for *us*.)

8 (7.) *God hath spoken in his holiness* (and therefore) *I will triumph, I will divide Shechem, and the valley of Succoth I will measure.* See above, on Ps. lx. 8 (6), with which this verse agrees exactly.

9 (8.) *To me* (belongs) *Gilead, to me Manasseh, and Ephraim the strength of my head, Judah my lawgiver.* See above, on Ps. lx. 9 (7.) The only variation is the omission, in the verse before us, of the *and* after *Gilead.*

10 (9.) *Moab* (*is*) *my wash-pot; at Edom will I throw my shoe; over Philistia will I shout aloud.* See above, on Ps. lx. 10 (8.) At the end of this verse is the most material variation in the whole psalm, which, however, is evidently not fortuitous or by a later hand, but intentional and made by the original writer. *I will shout aloud*, as an expression of triumph over a conquered enemy.

11 (10.) *Who will bring me* (*to*) *the fortified city? Who leads* (or *has led*) *me up to Edom?* See above on Ps. lx. 11 (9.) The only variation is the change of one synonymous word for another, to express the idea of a fortified city.

12 (11.) (Is it) *not God, who hast cast us off, and wilt not go forth with our hosts?* See above on Ps. lx. 12 (10.) The only variation consists in the omission of the emphatic pronoun *thou*, which is expressed in the parallel passage, and only implied in the one before us. Some interpreters suppose a sudden change of construction from the third to the second person. *Is it not God*—(even thou who) *didst cast us off, etc.*

13 (12.) *Give us help from the enemy* (or from distress); *and*

(the rather because) *vain is the salvation of man*, meaning that which he affords. See above, on Ps. lx. 13 (11), which agrees with this exactly.

14 (13.) *In God we will make* (i. e. gain or gather) *strength, and he will tread down* (or *trample on*) *our adversaries* (persecutors or oppressors.) See above, on Ps. lx. 14 (12), between which and the verse before us there is not the slightest difference.

PSALM CIX.

This psalm consists of three parts; a complaint of slanderous and malignant enemies, vs. 1—5; a prayer for the punishment of such, vs. 6—20; and a prayer for the sufferer's own deliverance, with a promise of thanksgiving, vs. 21—31. According to the theory repeatedly referred to, this is the second psalm of a Davidic trilogy. See above, on Ps. cviii. This psalm is remarkable on two accounts; first, as containing the most striking instances of what are called the imprecations of the psalms; and then, as having been applied in the most explicit manner to the sufferings of our Saviour from the treachery of Judas, and to the miserable fate of the latter. These two peculiarities are perhaps more closely connected than they may at first sight seem. Perhaps the best solution of the first is that afforded by the second, or at least by the hypothesis, that the Psalmist, under the direction of the Spirit, viewed the sufferings of Israel, which furnished the occasion of the psalm, as a historical type of the Messiah's sufferings from the treachery of Judas, representing that of

Judah, and that with this view he expresses his abhorrence of the crime, and acquiesces in the justice of its punishment, in stronger terms than would have been, or are elsewhere, employed in reference to ordinary criminals.

1. *To the Chief Musician. By David. A Psalm. God of my praise, be not silent.* The first inscription was particularly necessary here because the psalm might otherwise have seemed to be a mere expression of strong personal feeling. See above, on Ps. li. 1. *God of my praise*, i. e. the object of it, whom I delight, or am accustomed, or have cause, to praise. *Be not silent* means not merely *do not refuse to answer*, but amidst the threats and railings of my enemies, let thy voice be heard also. See above, on Ps. xxviii. 1. xxxv. 22. xxxix. 13. (12.)

2. *For a wicked mouth and a mouth of deceit they have opened; they have spoken against me with a tongue of falsehood.* Compare Ps. xxxv. 11. lv. 4 (3.) The subject of the first verb is his enemies, and not the nouns preceding, as the verb translated *open* is elsewhere always active. *Against me*, literally, *with me*, implying that they charged him falsely to his face, a circumstance remarkably fulfilled in Christ. See Matth. xxvi. 59.

3. *And with words of hatred they have compassed me, and have fought against me without cause.* See above, on Ps. xxxv. 20. xxxvi. 4 (3.)

4. *In return for my love they are my adversaries—and I (am) prayer.* The first word in Hebrew strictly means *instead* or *in lieu of*. The unusual expression at the end can only mean, I am all prayer, I do nothing but pray, which some understand to signify, I bear their persecution meekly and continue my devotions undisturbed by their calumnies and insults. But as the whole context is descriptive, not of the sufferer's behaviour but of his

enemies', a more probable sense is, I am forced to be continually praying for protection against them and deliverance from them.

5. *They lay upon me evil instead of good and hatred instead of love.* The first verb literally means *they set* or *place. Instead of* the good and the love which they owed me, or *in return* for my kindness and love to them, as in v. 4.

6. *Appoint thou over him a wicked one, and let an adversary stand upon his right hand.* The first verb in Hebrew means to place one in authority or charge over another. See Gen. xxxix. 5. xli. 34. Num. i. 50 and compare Lev. xxvi. 16. Jer. xv. 3. *Wicked one* and *adversary* (*Satan*), although here used as appellatives or common nouns, are the very terms applied, in the later scriptures, to the Evil Spirit or the Devil. See Job i. 6. ii. 1. 1 Chr. xxi. 1. Zech. iii. 1, 2. In the place last cited he stands too at the right hand of the sinner to accuse him. The change of number in the verse before us might, in conformity with usage, be explained as a mere difference of form, the ideal person denoted by the singular being really the type and representative of the whole class denoted by the plural. But the constancy with which the change, in this case, is adhered to, rather favours the conclusion, that a real individual is meant, to whom the Psalmist turns from the promiscuous crowd of his oppressors. For a similar transition, see above, on Ps. lv. 13 (12.)

7. *When he is tried he shall go forth guilty, and his prayer shall be for sin.* The future meaning of the second verb is determined by the form of the third, which is not apocopated, as in vs. 12, 13. *When he is tried*, literally, in his being tried. The next phrase simply means that he shall be condemned ; the last clause, that his very prayer for mercy shall be reckoned as a new offence, a strong description of extreme judicial rigour and inexorable justice.

8. *Let his days be few—his office let another take.* The word translated *office* is a collateral derivative of the verb at the beginning of v. 6, and means commission, charge. This expression makes it still more probable that a real individual is referred to, as the possession of a charge or office could not be common to the whole class of malignant enemies. The Septuagint version is ἐπισκοπήν, oversight or supervision, corresponding exactly to the meaning of the Hebrew verb in v. 6. This translation is retained in Acts i. 20, where the verse before us is expressly quoted by Peter, as "written in the book of Psalms," and applied to the case of Judas Iscariot.

9. *Let his sons be orphans and his wife a widow.* He here passes from the person of the criminal to the sufferings of those dependent on him. See Ex. xx. 5.

10. *And wander—wander—let his sons and beg, and seek* (their food) *from* (among) *their ruins.* The emphatic repetition of the first verb is expressed, in the English Bible, by a paraphrase, *let his children be continually vagabonds.* The last clause is extremely graphic, representing them as creeping forth in search of food from amidst the ruins of their habitations.

11. *Let a creditor entrap all he has, and strangers plunder* (the fruit of) *his labour.* The first noun originally means a lender, but in usage has the accessory sense of a hard creditor, an extortioner. The verb means to *lay a snare for*, as in Ps. xxxviii. 13 (12.) *Strangers*, not his natural heirs, not members of his family. See Deut. xxv. 5.

12. *Let there be no one to him extending mercy, and let there be no one showing favour to his orphans.* The verb translated *extend* literally means *draw out, prolong*, and is applied to the continued indulgence both of hostile and amicable feelings. See

above, on Ps. xxviii. 3. xxxvi. 11 (10.) lxxxv. 6 (5.) *Showing favour*, exercising mercy, as in Ps. xxxvii. 21.

13. *Let his posterity be cut off; in the next generation, blottea out be their name.* The word for posterity strictly means futurity, after part, or latter end. See above, Ps. xxxvii. 37, 38. *Cut off*, literally, for cutting off. *The next* or *after generation*, as in Ps. xlviii. 14 (13.) The plural pronoun *their* refers to the collective noun *posterity*.

14. *Let the guilt of his fathers be remembered by Jehovah, and his mother's sin not blotted out.* This is perhaps the most fearful imprecation in the psalm, as it extends the consequences of transgression, not merely to the children, who might naturally be expected to partake of them, but to the parents. It is not to be forgotten, however, that in all such cases, the personal guilt of the implicated parties is presupposed, and not inferred from their connection with the principals. *Remembered by* (literally *to*) *Jehovah*, which may possibly mean brought to his remembrance, recalled to mind by another, perhaps by the accuser before mentioned.

15. *Let them be before Jehovah always, and let him cut off from the earth their memory.* The subject of the first clause is the *guilt* and *sin* mentioned in the verse preceding. *Before Jehovah*, in his sight, an object of attention to him. See above, Ps. xc. 8. With the last clause compare Ps. ix. 7 (6.) xxxiv. 17 (16.)

16. *Because that he did not remember to do mercy, and persecuted an afflicted and poor man, and one smitten in heart, to kill (him.)* There is an antithesis between the *remember* of this verse and the *remembered* of v.14. Though he did not remember mercy, God remembers guilt. The last phrase, *to kill*, denotes both the design and the extent of the malignant persecution, whicb

was deadly or to death. The object of the persecution is the psalmist himself, or the ideal person whom he represents. See v. 22.

17. *And he loved a curse, and it has come (upon) him; and he delighted not in blessing, and it has removed far from him.* This verse contemplates the event as actually past. The optative meaning, given to the verbs in the English Bible, is as inconsistent with the form of the original as the future meaning given in the Prayer Book and the ancient versions.

18. *And he has put on cursing as his garment, and it has come like water into his inside, and like oil into his bones.* There is an obvious climax in this verse. That which is first described as the man's exterior covering, is then said to be within him, first as water, then as oil or fat, first in the vessels of his body, then in his very bones. The general idea is that the curse, which he denounced and endeavoured to inflict on others, has taken possession of himself, both within and without. Compare Num. v. 22, 24, 27. The first clause admits of a different construction, which would make it descriptive of the crime and not the punishment. He put on cursing as his garment, and (now) it has come, etc. This construction introduces an antithesis, and there by adds to the point of the sentence, and is also recommended by the analogy of v. 17.

19. *Let it be to him as a garment* (that) *he wears, and for a belt let him always gird it.* This is not a mere reiteration of the figure in the first clause of v. 18, but conveys the additional idea of a habitual and constant presence. The word *belt* is used in the translation of the last clause, because the Hebrew word to which it corresponds is not the usual derivative of the verb that follows, but etymologically unconnected with it.

20. *(Be) this the wages of my adversaries from Jehovah, and*

of those speaking evil against my soul. The pronoun *this* in the first clause refers to the whole preceding series of denunciations. The word translated *wages* means originally *work*, and secondarily the price or recompense of work or labour, and is so used in the law of Moses. See Lev. xix. 13. It is here peculiarly appropriate because it represents the misfortunes of his enemies as the direct fruit of their own misconduct. No single word in English can express this double meaning of the Hebrew. Such is their *work* and such their *wages*. The word translated *adversaries* is a cognate form to that used in v. 6, and might suggest the idea of *my Satans;* but this would probably convey too much. *From Jehovah,* their reward or recompense to be expected from him, or already bestowed by him. The description in the last clause includes insult, slander, and malicious plotting.

21. *And thou, Jehovah, Lord, do with me for thy name's sake, because good is thy mercy, set me free.* The emphatic *thou* at the beginning indicates a contrast between God and his oppressors. *Do with me* is a common English phrase meaning *deal with me, dispose of me;* but no such idiom exists in Hebrew, and the best authorities regard the construction as elliptical and make it mean, *do kindness* (or *shew mercy*) *to me.* With the last clause compare Ps. lxiii. 4 (3.) lxix. 17 (16.)

22. *For afflicted and poor (am) I, and my heart is wounded within me.* This, though indefinite in form, is equivalent to saying, I am the afflicted and poor man whom the malignant adversary persecuted, as was said in v. 16. The word translated *wounded* strictly means pierced or perforated, a stronger expression than the one in v. 16. With the first clause compare Ps. xl. 18 (17.) lxix. 30 (29.)

23. *Like a shadow at its turning I am gone; I am driven away like the locust.* The first comparison is the same with that

in Ps. cii. 12. Our idiom enables us to imitate the phrase *I am gone*, a passive which in Hebrew occurs only here. The other verb is rare, but its meaning is sufficiently determined by usage. The allusion here is to the violence with which a cloud of locusts in the east is scattered by the wind. Compare Ex. x. 19. Joel ii. 20. Nah. iii. 17.

24. *My knees totter from fasting, and my flesh fails from fatness.* The last phrase is obscure but seems to mean *from being fat*, so that it is not fat; the privative usage of the preposition being very common. The sense thus put upon the verb is justified by the analogy of Isai. lviii. 11, where an equivalent expression is applied to failing waters. Some interpreters, however, insist upon retaining the strict sense both of verb and noun, and understand the clause to mean, my flesh lies or deceives the eye, by no longer appearing as it once did, or by seeming to exist when it is gone, *from oil*, i. e. from want of oil, because no longer taken care of and anointed. But no construction could well be more forced and far-fetched. It may also be objected that the external use of oil was to anoint the head on festive occasions, not to fatten the person or preserve the flesh.

25. *And I have been a reproach to them, they see me, they shake their head.* A *reproach*, an object of contempt, as in Ps. xxii. 7 (6.) xxxi. 12 (11.) As to the meaning of the gesture mentioned in the last clause, see above, on Ps. xxii. 8 (7.)

26. *Help me, Jehovah, my God, save me, according to thy mercy.* The renewed description of his sufferings, in vs. 22—25, is followed by a renewed petition for deliverance, corresponding to that in v. 21. *According to thy mercy*, i. e. in proportion to its greatness and the freeness with which it is exercised.

27. *And they shall know that this (is) thy hand; thou, Jehovah,*

hast done it. The optative construction, *let them know*, and the subjunctive one, *that they may know*, are really involved in the more exact translation, *they shall know.* The subject of the verb may be men in general, or the persecuting adversaries in particular, more probably the latter, because they are referred to, both before and after. *This is thy hand*, i. e. this deliverance is the product of thy power. Compare Ps. lix. 14 (13.)

28. *They will curse, and thou wilt bless; they have risen up, and shall be shamed, and thy servant shall be glad.* The first clause, expressed in our idiom, would be, *they may curse but thou wilt bless. Risen up*, i. e. against me, a favourite expression in the Psalms. *Shamed*, in the pregnant sense of being disappointed, defeated, confounded. *Thy servant*, i. e. I as such, in that capacity or character.

29. *Clothed shall my adversaries be with confusion, and dressed, as a robe, in their shame.* This is not the mere expression of a wish, like that in v. 18, which would here be out of place, but a confident anticipation, with which he concludes the psalm. Compare Ps. lxxi. 13. The word translated *robe* denotes a garment reaching to the feet, and expresses therefore still more strongly the idea that his foes shall be completely covered with confusion

30. *I will thank Jehovah greatly with my mouth, and in the midst of many will I praise him.* He vows that his thanksgiving shall not be merely mental or domestic, but audible and public. With the last clause compare Ps. xxii. 23 (22.)

31. *For he will stand at the right hand of a poor (man), to save (him) from the judges of his soul.* This assigns the special reason of his promised praise. The verse is in strong contrast to v. 6 above, especially if *Satan* be there taken as a proper name. The right hand here is not the place of honour but of protection.

A poor man, as in v. 16, means *this poor man*, i. e. me a poor man. Compare Ps. xxxiv. 7 (6) The last clause is correctly paraphrased in the common version, *those that condemn his soul.*

PSALM CX.

THIS is the counterpart of the Second Psalm, completing the prophetic picture of the conquering Messiah. The progressive development of the Messianic doctrine lies in this, that the Kingship of Messiah, there alleged and confirmed by a divine decree, is here assumed at the beginning, and then shown to be connected with his Priesthood, which is also solemnly proclaimed, and its perpetuity ensured by a divine oath. This constitutes the centre of the psalm, v. 4, to which all the rest is either introductory, vs. 1—3, or supplementary, v. 5—7. The repeated, explicit, and emphatic application of this psalm, in the New Testament, to Jesus Christ, is so far from being arbitrary or at variance with the obvious import of the psalm itself, that any other application is ridiculous. The chief peculiarity of form is a frequent change of person, not unlike that in Ps. xci.

1. *By David. A Psalm. Thus saith Jehovah to my Lord, Sit thou at my right hand, until I make thine enemies thy footstool.* The ascription of the psalm to David is not only uncontradicted by external evidence, but corroborated by the internal character of the composition, its laconic energy, its martial tone, its triumphant confidence, and its resemblance to other undisputed psalms of David. In addition to all this, we have the authority of Christ himself, who not only speaks of it as David's, but founds an argument upon it, the whole force of which depends upon its having been composed by him. See Matt. xxii. 43.

Mark xii. 36. Luke xx. 42, and compare Acts ii. 34. As a further confirmation of the truth of this inscription, some allege the obvious relation of this psalm to those before it, as forming with them a Davidic trilogy. See above, on Ps. cviii. 1. *Thus saith Jehovah*, or more exactly, *a dictum* (or *saying*) *of Jehovah.* For the origin and usage of this formula, used only in prophetic declarations, see above on Ps. xxxvi. 2 (1.) *My Lord*, i. e. David's, as our Saviour explicitly declares in the passages already cited, yet not of David merely as a private person, nor even as an individual king, but as representing his own royal race and the house of Israel over which it reigned. The person thus described as the superior and sovereign of David and his house and of all Israel, could not possibly be David himself, nor any of his sons and successors except one, who, by virtue of his twofold nature, was at once his sovereign and his son. See Rom. i. 3, 4. That the Lord here meant was universally identified with the Messiah by the ancient Jews, is clear, not only from their own traditions, but from Christ's assuming this interpretation as the basis of his argument to prove the Messiah's superhuman nature, and from the fact that his opponents, far from questioning this fact, were unable to answer him a word, and afraid to interrogate him further (Matt. xxii. 46.) The original form of expression, in the phrase *Sit at my right hand*, is the same as in Ps. cix. 31. A seat at the right hand of a king is mentioned in the Scriptures as a place of honour, not arbitrarily, but as implying a participation in his power, of which the right hand is a constant symbol. See above, on Ps. xlv. 10 (9), and compare Matt. xix. 28. The sitting posture is appropriate to kings who are frequently described as sitting on their thrones. See above, on Ps. xxix. 10. In this case, however, the posture is of less moment than the position. Hence Stephen sees Christ *standing* at the right hand of God (Acts vii. 55, 56), and Paul simply says he *is* there (Rom. viii. 34.) The participation in the divine power, thus ascribed to the Messiah, is a special and extraordinary one, having reference to the total subjugation of his enemies. This idea is expressed by the figure of their being made his footstool, perhaps with allusion to the ancient practice spoken of in Josh. x. 24. This figure itself, however, presupposes the act of sitting on a throne. It does not imply inactivity, as some suppose, or mean that Jehovah would conquer his foes for him, without any intervention of his own. The idea running through the whole psalm is, that it is in and through him that Jehovah acts for the destruction of his enemies, and that for this very end he is invested with almighty power, as denoted by his session at the right hand of God. This session is to last until the total subjugation of his enemies, that is to say, this special and extraordinary power of the Messiah is then to terminate, a representation which agrees exactly with that of Paul in 1 Cor. xv. 24—28, where the verse before us is distinctly referred to, although not expressly quoted. It is therefore needless, though grammatical, to give the *until* an inclusive meaning, namely, until then and afterwards, as in Ps. cxii. 8 below. This verse, it has been said, is more frequently quoted or referred to, in the New Testament, than any other in the Hebrew Bible. Besides the passages already cited, it lies at the foundation of all those which represent Christ as sitting at the right hand of the Father. See Matt. xxvi. 64. 1 Cor. xv. 25. Eph. i. 20—22. Phil. ii. 9—11. Heb. i. 3, 14. viii. 1. x. 12, 13. 1 Pet. iii. 22, and compare Rev. iii. 21.

2. *The rod of thy strength will Jehovah send forth from Zion; rule thou in the midst of thine enemies.* The Psalmist now addresses the Messiah directly. The idea latent in the figures of the first verse, namely that of power, is here expressed. The word (מַטֶּה) translated *rod* never means a *sceptre*, as the synonymous term (שֵׁבֶט) sometimes does, from which it is distinguished by Ezekiel (xix. 11), but a rod of correction and of chastisement. See Jer. xlviii. 12, and compare Isai. ix. 3 (4.) x. 5, 15, xiv. 4, 5. Ez. vii. 10, 11. It is here named as the instrument with

which the foes are to be subdued. Compare Ps. ii. 9. There may be an allusion to the rod of Moses. See Ex. xiv. 16, 21, and compare Isai. x. 24, 26. The *rod of thy strength*, or thy rod of strength, thy strong rod, or rather the rod by means of which thine own strength is to be exerted. As this strength is not human but divine, it is said to be sent forth by Jehovah out of Zion, considered as his earthly residence, the seat of the theocracy. See above, on Ps. xx. 3 (2.) The verb translated *rule* is not applied in usage to a peaceful reign, but to coercive or compulsory dominion over conquered enemies. See above, on Ps. xlix. 15 (14), and compare Num. xxiv. 19. The imperative here involves prediction in its strongest form. As if he had said: All is ready for the conquest; there is no resistance; there can be no doubt of the result; rule, therefore, in the midst thine enemies, i. e. over the very enemies by whom thou art surrounded, and who threatened to dethrone thee.

3. *Thy people* (are) *free-will-offerings in the day of thy power, in holy decorations, from the womb of the dawn, to thee* (*is*) *the dew of thy youth.* Every member of this very obscure verse has been a subject of dispute and of conflicting explanations. The common version of the first words (*thy people shall be willing*) is entirely inadmissible as an exact translation, since the word translated *willing* is a plural substantive of the feminine gender, and not an adjective agreeing with the masculine singular noun *people.* The idea, however, is the same, but expressed with far more strength and beauty. The plural noun just mentioned is the one used to denote spontaneous gifts, or freewill-offerings, under the law of Moses. See above, on Ps. liv. 8 (7), and compare Ex. xxv. 2. xxxv. 29. xxxvi. 3. Lev. xxii. 23. By supplying the correlative verb, which may be considered as latent in the noun, we obtain the sense, *thy people* (offer) *voluntary gifts.* But by supplying the substantive verb, which is far more natural and common, we obtain the still more striking sense, thy people are

themselves such gifts, i. e. they freely consecrate themselves to God. In this sense of voluntary self-dedication the reflexive form of the verbal root is used even in historical prose (1 Chr. xxix. 14, 17), especially in reference to military service (Judg. v. 2, 9. 2 Chr. xvii. 16.) *The day of thy power*, the day in which it is exerted and displayed in the subjugation of thine enemies. The next phrase literally means, *in beauties* (or *ornaments*) *of holiness*, which may either have its obvious spiritual sense, as in Ps. xxix. 2, or that of *holy decorations*, with allusion to the sacerdotal dress, which is expressly called *garments of holiness*, Lev. xvi. 4. The last is the sense put by the modern interpreters upon the phrase, which then means that the people, when they make this solemn offering of themselves to God, appear clothed in sacerdotal vestments, as the servants of a priestly king (v. 4 below), and themselves a "kingdom of priests" (Ex. xix. 6.) *The womb of the dawn* (or *day-break*) is a very strong poetical description of the origin or source of the *dew* which immediately follows, and the sense of which must determine that of the whole clause. The most probable opinions as to this point are the following. Some suppose the clause to be descriptive of the multitude of warriors who devote themselves to the Messiah, and who are then described as no less numerous than the drops of dew born from the womb of morning. The objection to this is, that it lays too much stress upon mere numbers, and expresses that idea by a figure neither common nor altogether natural. Another explanation makes the point of the comparison with dew, not numbers, but beauty, brilliancy thus corresponding to the holy decorations of the other clause. Here again the comparison selected is by no means obvious, much less familiar. Lovely or beautiful as dew is not a combination likely to occur to the mind of any writer. In the two interpretations which have now been given, *youth* must be taken in the sense of *young men*, like the Latin *pubes* and *juventus*, when applied to a youthful soldiery, or made to qualify the noun before it, *youthful dew*, still meaning the young warriors. But of such a figure there is not a trace in Hebrew usage, and in the only other place where the word (יַלְדוּת) occurs, it evidently means *youth*, as a period of human life (Ecc. xi. 9, 10.) Free from all these objections is the supposition, that the clause relates not to the numbers or the beauty of Messiah's people, but to their perpetual succession, expressed by a fine poetical comparison with dew, engendered afresh daily from the womb of the morning. *Youth* will then have its proper sense, as denoting the perpetual youth of the Messiah, whose body is thus constantly renewed by the successive generations of his people. This construction also enables us to divide the clause more equally than in the masoretic interpunction, which, at all events, is either incorrect or rather musical than logical.

4. *Sworn hath Jehovah, and will not repent, Thou (shalt be) a priest forever, after the order of Melchizedek.* The declaration in the last clause of v. 3 is here repeated in another form, and with a statement of the ground or reason upon which it rests. What was there poetically represented as the perpetual youth of the Messiah is here more solemnly described as a perpetual priesthood, indissolubly blended with a perpetual kingship, both secured by the oath of God himself. *He will not repent*, there is no fear or even possibility of his breaking or retracting this engagement, for such it is, and not a mere declaratory attestation of the present fact or general truth, as it might seem to be from the common version, not only here but in Heb. v. 6. vii. 17, 21, in every one of which places the Greek conforms exactly to the Septuagint version and the Hebrew text, the *art* being constantly supplied by the translators. That the clause is a promise, and as such relates directly to the future, is clear from the whole tenor of the psalm as a prophetic one, as well as from the oath, which is not used in Scripture to attest mere matters of fact, but to confirm the divine promise and threatenings. The indefinite expression, *a priest*, is intended to describe the office in itself considered, without reference to

temporary distinctions and gradations. It therefore comprehends whatever appertained to the office of the High Priest, as the head and representative of all the rest. *After the order*, i. e. according to the manner, character, or institution. It is remarkable that this phrase (like יַלְדוּת in v. 3) is almost peculiar to this psalm and the book of Ecclesiastes, being found besides in only one place (Job v. 8.) In all the direct quotations of the verse in Hebrews, the Septuagint version of this word (τάξιν) is retained. But in one of the more indirect citations (Heb. vii. 15) another word (ὁμοιότητα) is substituted, showing that the essential idea is that of likeness or resemblance. This likeness consists primarily in the union of the regal and sacerdotal offices. See Gen. xiv. 18. The meaning of the verse in its original connection is, that this royal conqueror is also a priest, who makes atonement for the sins of his people, and thus enables and disposes them to make the dedication of themselves described in the preceding verse. The perpetuity of this relation, and its confirmation by the oath of God, are attendant circumstances but essential, and as such insisted on by the apostle, Heb. vii. 20—24. The coincidences founded on the meaning of the names Melchizedek and Salem (Heb. vii. 2), and on the want of hierarchical succession in both cases (Heb. vii. 3), are perfectly legitimate but not essential to the understanding of the verse in its original connection. The inspired commentary on this sentence, which occupies the whole seventh chapter of Hebrews, is not intended merely to explain its meaning, but also to make use of its terms, and the associations coupled with them, as a vehicle of other kindred truths, belonging to the Christian revelation, and not necessarily suggested by the Psalm to its original readers.

5. *The Lord on thy right hand has smitten, in the day of his anger, kings.* Some suppose this to be addressed to Jehovah, and *the Lord* to mean Messiah, on the ground that they could not each be on the right hand of the other. See above, v. 1. That they

could be so, however, only shows that the whole description is a figurative one, and that the principal figure has a two-fold meaning. *On the right hand* has precisely the same meaning here as in Ps. cix. 31, where it denotes the place of protection or assistance, the figure being probably derived from the usages of war, in which one who succours or protects another may be said to strengthen his right hand, as the member which he uses in his own defence. In one sense, therefore, the Lord is at the right hand of Jehovah; in another sense, Jehovah is at his. This assistance, far from excluding, presupposes his own action, or rather, what Jehovah is described as doing for him he does through him. See above, on v. 1. The word translated *smite* is very strong and has repeatedly occurred before. See above, on Ps. xviii. 39 (38.) lxviii. 22, 24 (21, 23.) The day of Jehovah's wrath is coincident with that of the Lord's strength in v. 3. The strength of the Messiah, as a conqueror, is to be exerted in giving effect to Jehovah's wrath against his enemies. The position of the word *kings* at the end of the sentence, although harsh and almost ungrammatical in English, is retained in the translation for the sake of its effect upon the emphasis and point of the description. The objects of Jehovah's wrath and the Messiah's strokes are not to be mere ordinary men, but kings, if they continue to oppose themselves. See above, on Ps. ii. 2, 10. The tense of the verb may be regarded as an instance of *praeteritum propheticum*, describing what is certainly to happen as already past.

6. *He will judge among the nations—he has filled* (*them*) *with corpses—he has smitten the head over much land* (or *over the wide earth.*) By another sudden change of form, the Messiah is again spoken of as a third person. The judgment here ascribed to him is only another name and figure for the conquest just described. The form of expression in the last clause is unusual and obscure. The common version makes both *head* and *land* collectives, *the heads over many countries.* Some interpreters explain the second

word in this way, but the first more strictly, as denoting a single ruler over many countries. Others invert the terms and understand by *head* the various chiefs of nations, but by *earth* the whole earth with its qualifying epithet of *great* or *wide.* Amidst these questions of construction or minute interpretation, the general idea is clear enough, to wit, that of universal conquest on the part of the Messiah, and extending to all earthly principalities and powers.

7. *From the brook in the way he will drink, therefore will he raise the head.* According to the masoretic interpunction, *in the way* does not qualify *the brook* but *he will drink*, a distinction of little exegetical importance. Unlike the foregoing verse, the one before us is perfectly clear in its particular expressions, but obscure in its general import and relation to the context. The most probable meaning of the first clause is, that he shall not be exhausted like those wandering in the desert (Ps. cii. 24. cvii. 4, 5) but refreshed and strengthened, with a reference, as some suppose, to the relief experienced by Samson (Judg. xv. 18, 19.) The raising of the head, in the last clause, is an obvious and intelligible figure for exhilaration, or relief from dejection and depression, which is naturally indicated by the hanging of the head. The only question is whether this effect is here supposed to be produced in the conqueror himself or in others. In favour of the former explanation is the parallel clause, which represents him as assuaging his own thirst. In favour of the other is the analogy of Ps. iii. 4 (3) xxvii. 6, where God is said to raise the head of man. As in other doubtful cases, where the senses are not incompatible or exclusive of each other, it is safe, if not entirely satisfactory, to leave them side by side, the rather as the words could probably not fail to suggest both ideas to the Hebrew reader.

PSALM CXI.

This is an alphabetical psalm, in which the Hebrew letters mark the beginning not of verses but of clauses. The first eight verses contain each two clauses; the last two consist of three. The psalm begins with an invitation to the public praise of God, v. 1, then assigns, as the ground and object of this praise, his dealings with his people, vs. 2—9, and ends with the conclusion, that the fear of the Lord is the beginning of wisdom, v. 10. There is nothing in the psalm itself to determine its date or its historical occasion. According to Hengstenberg, it is the first psalm of a trilogy, added to the ancient one preceding (Ps. cviii—cx.) after the return from exile.

1. *Hallelujah! I will thank Jehovah with a whole heart, in the company of the upright and in the congregation.* The *Hallelujah* (*praise ye Jah*) marks the designation of the latter psalms for permanent use in public worship, as the inscription *to the chief musician* does that of the older ones. *With a whole heart*, or *with all* (*my*) *heart*, as it is fully expressed in Ps. lxxxvi. 12. Compare Ps. cxix. 2. The word translated *company* means properly a circle of confidential friends. See above, on Ps. xxv. 14. lv. 15 (14.) lxiv. 3 (2.) lxxxiii. 4 (3.) It is here applied to the church or chosen people, as constituting such a company or circle, in opposition to the world without. It is not therefore really distinct from the *congregation* mentioned in the last clause, but another name for it. The *upright* (or *straightforward*) is a title given to the true Israel, from the days of Balaam downwards. See Num. xxiv 10.

2. *Great are the works of Jehovah, sought* (*according*) *to all*

their desires. The common version of the last phrase, *all them that have pleasure therein*, supposes the text to be differently pointed, as in Ps. xl. 15 (14,) lxx. 3 (2.) The received text can only mean *to (for* or *according to*) *all their wishes.* The antecedent of the pronoun (*their*) seems to be *the upright* in v. 1. For a similar construction of the same pronoun, see below, on v. 10 The clause, thus construed, is obscure, but may be understood to mean, that when the works of God are *sought out*, investigated, or explored, their greatness fully satisfies the hopes and wishes of his people. Another possible sense is, that they are *sought for*, i. e. the experience or knowledge of them eagerly desired, *with* (literally *as to*) *all their wishes*, i. e. with avidity, or, as it is expressed in the preceding verse, *with all the heart.*

3. *Honour and majesty* (*is*) *his work—and his righteousness standing forever.* In the first clause, *work* is the subject of the proposition, *honour and majesty* the predicate. *His work is honour and majesty*, i. e. all that he does is noble and majestic, worthy of the great King, to whom these epithets are often applied elsewhere. See above, on Ps. civ. 1. *His work* means specifically here what he does for the protection and deliverance of his people. In the last clause, as in many other places, this work is referred to his *righteousness*, not his *justice*, in the technical and strict sense, but his *rectitude*, including his fidelity to his engagements, and securing the exercise of his covenanted mercy. This seems more natural than to explain it as meaning the practical justification of his people by his providential care of them. *Standing to eternity* (or *perpetuity*), not fitful or capricious, not confined or temporary, but perpetual and constant.

4. *A memory has he made for his wonderful works; gracious and compassionate* (*is*) *Jehovah.* The first clause, though not exactly rendered, is correctly paraphrased in the English Bible, *he hath made his wonderful works to be remembered*, and still

more freely in the Prayer Book version. The last clause shows that the *wonderful works* of the first are not the wonders of creation, nor those of providence in general, but those wrought for the benefit of Israel. The terms of this clause are borrowed from Ex. xxxiv. 6. See above, on Ps. ciii. 8.

5. *Prey hath he given to those fearing him; he will remember to eternity his covenant.* The first word properly denotes the food of wild beasts, and may here be either a poetical equivalent to *food, provision*, as in Prov. xxxi. 15. Mal. iii. 10, or intended to suggest the additional idea of food obtained at the expense of enemies. In either case there seems to be no reason for restricting the clause to the supply of Israel in the desert, although that would necessarily occur to every reader, as the great historical example of the general fact alleged, and in the last clause represented as a proof of God's fidelity to covenant engagements.

6. *The power of his works he has declared to his people,* (so as) *to give to them a heritage of nations.* He has shown them what powerful things he can do, by favouring them so far as to drive out nations from their seats, and make his people their successors and, as it were, their heirs. This refers to the conquest of Canaan, as the first in a long series of such dispossessions, including all the territories gained in war from the surrounding nations, till the death of David. The construction of *to give* as a gerund *(by giving)* is not a Hebrew idiom, and restricts the meaning of the clause unduly. See above, on Ps. lxxviii. 18.

7. *The works of his hands are truth and judgment; sure (are) all his precepts.* The second clause is not an iteration of the first, but an inference from it. If what God does himself is always done in faithfulness and justice to his people, then what he requires them to do must certainly be right and best, and his

requisitions therefore may be trusted and confided in, the true sense of the adjective or participle here employed.

8. *Settled for ever and ever, done in truth and right.* The subjects are the same as in v. 7, but presented in an inverse order, the first clause relating to the *precepts*, the last to the *works*, of God. The former are *settled*, firmly supported, founded, or established, not capricious and precarious. The latter, by which they are recommended and attested (see above, on v. 9), are works of faithfulness and rectitude. The last word in Hebrew is an adjective used as a neuter or abstract noun, in which respect the English *right* resembles it.

9. *Redemption he has sent to his people; he has ordained to eternity his covenant; holy and fearful is his name.* That this verse was intended to consist of three clauses, is clear from the fact that it contains three letters of the alphabet in regular succession. The same thing is true of the remaining verse. The first clause relates mainly, not exclusively, to the deliverance from Egypt. As in v. 5, the second clause affirms a general truth, attested and exemplified by the particular fact mentioned in the first. *Fearful*, not merely to his foes but to his people, who can never cease to worship him with holy awe.

10. *The beginning of wisdom is the fear of Jehovah; a good understanding (is) to all (those) doing them; his praise endureth forever.* This is the conclusion drawn from all that goes before. Since all God's dealings with his people are in faithfulness and truth, and his commands not only are but must be right, then the first step in wisdom, its first principle or element, is reverence for such a Being, proved by obedience to his will. The same sentiment occurs in Prov. i. 7. ix. 10. Job. xxviii. 28. The intimate connection of the verse, notwithstanding its proverbial or aphoristic form, with the foregoing context, is apparent from the refer-

ence of the pronoun *them* to the plural nouns of the preceding verses. *Endureth forever*, literally, (*is*) *standing to eternity*. This is equivalent to saying that he will and must be praised forever, corresponding to the *Hallelujah*, at the beginning of the psalm.

PSALM CXII.

Another alphabetical psalm of precisely the same character, coinciding with the one before it, even in the number of verses, and the number of clauses in each verse. This formal agreement shows the intimate connection of the two compositions, and makes it highly probable that they belong not only to the same age but to the same author, and were meant to form parts of one continued series or system. This psalm begins precisely where the one before it ends, i. e. with the happiness arising from the fear of God, v. 1, the blessed effects of which are then recounted under several particulars, vs. 2—9, and finally contrasted with the fate of the ungodly, v. 10.

1. *Happy the man fearing Jehovah, in his commandments delighting greatly.* There is here not only an obvious connection with the close of the preceding psalm, but an obvious advance upon it or progression of ideas. As the fear of the Lord is there declared to be the principle of all true wisdom, so here it is declared to be the source of all true happiness. The second clause defines the meaning of the first by showing, that the fear there mentioned is a fear consistent with, or rather necessarily involving, a complacent acquiescence in God's will, thus entirely exclud-

ing a mere slavish dread, which is incompatible with such a disposition.

2. *Mighty in the earth shall be his seed; the race of the upright shall be blessed.* The first phrase is borrowed from Gen. x. 8, and would at once suggest to every Hebrew reader the idea of a mighty man like Nimrod and the other ancient heroes. Now a promise of personal heroism is perhaps without analogy, especially as given to the son, to the exclusion of the father. This anomaly can be avoided only by assuming, what is probable enough in itself, that the ideal person here described represents the chosen people, the *upright* of the other clause, each successive generation of whom might be expected to excel its predecessors in heroic eminence.

3. *Wealth and riches (are) in his house, and his righteousness endureth forever.* Not only in his dwelling but in his family, so that his wealth or prosperity might have been said to endure forever as well as his righteousness, i. e. his recognition and reception as a righteous person, his justification. *Endureth*, literally, (*is*) *standing*, the same expression that is used in Ps. cxi. 3 of God himself. There is also an analogy, at least in form, between the *majesty and honour* of the righteous God and the *wealth and riches* of the righteous man.

4. *There arises in the darkness light to the upright—kind and compassionate and righteous.* The figure in the first clause is a natural and common one, denoting relief from deep distress. See above, on Ps. xcvii. 11. In the last clause we have another instance of the singular way in which terms applied to God in the preceding psalm are copied and applied to man in this. The first two epithets in this clause are employed above in Ps. cxi. 4. The principle involved may be the same as in Luke vi. 36, "be ye therefore merciful as your Father also is merciful." Compare

Matt. v. 48. To these two epithets is added that of *righteous*, in the wide sense including both the others. The construction of the sentence is unusual and doubtful; but most probably the second clause sustains the same relation to the other as in v. 1; that is to say, it limits and defines the general description *upright*, by confining it to such as have the qualities expressed by the three adjectives that follow. The alternation of the numbers is familiar where the singular denotes an ideal individual including many real ones.

5. *Happy the man showing favour and lending; he shall sustain his affairs by justice.* The first word in Hebrew, which means *good*, is here descriptive not of character but of condition, and denotes good fortune. It is used in the same sense by Isaiah (iii. 10) and Jeremiah (xliv. 17.) The common version (*a good man*) is forbidden by the Hebrew collocation. *Lending*, not as a financial or commercial operation, but as an act of charity, lending to the poor. The verb in the last clause strictly means to provide for or sustain, especially with food. See above, on Ps. lv. 23 (22.) It is here applied to the control and management of all one's interests. *Affairs*, literally, *words*, but in the wider sense of that which words denote, namely, things, affairs, in which sense it is sometimes applied to causes or suits at law. The last word is commonly translated *judgment*, not in the sense of *discretion*, given in the English versions, but in that of practical justice, righteous conduct. He shall best secure his own interests by treating those of others justly and generously.

6. *For to eternity he shall not be moved; to the memory of eternity he shall be righteous.* The *for* assigns the reason for his being pronounced happy. *Moved*, i. e. from his prosperous condition, or from his position as a righteous man. The construction of the last clause in the English versions (*the righteous shal. be in everlasting remembrance*) is grammatical, and yields a gooc

sense; but the latest interpreters prefer another, which makes *to everlasting remembrance* mean the same as *to eternity.* As long as he shall be remembered, he shall be remembered as a righteous man. This construction has the advantage of making the parallelism more exact.

7. *From evil tidings he shall not fear; fixed is his heart, trusting in Jehovah.* The first Hebrew noun is in the singular number, and is properly a participle passive meaning *heard*, used absolutely as a noun denoting what is heard, a rumour or report, news or tidings. The common version (*he shall not be afraid of evil tidings*) seems to confine the negation to the mere apprehension or anticipation of bad news, whereas the original expression comprehends, and indeed more properly denotes, being frightened when the evil tidings are heard. A *fixed heart* is the negation both of fickleness and cowardice. See above, on Ps. li. 12 (10.) lvii. 8 (7.) cviii. 1. Instead of the active participle *trusting*, the Hebrew has the passive *trusted*, analogous to that in Ps. ciii. 14.

8. *Settled (is) his heart, he shall not fear, until he look upon his foes* (with triumph.) The first word is another expression borrowed from the foregoing psalm, but applied in a manner altogether different. See Ps. cxi. 8, where the plural of the same participle is applied to God's commandments. The construction in the last clause is the idiomatic one of the verb *see* with the preposition *in*, which usually means to see with strong emotion, and especially with joy or triumph. See above, on Ps. l. 23. liv. 9 (7.) *Until* does not imply that he shall then fear, but that there will then be no occasion so to do. See above, on Ps. cx. 1.

9. *He has scattered, he has given to the poor, his righteousness endureth forever, his horn shall be high with honour.* The first

verb denotes profuse munificence, as in Prov. xi. 34. This is alleged not as the cause but the effect, and therefore as the evidence of his being righteous. The next clause is the same as the last of v. 3. With the last clause compare Ps. lxxv. 5 (4.) lxxxix. 18 (17.)

10. *The wicked shall see and fret; his teeth he shall gnash, and shall melt away; the desire of the wicked shall perish.* He shall see, but not with triumph or delight, like the righteous in v. 8. The word translated *fret* means both to grieve and be angry, and has no exact equivalent in English. See above, on Ps. vi. 8 (7.) x. 14, xxxi. 10 (9.) *Gnash with his teeth*, a strong expression of impotent malignity. See above, on Ps. xxxv. 16, xxxvii. 12. *Melt away*, literally, be melted, i. e. waste or decay. See above, on Ps. xxii. 15 (14.) lxviii. 3 (2.) The *desire of the wicked* is his wish to see the righteous perish. Compare Prov. x. 24, 28. Job viii. 13, and the contrary promise to the humble, Ps. ix. 19 (18.)

PSALM CXIII.

The Psalmist celebrates the majesty of God, vs. 1—5, in contrast with his gracious condescension to his suffering creatures, vs. 6—9. According to a Jewish usage, which appears to have existed even in the time of Christ, the six psalms beginning with this one constitute the *Greater Hallel*, sung at the annual festivals, especially the Passover and the Feast of Tabernacles. According to Hengstenberg's arrangement, this psalm closes a second trilogy, added to the Davidic one (Ps. cviii—cx) after the return from Babylon.

1. *Hallelujah! Praise, oh ye servants of Jehovah, praise the name of Jehovah!* As the title, *Servant of Jehovah*, is applied to eminent leaders of the chosen people (Ps. xviii. 1. xxxvi. 1. xc. 1. cv. 6), so the plural, *Servants of Jehovah*, designates the chosen people itself. See above, Ps. xxxiv. 23 (22.) lxix. 37 (36), and below, Ps. cxxxvi. 22, and compare Ezra v. 11. Neh. i. 10, from which last places it appears, that this was a familiar form of speech with the returned exiles.

2. *Be the name of Jehovah blessed, from now and even to eternity.* In this as well as the preceding verse, the *name of Jehovah* involves the usual allusion to the manifestation of his nature in his former acts. See above, on Ps. v. 12 (11.) The wish expressed in this verse implies a perpetual continuation or renewal of the evidence already furnished.

3. *From the rising of the sun even to its setting, (to be) praised (is the) name of Jehovah.* With the first clause compare Ps. l. 1. The last clause might be grammatically construed as a wish, like that in the preceding verse, *praised (be the) name of Jehovah.* It is more probable, however, that the passive participle (*laudatus*) was meant to have the force of a gerundive (*laudandus.*) See above, on Ps. xviii. 4 (3.)

4. *High above all nations (is) Jehovah; above the heavens (is) his (glory.)* The two clauses are declaratory of his infinite superiority, both to the animate and inanimate creation, each being represented by its noblest part; the former by mankind, and that considered not as individuals but nations; the latter by the heavens. This is certainly more natural, and yields a better sense, than to give the preposition (עַל) a different meaning in the two clauses, in the first that of *above*, in the second that of *on*, in

which case it is necessary to explain *on heaven* as meaning *in heaven*, just as *on the earth* and *in the earth* are convertible expressions. See above, on Ps. lvii. 6 (5.)

5. *Who is like Jehovah, our God, the* (*one*) *dwelling high?* The verb denotes not merely *dwelling*, but *sitting enthroned*, sitting as a king. The original construction of the last clause is peculiar, *the* (*one*) *making high to sit* (or *dwell.*)

6. *The one seeing deep—in heaven and in earth.* The construction of the first clause is precisely the same with that of the last clause in v. 5, and must be explained in the same manner. As *making high to dwell* means *dwelling high*, so *making low* (or *deep*) *to see* must mean *seeing deep*, i. e. far below. It also follows from the exact correspondence of these clauses, that the remaining words of v. 6 are to be connected with the first words of v. 5. *Who is like Jehovah, our God......in heaven and in earth?* The rest will then be read as a parenthesis. This construction is confirmed by the analogy of Deut. iii. 24.

7. *Raising from the dust the poor—from the dunghill he will lift the needy.* The mention of God's seeing far below him suggests the idea of his condescension to the humblest objects which he thus beholds. The word translated *poor* is one of wide signification, meaning sometimes poor in flesh and sometimes poor in purse. See above, on Ps. xli. 2 (1.) The parallel term means *poor* in the strict sense, i. e. needy, destitute. *Dust* and *dunghill*, common figures in all languages for a degraded social state. The terms are borrowed from the prayer of Hannah, 1 Sam. ii. 8. Compare Ps. xliv. 26 (25.)

8. *To make him sit with nobles, with the nobles of his people.* Not merely *to dwell*, which is too vague, but *to sit* with them, as their equal and associate. There is also a climax in the last clause.

He not only raises the poor to an equality with nobles in general, but with the nobles of his people, i. e. with the noblest of mankind. See again, 1 Sam. ii. 8.

9. *Making the barren (one) of the house to sit a joyful mother of children. Hallelujah!* The common version (*to keep house*) is founded upon Ps. lxviii. 7 (6), but is here at variance both with Hebrew usage and the masoretic accents, which require (עֲקֶרֶת) *barren* and (הַבַּיִת) *the house* to be closely united in construction, as above. The form of expression is like one in Ps. lxviii. 13 (12.) *To sit* might be rendered *to dwell* without any material change of sense; but the former keeps up the uniformity with vs. 5, 8, where the same Hebrew word is used. The historical allusion is to Hannah who, with other long childless mothers mentioned in the sacred history, was a type of the Church in its low estate, and more especially in exile. Compare Isai. liv. 1.

PSALM CXIV.

As the preceding psalm encouraged the people of God, in a time of trial, by reminding them that, although infinitely exalted, he condescends to notice and relieve the sufferings of his creatures, so the one before us is intended to produce the same effect, by bringing to their recollection what he actually did for Israel in the period of the exodus from Egypt. By that deliverance he acknowledged Israel as his chosen people, vs. 1, 2, and attested the acknowledgment by miracle, vs. 3, 4. Nature herself, whose course was interrupted, is appealed to as a witness, vs. 5, 6, that she is subject to the God of Israel, vs. 7, 8. There is no improbability in the opinion that this psalm, with those which immediately follow, was intended to continue the series begun in the two preceding trilogies (Ps. cviii—cx, cxi—cxiii), and intended to sustain the hopes of the Jewish Church after its return from Babylon.

1. *In the coming forth of Israel from Egypt, of the house of Jacob from a people of strange language.* The first phrase is not to be restricted to the very act or moment of the exodus, but comprehends the whole Mosaic period, of which this was the characteristic and critical event. The *house of Jacob* is a phrase peculiarly appropriate to those who entered Egypt as a family, and left it as a nation. *Of strange language* is a paraphrase of one Hebrew word, apparently a participle and occurring only here; but according to its obvious etymological affinities, it probably means *stammering*, and then, by an association common in antiquity, *speaking barbarously*, i. e. in a foreign language. All such expressions may perhaps involve an allusion to the pre-eminence of Hebrew, as the primitive and sacred language. It was no small part of the humiliation to which Israel was subjected in Egypt, that the people of God should sustain for ages a relation of dependence to a nation who did not even speak the sacred language, much less profess the true religion, so inseparably blended with it. See above, on Ps. lxxxi. 6 (5), and compare my note on Isai. xxxiii. 19.

2. *Judah became his sanctuary, Israel his dominion.* Judah is put as an equivalent to Israel, not only because it had really become so when the psalm was written, but because it was destined to become so from the first. See Gen. xlix. 10. *Became*, literally, *was for*, which might mean nothing more than *served as* or *was treated as*; but this construction of the verb *to be* with *to* or

for is the only representative in Hebrew of our word *become*. The sense thus obtained is entirely consistent with the calling of Abraham, because what is here meant is that Israel, as a nation, was now publicly declared to be the chosen or peculiar people, an idea expressed by the phrase *his sanctuary* or *holy thing*, i. e. something set apart exclusively to his use and service. The parallel word in the original is plural, *dominions* or *domains*, in reference, as some suppose, to the plurality of tribes, but according to others, in contrast with the lordships and dominions of the world, to all which Israel is described as more than equipollent, just as the infinite superiority of the true God to all false gods is expressed or suggested by the plural name *Elohim*. Here, as in Ps. lxxxvii. 1, the pronouns are without an antecedent in the sentence. The reference to God is so self-evident, that the only question has respect to the unusual form, which some explain by supposing that the psalm was originally part of the preceding one, or at least designed to be always read or sung directly after it. The latest interpreters prefer the explanation, that the name of God was designedly suppressed, in order that the questions in vs. 5, 6, might appear more natural and yet more striking.

3. *The sea saw and fled—the Jordan turns back*. By supposing the conversive prefix to affect both verbs, we may render the last also as a preterite, *turned back*. The historical allusion is to Ex. xiv. 21. Josh. iii. 14—17. At the same time, as seas and rivers are familiar emblems of the world and its nations, the reminiscence is adapted to suggest the hope, that other seas and other rivers may be yet controlled by the same power. See above, on Ps. lxxvii. 17 (16.) xciii. 3. cvii. 23.

4. *The mountains skipped like rams*, (*the*) *hills like the young of sheep*. As the Psalmist is reciting actual events, to be used as symbols and pledges of others, this cannot be explained as a poetical figure, but must be understood as referring to the concus-

sion of Sinai, with its various peaks and neighbouring mountains See Ex. xix. 18. Judg. v. 4. Ps. lxviii. 9 (8.) xcvii. 4, 5. Hab. iii. 6. Here again, the familiar use of mountains to denote states and empires is suggestive of the same consolation as in v. 3.

5. *What aileth thee, oh sea, that thou fleest—oh Jordan* (*that*) *thou turnest back?* By a fine poetical apostrophe, the Psalmist, instead of simply stating the cause of these effects, puts the question to the natural objects which thus witnessed and attested the divine presence. The first phrase literally means, *what* (*is*) *to thee*, the nearest approach that the Semitic dialects can make to our expression, *what have you*, which in some languages, the French for instance, is the usual equivalent to *what ails you?*

6. *Ye mountains,* (*that*) *ye skip like rams—ye hills, like the young of sheep?* The sentence is continued from the foregoing verse, being still dependent on the question there asked. In this interrogation the terms of vs. 3, 4, are studiously repeated. *The young of sheep*, literally, *sons of the flock.*

7. *From before the Lord tremble, oh earth, from before the God of Jacob.* As in other cases of rhetorical interrogation, the writer or speaker answers his own question. The imperative mood is here peculiarly significant, including both a recollection and prediction; as if he had said, the earth might well tremble at the presence of the Lord, and may well tremble at it still. *From before* is better than *at the presence of*, because the very form of the expression necessarily suggests the ideas of recoil and flight. *Before* is itself a compound term in Hebrew, meaning *to the face of*. The word translated *Lord* is the simple or primitive form of *Adhonai*, and is applied both to God and man, in the sense of lord or master. See Ex. xxiii. 17. Mal. iii. 1.

8. *Turning the rock* (into) *a pool of water, the flint to springs*

of water. This refers to the miraculous supply of water in the desert. See above, on Ps. cvii. 35, and compare Ex. xvii. 6. Num. xx. 11. Deut. viii. 15. xxxii. 13. Isai. xli. 18. The connection with the preceding verse is still more marked in the original, the first words of which strictly mean *the (one) turning*, etc. The reader is left to draw for himself the natural and obvious conclusion, that the God, who thus drew water from a flinty rock for the supply of Israel, can still educe the richest blessings from what seem to be the hardest and most inauspicious situations. When this thought is supplied, the psalm no longer seems unfinished or abrupt in its conclusion.

PSALM CXV.

God is entreated by his people to vindicate not their honour but his own, vs. 1, 2, which is contrasted with the impotence of idols and their worshippers, vs. 3—8, and urged as a reason why his people should trust in him, for a large increase, vs. 9—15, and a fulfilment of his purpose to glorify himself by the praises of the living not the dead, vs. 16—17, in the promotion of which end the church declares her resolution to co-operate forever, v. 18. The general tenor of the psalm, thus stated, and its particular contents, make it perfectly well suited to the state of things in which the series is supposed to have been written, namely, that succeeding the return from exile, but before the actual rebuilding of the temple.

1. *Not unto us, Jehovah, not unto us, but to thy name give*

glory, for thy mercy, for thy truth. The glory meant is not that of former but of future deeds. The implied petition is, that God would interpose for the deliverance of his people, not to do them honour but to glorify himself, and especially to vindicate his mercy and fidelity, which seemed to be dishonoured by his desertion of the chosen people. See above, on Ps. lxxix. 9, and compare Num. xiv. 15. Isai. xliii. 7, 25. xlviii. 9, 11. Dan. ix. 18. The favour sought is the completion of the work of restoration, still imperfect, though auspiciously begun.

2. *Why should the nations say, Where now is their God?* Why should they have occasion so to ask? The form of expression is borrowed from Ps. lxxix. 10, with the addition of (נָא) *now*, which is not a particle of time, but of entreaty, or, in this connection, of triumphant demand. *Where, pray, is their God?* This verse is explanatory of the one before it, by showing that there really was need of something to silence the reproaches of the heathen, a description exactly corresponding to the state of the Jews at the Restoration.

3. *And our God (is) in heaven; all that he pleased he has done.* The *and*, though foreign from our idiom, adds sensibly to the force of the expression. They ask thus, as if our God were absent or had no existence; and yet all the while our God is in heaven, in his glorious and exalted dwelling-place. Compare Ps. ii. 4. xi. 4. ciii. 19. The same phrase, but in the future tense, is used by Solomon (Ecc. viii. 3.) The same idea is expressed in other words, Gen. xviii. 14. Job. xxiii. 13.

4. *Their idols (are) silver and gold, the work of the hands of man.* Here begins the contrast between the true God and all others. *Their idols*, those of the Gentiles, who reproach us with the absence or indifference of our God. For the associations coupled with the word for *idols*, see above, on Ps. cvi. 38

Hands of man, not of *a man*, but of *mankind*, i. e. human hands. With this whole passage compare Isai. xl. 18—20. xli. 7. xliv. 9—20. xlvi. 5—7. Jer. ii. 28. x. 3—15.

5. *They have a mouth and speak not ; they have eyes and see not* As the verb *to have* is wanting in the Hebrew and its cognate languages (see above, on Ps. cxiv. 5), it is not a literal translation of the original expression, (there is) *a mouth to them*, (there are) *eyes to them.* The futures include not only a simple affirmation, *they speak not*, *they see not*, but the future and potential sense, they never will or can speak or see.

6. *They have ears and hear not*, *they have a nose and smell not.* The antithesis is that expressed in Ps. xciv. 9, that God is the former of the eye and the planter of the ear in man ; much more then can he see and hear himself.

7. *They have hands and feel not ; they have feet and walk not ; they do not mutter in their throat.* The sameness of this long enumeration, the force of which is logical and not poetical, is partially relieved by a change in the form of the original, which cannot well be imitated in translation. *Their hands*, *and they feel not ; their feet*, *and they walk not.* Some make the first words in each clause nominatives absolute ; *their hands—they feel not ; their feet—they walk not.* But in the preceding parts of the description, the verbs relate not to the particular members, but to the whole person. It is better, therefore, to supply a verb—*their hands* (are there) *and* (yet) *they feel not—their feet* (are there) *and* (yet) *they go not.* The English *feel* is to be taken in its physical and outward sense, corresponding to the Latin *palpo*, here used by the Vulgate and Jerome. A less equivocal translation would be *touch.* The other verb denotes all progressive movements of the body, comprehended in the English *go.* See above, on Ps. civ. 3. The meaning of the last clause

is, that they cannot even make the faintest and most inarticulate guttural noise, like the lower animals; much less speak as men do. See above, on Ps. xxxv. 28. lxxi. 24.

8. *Like them shall be those who make them, every one who trusts in them.* The last clause forbids the application of the first to the mere artificers, as such, and fastens it on those who trust in idols, whether made by them or by others for them. However formidable now, they shall hereafter be as powerless and senseless as the gods they worship. The translation *are* is contrary to Hebrew usage, which requires the present tense of the substantive verb to be suppressed.

9. *Oh Israel, trust thou in Jehovah; their help and their shield* (*is*) *He.* This is the practical application of the contrast just presented. Since idols are impotent and God almighty, it is folly to fear them or their servants; it is worse than folly not to trust in Him. The last clause is borrowed from Ps. xxxiii. 20. After addressing Israel directly in the first clause, he resumes the third person in the second, and, as if speaking to himself, assigns the reason for the exhortation. The first clause is, as it were, uttered in a loud voice, and the second in a low one.

10. *Oh house of Aaron, trust ye in Jehovah; their help and their shield* (*is*) *He.* Before the exile this particular address to the priests would have been surprising. It is perfectly natural, however, after the return from Babylon, when the priests bore so large a proportion, not only to the other levites, but to the whole nation, and naturally exercised a paramount influence in its affairs.

11. *Fearers of Jehovah, trust ye in Jehovah; their help and their shield* (*is*) *He.* He turns again to the people at large, who are here described as fearers of Jehovah, not in reference to the

actual character of all the individual members, but to the high vocation of the body. See above, Ps. xxii. 24 (23.) cxi. 5.

12. *Jehovah hath remembered us; he will bless, he will bless the house of Israel; he will bless the house of Aaron.* The exhortation to confide in God does not imply that he has yet done nothing. He has already shown his gracious recollection of us by beginning to bless us, and he will still go on to bless us; an idea simply but beautifully expressed by the repetition of the verb, the effect of which is spoiled in the common version by needlessly supplying *us*.

13. *He will bless the fearers of Jehovah, the small with the great.* There is no need of explaining *the great* to be the priests and *the small* the laity. It is much more natural to understand this as an instance of a common Hebrew idiom, which combines *small* and *great* in the sense of *all*, just as *neither good nor evil* means neither one thing nor another, i. e *nothing*. Compare 2 Kings xviii. 24. Jer. xvi. 6. Rev. xiii. 16. xix. 6.

14. *May Jehovah add to you, to you and to your children!* This implies a previous diminution of the people, such as really took place in the Babylonish exile. The optative meaning of the verb, both here and in Gen. xxx. 24, is clear from Deut. i. 11. 2. Sam. xxiv. 3. The Hebrew preposition strictly means *upon* you, and conveys the idea of accumulation much more strongly. See above, on Ps. lxxi. 14, where we have an example of the same construction.

15. *Blessed are ye of Jehovah, Maker of heaven and earth.* Ye are the people blessed of old in the person of your father Abraham, by Melchizedek, priest of the Most High God, saying, " Blessed be Abraham of the Most High God, creator of heaven and earth," Gen. xiv. 19. *Of Jehovah*, literally, *to Jehovah*, as an object of benediction to him. Or the Hebrew preposition, as

in many other cases, may be simply equivalent to our *by*. The creative character of God is mentioned, as ensuring his ability, no less than his willingness, to bless his people.

16. *The heavens (are) heavens for Jehovah, and the earth he has given to the sons of man.* This verse suggests another reason why God would increase them, namely, that although he reserved heaven for himself, he designed the earth to be filled and occupied by man, and hence in the primeval blessing on mankind, as originally uttered, and as repeated after the flood (Gen i. 28. ix. 1), the command to increase is coupled with that to fill the earth. Now if it is not God's will that the race should be diminished and reduced to nothing, much less can such be his intention with respect to his own people. The form of expression in the first clause is unusual. The construction given in the English Bible (*the heaven, even the heavens, are the Lord's*) is entirely gratuitous, the distinction of numbers (*heaven, heavens*), and the emphatic *even*, being both supplied by the translators. The Hebrew word is plural in both cases, and is indeed used only in that number.

17. (It is) *not the dead* (that) *are to praise Jah, and not all* (those) *going down to silence.* This may be regarded as a further reason for expecting the divine protection. God has chosen a people, from among the nations of the earth, to praise him, not when dead but living, not in the silence of the grave, but with their voices in the present life. Thus understood, the verse teaches nothing as to the employments of the disembodied spirit, or of soul and body in the future state. All that is affirmed here (and perhaps in other places like it) is that the praises of the chosen people, as such, must be limited to this life. See above, on Ps. vi. 6 (5.) xxx. 10 (9.) lxxxviii. 11—13 (10—12), and compare Isai. xxxviii. 18. *Silence*, a poetical description of the grave or the unseen world, as in Ps. xciv. 17.

18. *And* (therefore) *we will bless Jah from now even to eternity. Hallelujah!* As it is not the dead who are to do it, and as we are still preserved alive, let us answer our vocation and the very end of our existence. The insensible transition from temporal to eternal praise is altogether natural. The *hallelujah* refers back to the expression *praise Jah (yehallelujah)* in v. 17. As if he had said: let us do what the dead can not, shout Hallelujah!

PSALM CXVI.

THE Church declares her resolution to praise Jehovah for the deliverance which she has experienced, vs. 1, 2, and which is then described with some particularity, vs. 3—10, followed by a declaration of the way in which the Church means to express her gratitude, vs. 11—19. The Septuagint and Vulgate, which combine the two preceding psalms as one, divide the one before us into two, with as little reason in the one case as the other. The state of things referred to in this psalm, as one of mingled joy and grief, and its peculiarities of language, all combine to fix its date immediately after the return from Babylon.

1. *I love—because Jehovah hears my voice, my supplications.* The common version gives the sense correctly, but by a transposition of *Jehovah*, avoids the singular peculiarity of form in the original. The object of the verb *I love* is easily supplied from the remainder of the sentence. Compare Ps. xviii. 2 (1.) Deut. vi. 5. Both verbs may be translated in the present, though of different tenses in the Hebrew. The preterite form of the first

(*I have loved*) implies that the occasion had already been afforded; the future form of the second (*he will hear*), that it was continued and would be continued. The last word, according to its etymology, means prayers for grace or favour.

2. *For he has inclined his ear to me, and in my days I will call* (*upon him.*) The original idea of the figure in the first clause seems to be that of leaning forward to catch a sound otherwise too faint to be distinctly audible. See above, on Ps. xxxi. 3 (2), and compare Ps. xvii. 6. lxxi. 2. lxxxviii. 1. cii. 3. *In my days* is commonly understood to mean through all the days of my life, or as long as I live. Compare Isai. xxxix. 8, and see above, on Ps. civ. 33. *I will call* might be understood to mean, I will still pray to him who has hitherto answered my petitions. But *to call upon God* is applied not only to prayer but to thanksgiving, as appears from v. 13 below, where indeed we have the execution of the purpose here avowed.

3. *The bands of death enclosed me, and the pangs of hell found me; distress and grief I find.* Here begins the description of the sufferings from which God had delivered him. The expressions are borrowed from Ps. xviii. 5, 6, (4, 5.) The twofold use of the verb *find* in this verse is analogous to that of the synonymous verbs *catch* and *seize* in English, when a man is said to catch a disease, and the disease is said to seize the man. Compare Ps. cxix. 143 with Prov. vi. 33. *Hell*, in the wide sense corresponding to *sheol*, the grave, death, or the state of the dead. See above, on Ps. vi. 6 (5.)

4. *And on the name of Jehovah I call: ah now, Jehovah, deliver my soul!* The future in the first clause may be strictly translated (*I will call*) as expressing the determination which he formed in the midst of his distress. See above, on Ps. xviii. 5, 7 (4, 6.) *Ah now* corresponds exactly, both in origin and mean-

ing, to the intensive particle of entreaty (אָנָּה for אָנָּא from אָהּ and נָא), which the common version paraphrases, *I beseech thee.* One of the elements of which it is compounded occurs above, Ps. cxv. 2.

5. *Gracious (is) Jehovah and righteous, and our God shows pity.* With the first clause compare Ps. cxi. 4. cxii. 4. The last word in Hebrew is the active participle of the verb to *pity*, to *compassionate*, and is here used to denote a habit as distinguished from a momentary feeling.

6. *A preserver of the simple (is) Jehovah; I was brought low, and to me he brought salvation.* Here again the first word is an active participle, *keeping the simple*, i. e. habitually watching over them. For the meaning of *the simple*, see above, on Ps. xix. 8 (7.) The word *brought*, twice used in translating this verse, has nothing distinctly corresponding to it in the Hebrew, but by a fortuitous coincidence, enters into two English phrases, by which the original verbs may best be represented. The verb translated *brought low* means to be reduced, in person, strength, or circumstances. See above, on Ps. lxxix. 8, and compare the cognate adjective in Ps. xli. 2 (1.) The other is the common Hebrew verb *to save*, here expressed by a circumlocution, for the purpose of retaining the original construction with the preposition *to*, which also occurs above, Ps. lxxii. 4. lxxxvi. 16.

7. *Return, oh my soul, unto thy rest, for Jehovah hath bestowed upon thee* (favour.) By calling on his soul, which had been agitated and alarmed, to return to its repose, he implies the cessation of the danger. *Rest*, literally, *rests* or *resting-places*, implying fulness or completeness of repose. See above, on Ps. xxiii. 2. For the sense and usage of (גָּמַל) the last verb, see above, on Ps. xiii. 6 (5), and compare Ps. vii. 5 (4.) ciii. 10. The unusual grammatical forms in this verse are similar to those in Ps. ciii. 2, 5.

8. *For thou hast delivered my soul from death, my eye from weeping, my foot from falling.* By a sudden apostrophe, God is now addressed directly. The first and last members of the sentence are borrowed from Ps. lvi. 14 (13.) The second bears some resemblance to Ps. lvi. 9 (8) and Jer. xxxi. 16.

9. *I will walk before Jehovah in the land of life* (or *of the living.*) This is also borrowed from Ps. lvi. 14 (13), with the substitution of *land* (literally *lands*) for *light*. Compare Ps. xxvii. 13. The hope here expressed is in contrast with Ps. cxv. 17.

10. *I believed, for* (thus) *I speak; I was afflicted greatly.* I must have exercised faith, or I could not thus have spoken. The Septuagint version, retained in the New Testament (2 Cor. iv. 13), clothes the same essential meaning in a different form, *I believed, therefore have I spoken.* It was because his faith enabled him to speak, so that his speaking was a proof of faith.

11. *I said in my terror, All mankind* (*are*) *false.* The form of expression in the first clause is borrowed from Ps. xxxi. 23 (22.) But instead of being a confession of error it is here rather a profession of faith. Even in the midst of his excitement, terror, panic, he could turn away from all human aid and trust in God alone. The proposition, *all mankind are false*, i. e. not to be trusted or relied upon, implies as its complement or converse, therefore God alone is to be trusted. See the same contrast stated more explicitly in Ps. cxviii. 8, and compare Ps. lxii. 9, 10 (8, 9.) cviii. 13 (12.) cxlvi. 3, 4.

12. *How shall I requite to Jehovah all his bestowments upon me.* Between this verse and that before it, we must supply the thought that his faith was rewarded and justified by the event. This is indeed implied in the interrogation now before us. *How*, liter-

ally *what*, i. e. (*in*) *what* (*way*), or (*by*) *what* (*means*)? See Gen. xliv. 16. The unusual word *bestowments* is here used to represent a Hebrew one occurring only here, but evidently formed from the verb (גָּמַל) to confer or bestow upon, employed in v. 7 above. The peculiar form both of the noun and pronoun (תַּגְמוּלוֹהִי) is regarded by the highest philological authorities as fixing the date of the composition after the Captivity.

13. *The cup of salvations I will take up, and on the name of Jehovah will call.* This is commonly explained by a reference to the Jewish tradition of a cup of thanksgiving which accompanied or followed the thank-offerings. But we read of no such cup in Scripture, and its origin may probably be traced to the rabbinical interpretation of this very passage. Interpreted by Scriptural analogies it simply means, I will accept the portion God allots me. For this figurative use of *cup*, see above, on Ps. xi. 6. xvi. 5. The plural form, *salvations*, denotes fulness or completeness, as in Ps. xviii. 52 (51.) liii. 7 (6.) *Take up*, as if from the table where the hand of God has placed it; or *lift up*, towards heaven, as a gesture of acknowledgment.

14. *My vows to Jehovah will I pay—in the presence of all his people.* The word *now*, in the common version, misleads the English reader, who can scarcely fail to understand it as an adverb of time, meaning *at present*, *immediately*, *without delay*, whereas it is the particle of entreaty (נָא) used in Ps. cxv. 2, and here employed to modify the bold avowal of a purpose, by making it dependent on divine permission. As if he had said: my vows to Jehovah I will pay—let me do it in the presence (I entreat) of all his people. The same meaning is attached by some to the augmented or paragogic form of the word translated *presence*, and which strictly means the front or forepart. Both these peculiarities are reckoned among the indications of a later age of Hebrew composition.

15. *Precious in the eyes of Jehovah (is) the death of his gracious ones* (or *saints.*) The idea and expression are borrowed from Ps. lxxii. 14, where the same thing is said of their blood. The word for *death* has the same peculiarity of form as that for *presence* in v. 14, and is construed in the same way with the preposition *to*, *the death to his saints*, i. e. the death belonging to them, which they die. These are regarded by the critics as additional tokens of the age in which the psalm was written. The verse assigns the reason for the preceding vow, to wit, that God counts the death of his people too costly to be lightly or gratuitously suffered.

16. *Ah now Jehovah—for I (am) thy servant, I (am) thy servant, the son of thy handmaid; thou hast loosed my bonds.* The expression of entreaty at the beginning has reference to some thing not expressed, though easily supplied, namely permission thus to testify his gratitude. Ah now Lord (suffer me thus to do) for I am thy servant, etc. The additional phrase, *son of thy handmaid*, is much stronger than *thy servant*, and describes him as a home-born slave. See above, on Ps. lxxxvi. 16. In the last clause we have another instance of a preposition (ל) interposed between the active verb and its object, in a way unknown to the older Hebrew. It is possible, however, to translate the words, *thou hast freed (me) as to* (i. e. from) *my bonds.*

17. *To thee will I sacrifice a sacrifice of thanks, and on the name of Jehovah will I call.* The sense is not, I will offer thanks instead of an oblation, but an oblation really expressive of thanksgiving and appointed for that purpose.

18. *My vows to Jehovah will I pay in the presence* (I entreat) *of all his people.* An exact repetition of v. 14, with all its singularities of form.

19. *In the courts of the house of Jehovah, in the midst of thee, Jerusalem. Hallelujah!* This verse completes the one before it, and explains the phrase, *before all his people.* Some regard it as a proof that the psalm was composed after the actual rebuilding of the temple. But in Ezr. ii. 68. iii. 8, we find the designation *house of God* applied to the consecrated site. The use of the word *courts* is still more natural, because it originally means *enclosures*, which might be and no doubt were defined, long before the temple was rebuilt. This explanation seems to be confirmed by the addition of the last clause. In the courts of the Lord's house, that is, on the consecrated spot in the midst of thee, oh Jerusalem, the Holy City.

PSALM CXVII.

This, which is the shortest psalm in the collection, has evidently no independent character or even meaning of its own, but was designed to be a chorus or doxology to a longer composition. Its position is sufficiently accounted for by the assumption, that it was primarily meant to serve the purpose just described with reference to the psalm or to the trilogy immediately preceding; while its being separately written as an independent psalm may have arisen from the purpose to use it sometimes in a different connection, with which view it would naturally be left moveable, like the doxologies in our modern books, which may be attached to any psalm or hymn, at the discretion of the person who conducts the service.

1. *Praise Jehovah, all ye nations; laud him all ye peoples.*

The last word is a different plural form from that in Gen. xxv. 16. Num. xxv. 15, and belongs no doubt to the later Hebrew. Here, as in Ps. xlvii. 2 (1.) lxvi. 8. xcviii. 4. the whole world is invited to praise God for his favours shown to Israel.

2. *For mighty over us has been his mercy, and the truth of Jehovah (is) to eternity. Hallelujah!* The verb at the beginning means not merely to be great, but tc be strong or powerful. See above, on Ps. ciii. 11. The preposition *over* suggests the idea of protection, or, if translated *on,* that of favour descending from above.

PSALM CXVIII.

After an invitation to praise God for his goodness to his people, vs. 1—4, the occasion of this praise is more particularly stated, namely, that he has delivered Israel from great distress, and thereby proved himself worthy of their highest confidence, vs. 5—14. After another statement of the favour just experienced, vs. 15—18, the people are described as entering the sanctuary, there to give thanks and implore the divine blessing on the enterprise in which they are engaged, vs. 19—29. The ideal speaker, throughout the psalm, is Israel, as the Church or chosen people. The deliverance celebrated cannot be identified with any one so naturally as with that from the Babylonish exile. Some, on account of supposed allusions to the temple as already built, refer the psalm to the times of Nehemiah. Others, with more probability, though not with absolute conclusiveness, infer from the tone of lively joy and thankfulness, pervading the whole composition, that it was written and originally sung soon after the return; and from the allusions in vs. 22, 25, that it has reference to the founding of the second temple, and is the very psalm, or one of the psalms, mentioned in the history, Ezra iii. 10, 11, where its first and last words are recited. The mention of David in that passage is accounted for by the assumption that this psalm was sung only as a part of the whole series, which opens with a Davidic trilogy, Ps. cviii—cx.

1. *Give thanks unto Jehovah, for (he is) good, for unto eternity (is) his mercy.* The opening formula is common to this psalm with Ps. cvi and cvii. Its elements are also found, combined with others, in Ps. c. 4, 5. With the second member of the sentence compare Ps. xxv. 8. lxxiii. 1.

2. *Oh that Israel would say—for unto eternity (is) his mercy.* The first clause of this translation is a paraphrase of the original, to which the particle of entreaty (נָא) gives a strong optative meaning. Here, as in Ps. cxvi. 14, 18, the common version (*now*) is equivocal. That version also has *that* instead of *for*, in the last clause of this and the two next verses. This translation is perfectly grammatical, and makes the sentence more complete in itself. But besides that it breaks the studied uniformity of the context by varying the version of the particle (כִּי), the dependence of the clause on the preceding verse, required and denoted by the use of the word *for*, is really essential to the writer's object. It is as if he had said: the reason for thus urging man to praise Jehovah is because his mercy endureth forever, and oh that Israel would join in affirming this reason. *Oh that Israel would say* (I will give thanks) *for his mercy endureth forever.*

3, 4. *Oh that the house of Aaron would say—'for unto eternity (is) his mercy.' Oh that the fearers of Jehovah would say—'for unto eternity (is) his mercy.'* The succession of Israel, the house of Aaron, and the fearers of Jehovah, in this and the following verses, is the same as in Ps. cxv. 9—11. This and the trine repetitions in vs. 10—12, 15—16, compared with that in Ps. cxv. 12—13, are corroborations of the assumed affinity between the psalms of this whole series, both in origin and purpose.

5. *Out of anguish I invoked Jah; heard me in a wide place Jah.* The first noun is a rare one, common to this place and Ps. cxvi. 3, another indication of affinity. *Heard*, in the pregnant sense of heard favourably, heard and answered. See above, on Ps. xxii. 22 (21.) As the word translated *anguish* originally means pressure, confinement, the appropriate figure for relief from it is a wide room, ample space, enlargement. See above, on Ps. iv. 2 (1.) To *answer in a wide place* is to grant his prayer by bringing him forth into such a place.

6. *Jehovah (is) for me; I will not fear; what can man do to me?* Instead of *for me*, i. e. in my favour, on my side, the Hebrew (לִי) may also be translated *to me*, i. e. is or belongs to me, is mine. See above, on Ps. lvi. 5, 10, 12 (4, 9, 11.) *Man* does not here mean *a man*, but *mankind*, or Man as opposed to God.

7. *Jehovah is for me, among my helpers, and I shall look upon my haters.* Here again, the first clause may be rendered, *Jehovah is to me (or I have Jehovah) among* or *with my helpers.* With this last expression compare Ps. xlv. 10 (9.) xcix. 6. The construction in the last clause is the idiomatic one meaning to see with joy or triumph, or to see their punishment and subjugation. See above, on Ps. liv. 9 (7), and with the whole verse compare Ps. liv. 6 (4.) As the ideal speaker is the ancient church or

chosen people, the haters or enemies here meant are primarily heathen persecutors and oppressors.

8. *It is good to confide in Jehovah* (more) *than to trust in man.* This and the next verse affirm clearly and fully what is more obscurely intimated in Ps. cxvi. 11. As the Hebrew has no distinct form of comparison, this is the nearest possible approach to saying, *it is better.* *Than*, literally *from*, *away from*, implying difference, and then comparison, but not expressing it. The verb *confide* is the expressive one originally meaning to take refuge or find shelter. See above, on Ps. ii: 12.

9. *It is good to confide in Jehovah* (more) *than to trust in nobles.* This merely strengthens the foregoing declaration, by rendering it more specific and emphatic. The Lord is more to be confided in, not merely than the mass of men, but than their chiefs. *Nobles* is a better translation than *princes*, because it keeps up the association with the adjective sense *noble*, generous, liberal, spontaneous, which is otherwise lost sight of. See above, on Ps. li. 14 (12.) Even the Persian patrons and protectors of the Jews had not entirely deserved their confidence; nor at all, in comparison with Jehovah their covenanted God.

10. *All the nations surround me; in the name of Jehovah—that I will cut them off.* The hyperbolical expression, *all the nations*, is less strange than it might otherwise appear because (גּוֹיִם) *nations* had now begun to be familiarly applied to the gentiles or heathen, not as organized bodies merely, but as individuals, especially when numerous. There is nothing unnatural, therefore, in the use of this expression to describe the heathen adversaries of the Jews at the period of the Restoration, not excepting the Samaritans, who, though they claimed to be a mixed race, were really heathen, both in origin and character. Another way in which the hyperbole may be explained, or rather done

away, is by supposing the first clause to be substantially although not formally conditional. *Should all nations* (or *though all nations should*) *surround me.* The strongest sense may then be put upon the words *all nations*, as the act ascribed to them is merely hypothetical. The construction of the last clause is unusual and doubtful. Some arbitrarily make the כִּי a particle of affirmation, yea, yes, verily, etc. Others gain the same sense by explaining the whole phrase to mean, (it is true, or it is certain) *that I will cut them off*. The same use of the particle is thought to be exemplified in Isai. vii. 9. Perhaps the best solution is the one afforded by the Hebrew usage of suppressing the principal verb in oaths or solemn affirmations. If this may be omitted even when there is nothing to denote the character of the expression, and when the form of the expression itself is liable to misconstruction, as for instance in the formula with *if*, much more may it be omitted where the sense of the expression is quite clear, and its juratory or imprecatory character denoted by accompanying words. The sense will then be, *in the name of Jehovah* (I swear or solemnly affirm) *that I will cut them off*. This last verb always means *to cut*, and except in Ps. xc. 6, where one of its derived forms is used, *to circumcise*. It was here used, as some suppose, to suggest that the uncircumcised enemies of Israel, as they are often called, should be cut or cut off in another sense. Compare the play upon the corresponding Greek words in Phil. iii. 2, 3.

11. *They surround me, yea they surround me; in the name of Jehovah* (I declare) *that I will cut them off*. The same sentence is repeated with a slight variation, which consists in the omission of the subject and the iteration of the verb, rendered more emphatic by a change of form. The word translated *yea* means *also*, *likewise*, but cannot be so used in the English idiom. The climax indicated may be, that the act described is no longer hypothetical but actual. They surround me, yes, they really, in fact, surround me.

12. *They surround me like bees; they are quenched as a fire of thorns; in the name of Jehovah* (I declare) *that I will cut them off.* This completes the trine repetition so characteristic of these psalms. The point of comparison with bees is their swarming multitude and irritating stings. Compare Deut. i. 44. That with thorns is the rapidity and ease with which they are both kindled and extinguished. See above, on Ps. lviii. 10 (9.)

13. *Thou didst thrust, thrust at me, to* (make me) *fall, and Jehovah helped me.* By a lively apostrophe, the enemy is here addressed directly, that is, the hostile heathen power, from whose oppressions Israel had just been rescued. See above, on v. 7. The verb to *thrust* or *strike at* is the root of the noun translated *falling* in Ps. lvi. 14 (13.) cxvi. 8.

14. *My strength and song (is) Jah, and he has become my salvation.* These words are from Ex. xv. 2. The first clause is also borrowed by Isaiah (xii. 2.) *My strength and song*, my protection or deliverer, and as such the object of my praise. *Become my salvation*, literally, *has been to me for salvation*, a stronger though synonymous expression for *my saviour*.

15. *The voice of joy and salvation in the tents of the righteous—the right hand of Jehovah has made strength.* The word translated *joy* means properly the audible expression of it by shout or song, and is sometimes applied even to a cry of distress. Compare Ps. xxx. 6 (5.) xlii. 5 (4.) xlvii. 2 (1) with Ps. xvii. 1. lxi. 2 (1.) *Joy and salvation* are related as cause and effect, joy occasioned by salvation. *Tents*, a poetical expression for dwellings. See above, on Ps. xci. 10. *The righteous*, the true Israel, the people of God, as such considered. See above, on Ps. xxxiii. 1. The substantive verb (*is*) may be supplied in this verse, so as to make it a complete proposition; or it may be a kind of exclamation, as if he had said, Hark! the voice of joy, etc. Compare

Isai. xl. 3, 6. The last clause may then be understood as containing the words uttered by the voice. The idiomatic phrase at the end may either mean that God has acquired or exerted strength. See above, on Ps. lx. 14 (12.) cviii. 14.

16. *The right hand of Jehovah is raised, the right hand of Jehovah makes strength.* This, with the last clause of v. 15, makes another of the triplets or trine repetitions, which are characteristic of these psalms. See above, on vs. 2—4, 10—12. Instead of *is raised* some read *raises* or *exalts*, which is equally grammatical, as the active and passive forms in this case are coincident. The meaning then is, that his right hand raises or exalts his people, as the other clause says that his right hand gains or exercises strength in their behalf. It seems more natural, however, to explain it as an instance of a common figure which describes God's hand as raised, when he exerts his power.

17. *I shall not die but live, and recount the works of Jah.* The existence thus to be preserved is that of Israel, and the last clause describes the final cause of that existence, which is here stated as a ground of confidence, and is elsewhere urged as an argument in prayer. See above, on Ps. cxv. 17. cxvi. 9, 15, and compare Ps. lxxi. 20. The original construction of the first clause is, *I shall not die, for I shall live.*

18. *Sorely has Jah chastened me, but to death did not give me.* This verse, though simple in its structure and transparent in its meaning, is highly idiomatic in its form. The adverb used in the translation represents the emphatic repetition of the verb in Hebrew, which is sometimes imitated in the English Bible (*chastening has Jah chastened me*), but seldom so as to convey the whole idea. Of such a repetition we have had an instance in v. 13. Another unavoidable departure from the original form consists in using *but* for *and*, at the beginning of the second clause. Did

not *give*, give up, give over or abandon. The chastisement here mentioned must be the calamity from which the people had been recently delivered, and in which we have already seen good grounds to recognize the Babylonish conquest, domination and captivity.

19. *Open ye to me the gates of righteousness, I will come in by them, I will thank Jah.* This may have been intended to accompany the entrance of the priests and people into the sacred enclosure, for the purpose of laying the foundation of the temple, as when David pitched the tabernacle on Mount Zion. See above, on Ps. xxiv.

20. *This (is) the gate* (that belongs) *to Jehovah; the righteous shall come in by it.* Or the meaning may be, since this is the Lord's gate, let the righteous (and no others) enter at it. Many interpreters find obvious indications here of double or responsive choirs, by which the psalm was to be sung. But this, though possible, is not a necessary supposition, nor is there any certain trace of such a usage or arrangement elsewhere in the book of Psalms. See above, vol. i. pp. 198, 200, 203.

21. *I will thank thee, for thou hast answered me, and hast become my salvation.* This verse assigns the reason for their entrance. *Answered*, in the specific sense of answering or granting prayer. See above, on v. 5. The last clause is from v. 14.

22. *The stone (*which*) the builders rejected has become the head of the corner.* This is a proverbial expression, and as such applicable to any case, in which what seemed to be contemptible has come to honour. This mode of expressing the idea was most probably suggested by the founding of the temple. There is no need, however, of supposing any actual dispute among the Jewish builders in relation to the corner stone of the sacred edi-

fice. The sight of the stone, or the act of laying it, would be sufficient to suggest the proverb and its application to the happy change experienced by Israel, so lately blotted from the list of nations, and regarded by the heathen as unworthy even of an humble place in the proud fabric of consolidated empire, but now restored not only to a place but to the highest place among the nations, not in point of power, wealth, or worldly glory, but as the chosen and peculiar people of the Most High God. As this psalm was sung by the people at the last Jewish festival attended by our Saviour, he applied this proverb to himself, as one rejected by the Jews and by their rulers, yet before long to be recognized as their Messiah whom they had denied and murdered, but whom God had exalted as a Prince and a Saviour, to give repentance to Israel and remission of sins (Acts v. 31.) This, though really another application of the proverb in its general meaning, has a certain affinity with its original application in the verse before us, because the fortunes of the ancient Israel, especially in reference to great conjunctures, bore a designed resemblance to the history of Christ himself, by a kind of sympathy between the Body and the Head. Even the temple, which suggested the original expression, did but teach the doctrine of divine inhabitation, and was therefore superseded by the advent of the Son himself. *The head of the corner* means the chief or corner stone of the foundation, even in Zech. iv. 7, where it is translated *head-stone.* The application of the verse before us made by Christ himself (Matt. xxi. 42) is renewed by Peter (Acts iv. 11.)

23. *From Jehovah is this; it is wonderfully done in our eyes.* This signal revolution in the condition of the chosen people is not the work of man but of God. *From the Lord*, i. e. proceeding from him as its author. *Is this*, literally, *has been*, i. e. happened, come to pass. In the last clause it is said to be not merely *wonderful*, but *wonderfully done*, the Hebrew word being a passive participle, which strictly means distinguished, made tc differ,

made strange, strangely done. Its plural is continually used as a noun in application to God's wondrous works or doings. This, no less than the proverb to which it is attached, was as appropriate to the case of the Messiah as to that of his people, and is accordingly applied in the same manner by himself (Matt. xxi. 42.)

24. *This is the day Jehovah has made, we will rejoice and triumph in it.* By the day we are here to understand the happier times which Israel, through God's grace, was permitted to enjoy. This day he is said, as the author of this blessed revolution, to have made, created. Some understand by *day* the festival or celebration, at which the psalm was intended to be sung. The *day*, in this sense, God is said to have *made* or instituted, not so much by positive appointment as by having providentially afforded the occasion for it. In a still higher sense, the words may be applied to the new dispensation, as a glorious change in the condition of the church, compared with which the restoration from captivity was nothing, except as a preliminary to it and a preparation for it. There is no allusion to the weekly Sabbath, except so far as it was meant to be a type of the rest of the church from the heavy burdens of the old dispensation.

25. *Ah now, Jehovah, save, we beseech thee! Ah now, Jehovah, prosper, we beseech thee!* The circumlocution, *we beseech thee*, is the only form in which the force of the supplicatory particle (נָא) can be expressed, without the risk of its being mistaken for an adverb of time. The whole phrase (הוֹשִׁיעָה נָּא), *save we pray*, became a standing formula of supplication with reference to great public interests or undertakings, and reappears in the New Testament under the form *Hosanna.* See Matt. xxi. 9, where we find it, in the acclamations of the multitude, combined with other expressions from this same psalm which, as we have seen, they were accustomed to sing at their great festivals. See above, on v. 22.

26. *Blessed be he that cometh in the name of Jehovah! We bless you from the house of Jehovah.* According to the accents, the construction of the first clause is, *blessed, in the name of Jehovah, be he that cometh.* This agrees exactly with the frequent mention of blessing in the name of Jehovah. See below, Ps. cxxix. 8, and compare Num. vi. 27. Deut. xxi. 5. 2 Sam. vi. 18. *He that cometh* is commonly and not improbably supposed to have meant primarily the people or their representatives, to whom, as they approached the sacred spot, these words were to be uttered. There were other thoughts, however, which the words could hardly fail to suggest, for example that of Israel coming back from exile, that of God coming back to his forsaken people, and at least in the most enlightened minds, that of the great Deliverer, to whose coming all the rest was but preparatory, to whom the name הַבָּא or ὁ ἐρχόμενος was afterwards given as a standing appellation, in allusion either to this passage or to Mal. iii. 1, or to both, and to whom this very sentence was applied by the multitude who witnessed and attended Christ's triumphal entrance into the Holy City. See Matt. xxi. 9.

27. *Mighty (is) Jehovah and hath given light to us. Bind the sacrifice with cords as far as the horns of the altar.* The first word does not express the general idea of divinity, but that of divine power, which is no doubt essential to the writer's purpose. It was the power of Jehovah which had turned the night of Israel to day, and illumined the darkness of their sore distress with the light of his returning favour. The figure is borrowed from the pillar of fire, the token of Jehovah's presence with his people in the wilderness. See Ex. xiii. 21. xiv. 20. Neh. ix. 12. The last clause has been the subject of a good deal of dispute. It is commonly admitted that (חַג) a Hebrew word, which properly denotes a periodical or stated festival, is here put for the victim offered at it, as in Ex. xxiii. 18 *the fat of my sacrifice* is in Hebrew the fat of my festival (חַגִּי), and in 2 Chron. xxx. 22,

another word for festival (מוֹעֵד) is used in precisely the same way, being governed by the verb to *eat*, although this singular expression is avoided in the English Bible, by the use of the word "throughout." Those who agree in this, however, are at variance in relation to the act required. As the word translated *cords* is sometimes applied to the thick boughs or branches of a tree (Ez. xix. 11. xxxi. 3, 10, 14), some understand the sense to be, Bind the sacrifice with branches, sacrificial wreaths. But this practice, and the meaning put upon the Hebrew word, are both denied by others who allege moreover the repeated combination of the same verb and noun in the sense of tying, making fast, with cords. See Judg. xv. 13. xvi. 11. Ez. iii. 25. The English Bible makes the clause refer to the fastening of the victim to the altar. To this it is objected that the preposition (עַד) means *as far as*, and implies a verb of motion, expressed or understood. To avoid this difficulty, some of the latest writers understand the words to signify the conducting of the victim bound until it reaches the altar as the place of sacrifice. Hold fast the sacrifice with cords, until it comes to the horns of the altar, poetically put for the altar itself, not only as its prominent or salient points, but as the parts to which the blood, the essential vehicle of expiation, was applied. Thus understood the clause is merely an invitation to fulfill the vow recorded in Ps cxvi. 14, 17, 18.

28. *My God art thou, and I will thank thee; my God, I will exalt thee.* The Hebrew words for *God* are not the same. The second is that commonly so rendered, while the first is that used in v. 27, and denoting the divine omnipotence.

29. *Give thanks unto Jehovah, for (He is) good, for unto eternity (is) his mercy.* In these words we are brought back to the point from which we started, and the circle of praise returns into itself.

PSALM CXIX.

There is no psalm in the whole collection which has more the appearance of having been exclusively designed for practical and personal improvement, without any reference to national or even to ecclesiastical relations, than the one before us, which is wholly occupied with praises of God's word or written revelation, as the only source of spiritual strength and comfort, and with prayers for grace to make a profitable use of it. The prominence of this one theme is sufficiently apparent from the fact, to which the Masora directs attention, that there is only one verse which does not contain some title or description of the word of God. But notwithstanding this peculiar character, the position of the psalm in the collection, and especially its juxtaposition with respect to Ps. cviii—cxviii, its kindred tone of mingled gratitude and sadness, and a great variety of minor verbal correspondences, have led some of the best interpreters to look upon it as the conclusion of the whole series or system of psalms, supposed to have been written for the use of the returned Jews, at or near the time of the founding of the second temple. The opinion, held by some of the same writers, that the ideal speaker, throughout this psalm, is Israel, considered as the church or chosen people, will never commend itself as natural or likely to the mass of readers, and is scarcely consistent with such passages as vs. 63, 74, 79, and others, where the speaker expressly distinguishes himself as an individual from the body of the people. The same difficulty, in a less degree, attends the national interpretation of the psalms immediately preceding. Perhaps the best mode of reconciling the two views is by supposing that this psalm was intended as a manual of pious and instructive thoughts, designed for popular improvement and especially for that of the younger generation after the return from exile, and that the person speaking is the individual believer, not as an isolated personality, but as a member of the general body, with which he identifies himself so far, that many expressions of the psalm are strictly applicable only to the whole as such considered, while others are appropriate only to certain persons or to certain classes in the ancient Israel. To this design of popular instruction, and especially to that of constant repetition and reflection, the psalm is admirably suited by its form and structure. The alphabetical arrangement, of which it is at once the most extended and most perfect specimen, and the aphoristic character, common to all alphabetic psalms, are both adapted to assist the memory, as well as to give point to the immediate impression. It follows, of course, that the psalm was rather meant to be a store-house of materials for pious meditation than a discourse for continuous perusal. At the same time, the fact of its existence in the Psalter is presumptive proof that it was used in public worship, either as a whole, or in one or more of the twenty-two stanzas into which it is divided, corresponding to the letters of the Hebrew alphabet, all the eight verses of each paragraph beginning with the same Hebrew letter.

1. *Happy the perfect of way*, i. e. blameless in their course of life, *those walking in the law of Jehovah.* There seems to be allusion to the precept in Lev. xviii. 4. The common version of the second Hebrew word (*undefiled*) is derived from the Vulgate (*immaculati*), which is itself too confined a version of the Septuagint (ἄμωμοι.) The essential idea is that of completeness or perfection. The form and construction of the first word are the same as in Ps. i. 1.

2. *Happy the keepers of his testimonies* (who) *with a whole heart seek him.* *Keepers*, observers, those obeying. *Testimonies*, the divine precepts, which bear witness against sin and in behalf of holiness. *With all the heart*, undivided affection. See above, Ps. cxi. 1, and compare 2 Kings xxiii. 3. *Seek him*, the knowledge of his will and the enjoyment of his favour.

3. (Who) *also do not practise wrong*, (but) *in his ways walk.* This verse both limits and completes the one before it, by showing that no zeal in seeking God can be acceptable, if coupled with a wicked life. *In his ways*, not in those of his enemies, nor even in their own.

4. *Thou hast commanded thy precepts, to be kept strictly.* Commanded, given them in charge, entrusted others with them. The literal meaning of the last clause is, *to keep very* (*much*), i. e. not formally or superficially, but really and thoroughly. Compare the use of (מְאֹד) as a noun in Deut. vi. 5.

5. *Oh that my ways were settled, to observe thy statutes!* The optative particle at the beginning occurs only here and, with a slight difference of pointing, 2 Kings v. 3. *My ways*, my customary modes of acting, my habits. *Settled*, fixed, confirmed, established, in opposition to capricious vacillation and unsteadiness. *To observe*, to watch, for the purpose of obeying. The word translated *statutes*, according to its etymology, means definite and permanent enactments.

6. *Then shall I not be shamed, in my looking unto all thy commandments.* The *then* at the beginning has respect to the time mentioned in the last clause. *Shamed*, put to shame, defeated, frustrated, disappointed in one's highest hopes. *In my looking* suggests the idea both of time and of causation, *when I look* and *because I look.* The act itself is that of looking towards

a mark to be attained, or towards a model, rule, or standard, to be followed and conformed to.

7. *I will thank thee with rectitude of heart, in my learning the judgments of thy righteousness.* It is only my experience of thy righteous judgments that enables me to praise thee as I ought; a sentiment peculiarly appropriate to the period of some great deliverance, for instance that of the return from exile, when the righteousness of God had been so signally displayed in the destruction of his enemies, and in the fulfilment of his promise to his people. Here again, *in my learning* does not mean merely *after I have learned*, but in the very act and in consequence of learning.

8. *Thy statutes I will keep; oh forsake me not utterly.* The fixed resolution to obey is intimately blended with a consciousness of incapacity to do so, unless aided by divine grace. *Utterly*, unto extremity or still more literally, *until very* (*much.*) The initial words of this first stanza are all different, except that vs. 1, 2, both begin with (אשרי) *happiness* or *happy.*

---

9. *By what* (means) *can a youth cleanse his path*, (so) *as to keep* (it) *according to thy word?* To *cleanse* is here to keep clean or pure from the stain of sin. Most interpreters regard the last clause as an answer to the question in the first. But this requires the infinitive to be construed as a gerund (*by keeping*), a construction too rare and doubtful to be anywhere assumed without necessity. See above, on Ps. lxxviii. 18. cxi. 6. It is much more simple and agreeable to usage to regard the whole as one interrogation, and the second clause as supplementary to the first. *To keep* may then mean to adhere to it, or rather, in accordance with the figure of the first clause, to preserve it clear or pure as God requires. The answer is suppressed, or rather left to be inferred from the whole tenor of the psalm, which is,

that men, and especially the young, whose passions and temptations are strong in proportion to their inexperience, can do nothing of themselves but are dependent on the grace of God. The omission of an answer, which is thus suggested by the whole psalm, rather strengthens than impairs the impression on the reader.

10. *With my whole heart have I sought thee; let me not err from thy commandments.* While the first clause alleges his sincerity in seeking God, the second and third owns his dependence on him for success and safety.

11. *In my heart have I hid thy saying, that I may not sin against thee.* The first phrase means *within me*, as opposed to a mere outward and corporeal possession of the written word. Not in my house, or in my hand, but in myself, my mind, with special reference, in this case, to the memory. *Hid*, not for concealment, but for preservation. The word *saying*, elsewhere used to signify God's promise, here denotes his precept, as it does in v. 67 below. *Against thee*, literally, *as to, with respect to thee.* See above, on Ps. li. 6 (4.)

12. *Blessed (be) thou, Jehovah! Teach me thy statutes!* The doxology seems designed to break the uniformity of this series of aphorisms, by an occasional expression of strong feeling. At the same time, it furnishes a kind of ground for the petition in the last clause. Since thou art the blessed and eternal God, have pity on my weakness and instruct me in the knowledge of thy will.

13. *With my lips have I recounted all the judgments of thy mouth.* I have not confined the knowledge of thy precepts to my own mind, but imparted it to others. See above, on Ps. xl. 10, 11 (9, 10.) *Judgments*, judicial decisions, determinations as to

what is right and binding, a description perfectly appropriate to the divine precepts. *Of thy mouth*, which thou hast uttered. There seems to be allusion to the phrase *with my lips* in the first clause.

14. *In the way of thy testimonies I rejoice as over all wealth.* Not merely in the knowledge of God's will, but in the doing of it, in treading the path which he prescribes for us. *Over* may be simply equivalent to *in*, or intended to suggest the additional idea of superiority, *above* (or *more than*) *all wealth*. *As over*, as I do over all the wealth I have, or as I should do over all wealth if I had it.

15. *In thy precepts will I meditate and look (at) thy paths.* Not only *of* thy precepts or concerning them, but *in* them, while engaged in doing them. *Look* has the same sense as in v. 6.

16. *In thy statutes I will delight myself; I will not forget thy word.* Delight or enjoy myself, seek my pleasure, find my happiness. Here ends the second stanza, in which all the verses except one (v. 12) begin not only with the same letter but the same word, the preposition (ב) *in*.

---

17. *Grant to thy servant* (that) *I may live, and I will keep thy word.* Grant to, bestow upon, thy servant this favour. See above, on Ps. xiii. 6 (5.) There may be an allusion to the way in which the law connects life and obedience. See Lev. xviii. 5. Deut. vi. 24.

18. *Uncover my eyes and I will look—wonders out of thy law!* The last clause is a kind of exclamation after his eyes have been uncovered. This figure is often used to denote inspiration or a special divine communication. *Out of thy law*, i. e. brought out to view, as if from a place of concealment.

19. *A stranger (am) I in the earth; hide not from me thy commandments.* A stranger, an exile, one without friends or home, a poetical description of calamity in general, not without allusion to the captivity both in Babylon and Egypt, and to the consequent mention of strangers in the Law as objects of compassion. The prayer in the last clause is, that God will not withhold from him the knowledge of his will.

20. *My soul breaketh with longing for thy judgments at every time.* The Hebrew verb occurs only here, but its meaning is determined by the cognate dialects. The word translated *longing* belongs also to the later Hebrew. Its verbal root occurs below in vs. 40, 174. *Judgments* includes God's precepts mentioned in v. 19 and his penal inflictions on the wicked mentioned in v. 21.

21. *Thou hast rebuked the proud, the accursed, those wandering from thy commandments.* Compare Ps. ix. 6 (5.) Rebuked, not merely by word but by deed, i. e. punished.

22. *Roll from off me reproach and contempt, for thy testimonies I have kept.* The first verse coincides in form with that at the beginning of v. 18, but is from a different root. There is an obvious allusion to the rolling off of the reproach of Egypt, Josh. v. 9.

23. *Also princes sat and at me talked together, and thy servant muses of thy statutes.* This is one of the expressions in the psalm not literally applicable to the individual believer, and regarded therefore as a proof of its national design and import. The princes are then the chiefs of the surrounding nations. The *also* (גַּם) seem to be inserted merely on account of the alphabetical arrangement which requires the letter gimel.

24. *Also thy testimonies (are) my delights, the men of my*

counsel. He calls them his counsellors, in opposition to the malignant counsels of the enemy. *Delights*, enjoyments, happiness, the plural form denoting fulness and completeness. Two of the verses in the stanza ending here begin with (גם) *also*, and two with (גל), though in different senses.

---

25. *My soul cleaveth unto the dust; quicken thou me according to thy word.* The first clause seems intended to suggest two consistent but distinct ideas, that of deep degradation, as in Ps. xliv. 26 (25), and that of death, as in Ps. xxii. 30 (29.) The first would be more obvious in itself, and in connection with the parallel referred to; but the other seems to be indicated as the prominent idea by the correlative petition in the last clause. *Quicken*, i. e. save me alive, or restore me to life, the Hebrew word being a causative of the verb *to live.* See above, on Ps. xxx. 4 (3.) *Thy word*, the promise annexed to thy commandment, as in v. 28 below.

26. *My ways have I recounted, and thou hast answered me; teach me thy statutes.* The first clause is not to be restricted to a confession of sin, though that may be included, but extended to a statement of his cares, anxieties, and affairs in general. Hence the correlative expression, *thou hast answered me*, the Hebrew verb being specially appropriated to the hearing or answering of prayer, i. e. granting what it asks. The last clause expresses a desire to testify his gratitude for God's compassion by obeying his commandments, with the usual acknowledgment that these cannot be executed without divine assistance, or even known without divine instruction.

27. *The way of thy precepts make me understand, and I will muse of thy wonders.* The first clause expreses the same wish, arising from the same consciousness of weakness, as in v. 26. The verb in the last clause is one of those in the usage of which the

ideas of speech and meditation run continually into one another See above, on Ps. lv. 18 (17.) lxix. 13 (12.) lxxiv. 4, 7 (3, 6.) cv. 2.

28. *My soul weeps from sorrow ; raise me up according to thy word.* The meaning of the first verb seems to be determined by Job xvi. 20, where the same thing is predicated of the eye. The oldest versions make it mean *to slumber* (LXX. ἐνύσταξεν. Vulg. *dormitavit*), which would make the clause remarkably coincident with Luke xxii. 45.

29. *The way of falsehood remove from me, and thy law grant unto me graciously.* The way mentioned in the first clause is that of unfaithfulness to God's covenant, or of apostasy from it. See above, v. 21. *Remove*, a causative in Hebrew, meaning *make to depart.* The common version of the last verb, as above given, is a correct paraphrase of the Hebrew verb (חָנַן) to be gracious, to act graciously, and here still more specifically, to give graciously, to bestow as a free favour. To give the law is still, as in the preceding verses, to make it known by a divine illumination.

30. *The way of truth have I chosen ; thy judgments have I set* (before me.) *Truth*, in the sense of faithfulness, fidelity to obligations, the opposite of the *falsehood* mentioned in v. 29. His own choice coincides with the divine requisitions. *Judgments*, as in vs. 7, 13, above. *I have set*, i. e. before me, as an end to be aimed at, and a rule to be followed. The Hebrew verb occurs above, Ps. xviii. 34 (33.) xxi. 6 (5.) lxxxix. 20 (19), and the full phrase, Ps. xvi. 8. The Septuagint renders it here, *I have not forgotten.*

31. *I have cleaved unto thy testimonies, oh Jehovah, put me not to shame.* The first verb is the same with that in v. 25. *Unto*, literally *in*, as if implying a complete absorption in the object.

See above, on Ps. i. 2. *Testimonies*, precepts, as in v. 2. *Shame me not*, suffer not my hopes to be disappointed and confounded The Hebrew verb is a causative of that in v. 6.

32. *The way of thy commandments will I run, for thou wilt enlarge my heart.* The verb to *run* expresses a more zealous obedience than the usual expression *walk*. To *enlarge* is sometimes to relieve from confinement. See above, on Ps. cxviii. 5. But the whole phrase, *to enlarge the heart*, seems, especially in this connection, to denote a change in the affections leading to more prompt obedience. Of the eight verses in this stanza five begin with the noun (דֶּרֶךְ) *way* or its plural, and two with the verb (דָּבַק) *to cleave.*

---

33. *Guide me, Jehovah,* (in) *the way of thy statutes, and I will keep it* (to the) *end.* The first verb is here used in its primary sense of showing or pointing out the way, from which is deduced the secondary one of teaching. *Keep it*, observe it, adhere to it, keep in it. The last word in Hebrew, which occurs above, in different senses and connections, Ps. xix. 12 (11.) xl. 16 (15.) lxx. 4 (3), is used adverbially here and in v. 112 below.

34. *Make me understand* (it) *and I will keep thy law, and will observe it with a whole heart.* The first verb is too vaguely rendered in the English versions (*give me understanding.*) It has here the same sense as in v. 27, and the object is to be supplied from the next member of the sentence. The form of the last verb is one expressing strong desire and fixed determination. *With a whole heart*, or *with all (my) heart*, as in v. 2.

35. *Make me tread in the path of thy commandments, for in it do I delight.* The first verb is the causative of that used in Ps. vii. 13 (12.) xi. 2. xxxvii. 14. xci. 13. *I delight*, have delighted, not at present merely but in time past.

36. *Incline my heart unto thy testimonies, and not to gain.* Here again the sense of absolute dependence or divine influence is strongly implied. *Testimonies*, as in v. 31. *Gain*, profit, lucre, as in Ps. xxx. 10 (9), but here put for overweening love of it, supreme devotion to it.

37. *Turn away my eyes from seeing falsehood; in thy ways quicken me.* The first verb strictly means to *cause to pass* (or *turn*) *away*. *Falsehood* is not the word so rendered in v. 29, but the negative term (שָׁוְא) meaning *vanity*, nonentity, and here applied to all objects of religious trust besides God. These the Psalmist desires not even to see, much less to gaze at with delight and confidence. See above, Ps. xxxi. 7 (6.) xl. 5 (4.) lx. 13 (11.) lxii. 10 (9.) *Quicken me*, save me or make me alive, as in v. 25. *In thy ways*, by leading me in the way of thy commandments.

38. *Make good to thy servant thy word which* (thou hast spoken) *to thy fearers.* The first verb means to cause to stand, to set up, to establish, to confirm, and in this connection to fulfill or verify. *To thy servant*, not merely *to me*, but *to me who am thy servant*, in a special and emphatic sense, which is applicable either to the chosen people as a whole, or to its individual members. *Thy word*, as in vs. 25, 28. *To thy fearers*, literally, *to thy fear*, the abstract being put for the concrete term; or it might be rendered *for thy fear*, that thou mayest be feared. See below, on Ps. cxxx. 4.

39. *Turn away my disgrace which I dread, for thy judgments* (*are*) *good.* The first word is the same with that in v. 37, meaning *make* (or *cause*) *to pass away*. In this connection it might either mean to remove or to avert; but the latter agrees better with the next phrase, *which I dread*. The original is not the common Hebrew word for *fear*, but one used by Moses in precisely the same sense as here. See Deut. ix. 19. xxviii. 60, and com-

pare Job ix. 28. *Thy judgments are good*, i. e. prompted and controlled by infinite goodness, and should therefore fall upon the wicked, not the righteous.

40. *Behold, I long for thy precepts ; in thy righteousness quicken me.* The first word is equivalent to *see* (or *thou seest*) that it is so, and involves an appeal to the divine omniscience. The first verb is the root of the noun *longing* in v. 20. To long for God's precepts is to long for the knowledge of them and for grace to obey them. The last clause prays that since God's judgments are good (v. 39), instead of killing they may make alive. See above, on vs. 17, 25, 37. In the stanza closing with this verse, only one initial word is repeated, namely (הַעֲבֵר) *cause to pass* or *turn away.*

---

41. *And let thy mercies come (unto) me, oh Jehovah, thy salvation, according to thy word.* That the stanzas were not meant to be regarded as distinct and independent compositions, is clear from the copulative (*and*) at the beginning of this verse. *Mercies*, suited to my various necessities. *Come to me*, or *upon me*, or *into me*, which are the ideas commonly expressed by this verb when construed directly with a noun. See above, Ps. xxxv. 8. xxxvi. 12 (11.) c. 4. *Salvation* is in apposition with *mercies*, being that in which all other gifts and favours are summed up and comprehended. With the last words compare v. 38 above.

42. *And* (then) *I will answer my reviler a word ; for I trust in thy word.* The best answer to the calumnies and insults of his enemies is that afforded by his manifest experience of God's favour, and the practical vindication thereby afforded. The addition of *word*, which in our idiom is superfluous, may have some reference to its use in the corresponding clause. As if he had said : only let thy word be fulfilled, and I shall have a word to say in answer to my enemies.

43. *And take not out of my mouth* (this) *word of truth utterly, for in thy judgments do I hope.* Deprive me not of this conclusive answer to my enemies, by withholding that providential vindication of my character and practical attestation of thy favour towards me, which I confidently look for. The first verb is used in its primary sense (Gen. xxxii. 12), from which comes the usual but secondary one of snatching out of danger, extricating, saving. For the literal meaning of the Hebrew phrase translated *utterly*, see above, on v. 8. The last phrase in the verse means, *for thy judgments I have waited*, i. e. confidently looked for their appearance.

44. *And I will observe thy law always, unto eternity and perpetuity.* Not merely for a time, or for the purpose of securing this triumph over his enemies, but forever, to express which idea the three strongest terms afforded by the language are combined. As the keeping of the law, so often mentioned in this psalm, has evident reference to the present life, the strong promise of perpetual obedience, in the verse before us, is considered by some writers as a proof that the ideal speaker is not an individual believer, but the church or chosen people.

45. *And I will walk in a wide place, for thy precepts have I sought.* Free from the pressure and confinement to which he had been previously subject. See above, on Ps. cxviii. 5. *Sought thy precepts*, i. e. sought to know them and to do them. Compare the combination, *keep and seek*, in 1 Chr. xxviii. 8.

46. *And I will speak of thy testimonies before kings and will not be ashamed.* Here again some eminent interpreters have found an indication of the national design and meaning of the whole psalm, as the individual believer could not be expected to bear witness to the truth in such a presence. He might however do so, as one of the component parts of the whole body. But

the words are really expressive only of a readiness to declare the divine testimony against sin, in any presence, even the most august, if it should be necessary. This passage seems to have been present to our Saviour's mind when he uttered the prediction in Matt. x. 18. *Ashamed* has here its strict sense, as denoting a painful feeling of humiliation.

47. *And I will delight myself in thy commandments which I love.* I will not obey them merely from a selfish dread of punishment or painful sense of obligation, but because I love them and derive my highest happiness from doing them. See above, on Ps. xix. 12 (11.) The first verb has the same sense as in v. 16. The past tense of the last verb (*I have loved*) represents his love to God's commandments as no new-born and capricious passion, but a settled habit and affection of his soul.

48. *And I will raise my hands to thy commandments which I love, and I will muse of thy statutes.* The raising of the hands is a symbol of the raising of the heart or the affections to some elevated object. See above, on Ps. xxviii. 2. *Which I love*, or *have loved*, as in v. 47, the terms of which are studiously repeated with a fine rhetorical effect, which is further heightened by the *and* at the beginning, throwing both verses, as it were, into one sentence. As if he had said: I will derive my happiness from thy commandments, which I love and have loved, and to these commandments, which I love and have loved, I will lift up my hands and heart together. For the meaning of the last clause, see above, on v. 27. The connective force of the conjunction *and* must not be urged in this verse, as it was needed to supply the initial *vau*, a letter with which scarcely any Hebrew words begin.

---

49. *Remember* (thy) *word to thy servant, because thou hast made me to hope.* The obvious meaning of the first clause

is, *remember the word* (spoken) *to thy servant.* But Hebrew usage makes it probable, that the first and last words of the clause are to be construed together, so as to mean *remember for thy servant*, i. e. for his benefit, as in Ps. xcviii. 3. cvi. 45. *Word* is then absolutely put for promise, as in Ps. lvi. 11 (10), and the meaning of the whole clause is, remember thy promise in compassion to thy servant. The common version of the last clause (*upon which etc.*) is forbidden by the facts, that the Hebrew verb is never construed elsewhere with the proposition *on*, and that Hebrew usage would require a different combination (אשר עליו) to convey the sense supposed. That the one here used (על אשר) may mean *because*, is clear from Deut. xxix. 24. 2 Sam. iii. 30. The same verb that means *to hope* in v. 43 is used as a causative, *to make hope*, here and in Ezek. xiii. 6.

50. *This (is) my comfort in my suffering, and thy word quickens me.* The reference to continued suffering in the first clause, and to its partial cessation in the second, agrees well with the condition of the chosen people when restored from exile. The terms, however, are so chosen as to be equally appropriate to personal afflictions, restorations, and deliverances. The word for *comfort* occurs elsewhere only in Job vi. 10, where it has precisely the same form. *Thy word* includes thy decree or order and thy promise. *Quickens*, saves alive, or restores to life, according to the prayer in vs. 25, 37, 40. The past tense (*has quickened*) implies that the conservative or restorative effect has already been experienced, though not yet perfected.

51. *Proud (ones) deride me greatly; from thy law I swerve not.* Both verbs are in the past tense, which would seem to indicate that the derision here complained of, although recent, had now ceased or been abated. The clause agrees well with the scorn excited in the heathen neighbours of the restored Jews by what seemed to be their mad attempt to build the temple.

The omission of a connective makes the antithesis more pointed. *Swerved*, declined, or turned aside. See above, on Ps. xliv. 19 (18), and compare Ps. xl. 5 (4.) The first word in the verse is one commonly applied to presumptuous high-handed sinners. See above, on Ps. xix. 14 (13.)

52. *I have remembered thy judgments from eternity, Jehovah, and consoled myself.* His faith and hope under present trials are sustained by recollection of the past. *Thy judgments*, not merely the punishments inflicted on thy enemies, but all the exhibitions of thy righteousness in outward act, including the deliverances of thy people. *From eternity*, or from an indefinite antiquity, which is the primary meaning of the Hebrew word. There is no reason for discarding the reflexive form of the last verb, as some versions do, especially as it suggests the idea, not of a mere passive reception of the comfort, but of an active effort to obtain it.

53. *Rage has seized me from wicked (men) abandoning thy law.* No English word is strong enough to represent the first one in the Hebrew of this verse except rage or fury. See above, on Ps. xi. 6. It here denotes the highest pitch of indignant disapproval. *From*, i. e. arising or proceeding from, because of. *Forsaking thy law*, not only refusing in practice to obey it, but avowedly abjuring its authority.

54. *Songs for me have been thy statutes in the house of my sojournings.* Instead of abjuring them as presumptuous sinners do, I make them the subject of my thankful and triumphant songs (Isai. xxiv. 16), even while I sojourn as a pilgrim and a stranger in a strange land. *The house of my sojournings, i. e.* the house where I sojourn, is an imitation of the phrase, *land of sojournings*, which occurs so often in the patriarchal history. See Gen. xvii. 8. xxviii. 4. xxxvi. 7. xxxvii. 1. *Pilgrimage* is less exact because it suggests the idea of locomotion rather than of

rest. The statutes of God are thus rejoiced in, not as mere requisitions, but as necessarily including promises.

55. *I remember in the night thy name, Jehovah, and observe thy law.* The night is mentioned as the natural and customary season of reflection and self-recollection, and also as the time when pains of every kind are usually most acute. See above, on Ps. xci. 5. With this clause and the verse preceding compare Job xxxv. 10. *Thy name*, i. e. all that is denoted by thy names, and more especially by the one here mentioned, thy eternal self-existence and thy covenant relation to thy people.

56. *This has been to me, for thy precepts I have kept.* The usual interpretations, *this I had because I kept thy precepts*, and *this I have* (namely) *that I keep thy precepts*, are almost unmeaning. When taken in connection with the one before it, the true sense of the verse appears to be, that what he was thus wont to promise or resolve, he had performed. The substantive verb is to be taken in the sense which it so often has in history. This has happened to me, come to pass, been verified in my experience. In the stanza which here ends, three verses begin with some form of the verb (זָכַר) *to remember*, and two with the pronoun (זאת) *this*.

---

57. *My portion, oh Jehovah, I have said, (is) to keep thy words.* This construction is rejected by Hengstenberg and others, as forbidden by the accents and the analogy of Ps. xvi. 5. lxxiii. 26. But as the same words may either express the sense here given or *my portion (is) Jehovah*, we are at liberty to choose the one best suited to the context, even in opposition to the accents, which cannot be regarded as an ultimate authority. In favour of the sense first given is its perfect agreement with the close of the preceding stanza. In reference to the resolution there recorded

and described as having been fulfilled, he here adds, thus have I said (declared my purpose) oh Lord to obey thy words.

58. *I have sought thy favour with all* (my) *heart; be gracious unto me according to thy word.* In the first clause we have a repetition of the singular and striking idiom used in Ps. xlv. 13 (12), and explained by some as meaning strictly to soothe or stroke the face, and by others to soften or subdue it, i. e. the hostility or opposition expressed by it. *With all (my) heart*, or *with a whole heart*, as in vs. 2, 34, above. *Thy word* or *saying*, i. e. thy promise. The original expression is not (דבר) the one so constantly employed in this psalm, but (אמרה) that used in vs. 10, 41, and derived from the verb (אמר) *to say*.

59. *I have thought on my ways, and turned back my feet to thy testimonies.* The first verb here means *thought over*, pondered, as in Ps. lxxvii. 6 (5.) *My ways*, i. e., as appears from the last clause, my departures from thy testimonies or commandments. See above, on vs. 2, 14, 31, 36, 46. The common version of the last verb (*turned*), although correct, is not sufficient to convey the full force of the Hebrew word, which is a causative meaning to bring back or make to return, and implying previous departure, whereas the primitive verb *turn* carries with it no such implication. While this verse is exactly descriptive of the process of personal conviction and conversion, it is also strikingly appropriate to the effects of the captivity on Israel, as a church and nation.

60. *I hastened, and delayed not, to observe thy commandments.* This continues the account of his conversion, begun in the preceding verse. The first clause exemplifies the idiomatic combination of a positive and negative expression of the same idea. The second verb is peculiarly expressive and seems to be applied, in the most ancient Hebrew books, to a trifling and unreasonable tarrying in great emergencies. See Gen. xix. 16. xliii. 10. Ex. xii

39. In this respect, as well as in relation to its singular reduplicated form, the Hebrew verb bears some analogy to certain familiar terms in English, which are colloquially used in the same manner.

61. *The bands of wicked men environed me,* (but) *thy law I did not forget.* As descriptive of personal experience, this may be translated in the present (*environ me, forget not*) ; but in order to include a reference to the Babylonish exile, and the preservation of the people from apostasy at that eventful crisis, the preterite forms of the original must be preserved. The figure of the first clause is borrowed from Ps. xviii. 5, 6 (4, 5), but with the substitution of a verbal form used only here, and represented by the word *environed.* The relation of the clauses, to denote which in English *but* has been supplied, is the same as in v. 51 above.

62. *At midnight I will rise to give thanks unto thee on (*account of*) the judgments of thy righteousness.* The first phrase, which literally means *the half* (or *halving*) *of the night*, is borrowed from the history of the midnight massacre in Egypt, Ex. xi. 4. xii. 29, to which there is also a historical allusion, as a signal instance of divine interposition and miraculous deliverance. A similar allusion may be traced in Job xxxiv. 20. *The judgments of thy righteousness*, thy judgments of righteousness, thy righteous judgments, cannot be altogether different in meaning from the very same words in v. 7, as supposed by some interpreters, who there explain the phrase to mean God's precepts or his requisitions, here his penal inflictions. The solution of the difficulty lies in this, that the words mean neither of these things specifically, but something which comprehends them both, viz. the actual manifestations of God's righteousness, in word or deed, by precept or by punishment.

63. *A fellow* (*am*) *I to all who fear thee, and to the keepers of*

thy precepts. Not merely a *companion* or frequenter of their company, but an associate, a congenial spirit, one of the same character. Compare the use of the same Hebrew word in Ps. xlv. 8 (7), where the plural is translated *fellows* in the English Bible. The verse before us is one of those which it seems most difficult to understand of Israel as a whole ; for in what sense was the church or chosen people a companion of those fearing God and keeping his commandments, when all the people in the world of that description were embraced within her own communion ? The force of this objection is so great that Hengstenberg applies the description to the pious ancestors of the returned Jews, and refers to Mal. iii. 24 (iv. 6.) The necessity of such a forced construction goes far to confirm the exegetical hypothesis, already stated as most probably the true one, that the psalm was intended to express the feelings of an individual believer, but that some of its terms are, from parity of circumstances, equally descriptive of what had been experienced by the house of Israel as a church and nation.

64. *Of thy mercy, oh Jehovah, full is the earth; thy statutes teach me.* Since thy mercy fills the whole earth, let it reach to me, enabling me to understand thy will and to obey it. The relation of the clauses is not unlike that in v. 12. The stanza closing with this verse is the first in which the initial words of all the verses are entirely different. See above, on vs. 8, 16, 24, 32, 40, 48, 56.

---

65. *Good hast thou done to thy servant, oh Jehovah, according to thy word.* The common version of the first clause (*thou hast dealt well with thy servant*) is equally correct and has the advantage of retaining the preposition *with*, which may be used in English after *deal* but not after *do.* The sense expressed by both translations is the same, to wit, thou hast treated him graciously or

kindly. *According to thy word*, i. e. the promise annexed to thy commandments, as in vs. 25, 28 (compare vs. 41, 58.) This verse is equally appropriate as a personal thanksgiving, and an acknowledgment of national deliverances, such as that from Babylon.

66. *Goodness of judgment and knowledge teach me, for in thy commandments I believe.* The first word in Hebrew is not (טוֹב) the adjective *good*, as in v. 65, but (טוּב) the corresponding abstract noun meaning *goodness*, as in Ps. xxv. 7. xxvii. 13. xxxi. 20 (19.) That it here denotes not moral but intellectual excellence, is determined by the addition of (טַעַם) a word originally meaning *taste*, and then transferred to reason, judgment, understanding. See above, on Ps. xxxiv. 1. *Teach me good judgment*, i. e. impart it by divine instruction. Judgment and knowledge may be here distinguished as in common parlance, the one denoting the faculty employed, the other the result of its exertion. The *knowledge* meant is that continually prayed for in this psalm, to wit, the knowledge of God's will. The connection of the clauses seems to be, that he has faith and would fain have knowledge ; he takes God's precepts upon trust, but then prays that he may understand them. To believe in God's commandments is to believe that they are his, and therefore right and binding.

67. *Before I suffered I (was) going astray, and now thy saying I observe.* Going astray, wandering, erring, i. e. habitually, ever straying. *And now* (on the contrary), where our idiom would require a *but*. The *saying* of God is what he says, including both commands and promises, which indeed are represented in the Old Testament, and especially in this psalm, as inseparable. *Observe*, attend to, keep in view, according to the nature of the object, trusting the promise, obeying the command. The last verb strictly means *I have observed*, implying that the salutary fruit of the

affliction was already realized and still continued. The sentiment of this verse has been echoed, and its very words repeated, by the godly sufferers of every age, a strong proof that it was meant to be so used. At the same time it furnishes an exquisite description of the effect produced upon the Jews, as a body, by the Babylonish exile, and especially the end which it forever put to their continual lapses into idolatry, by which their early history was characterized, and with respect to which the whole race might well have said, Before I suffered I was (ever) straying.

68. *Good* (*art*) *thou and doing good—teach me thy statutes!* Good, both essentially and actively or practically; good in thyself and good to others. The participle, as in v. 67, denotes habitual constant action, (*ever*) *doing good.* It is characteristic of this psalm, that the petition founded on the goodness of God's nature, on his beneficence, and even on his infinite perfection, si still, *teach me thy statutes!* Make me acquainted with thy will, and show me how to do it! See above, on vs. 12, 64.

69. *Proud* (*men*) *have forged a lie against me; I, with all* (*my*) *heart, will keep thy precepts.* Proud, presumptuous, overbearing sinners, as in v. 51. *Forged* expresses the essential meaning of the Hebrew word, but not its figurative form, which seems to be that of sewing, analogous to that of weaving, as applied to the same thing, both in Hebrew and in other languages. We may also compare our figurative phrase, *to patch up*, which however is not so much suggestive of artifice or skill as of the want of it. The connection of the clauses is, that all the craft and malice of his enemies should only lead him to obey God with a more undivided heart than ever. See above, on v. 58. With the same surprising skill and wisdom as in many other cases which have been already mentioned, this verse is so framed as to be equally well suited to such national and public evils as those described in the fourth chapter of Ezra, and to the sufferings of

the pious individual, arising from the pride and spite of wicked enemies.

70. *Fat as grease (is) their heart. I (in) thy law delight.* The connection of the clauses lies in the figurative use of fat to denote insensibility. See above, on Ps. xvii. 10. lxxiii. 7. While they are utterly insensible to spiritual pleasures, and especially to those springing from the knowledge of thy law, I find therein my highest happiness. The verb in the last clause is a cognate form to that in vs. 16, 47, and identical with that in Isai. xi. 8, where it means to play, sport, or enjoy one's self.

71. (It is) *good for me that I was made to suffer, to the end that I might learn thy statutes.* The prayer so frequently repeated, *teach me thy statutes,* is now proved to be sincere by a hearty acquiescence in the painful discipline by which it had been partially fulfilled already. *Good for me,* and therefore good on God's part. The idea of compulsory subjection to this salutary process is suggested by the passive causative form of the verb used in v. 67. *To the end* or *intent,* a phrase corresponding, both in form and meaning, to the Hebrew.

72. *Good for me is the law of thy mouth (more) than thousands of gold and silver. For me,* for my use as well as in my estimation. *The law of thy mouth,* that which thou hast uttered. See above, on v. 13. *Than,* literally, from, away from, as distinguished from, as compared with, which is just the meaning of the English *than.* The combination *good than,* or good from, is the nearest approach, of which the Hebrew idiom admits, to *better than.* The indefinite term *thousands* may refer to weight or number; to coin or bullion; to coins in general, or to shekels or talents in particular. While this verse primarily expresses the changed estimate which Israel learned in exile to put upon the law,

it is equally expressive of the feeling cherished by all true believers, in their best estate, as to the value of the word of God. Here ends the ninth stanza, of which five verses begin with the word (טוב) *good.*

---

73. *Thy hands made me and fashioned me; make me understand and let me learn thy commandments.* As I owe my existence to thy power, so too I rely upon thy grace for spiritual illumination. Compare Deut. xxxii. 6. *Fashioned*, literally, fixed, established, i. e. framed my constitution as it is.

74. *Thy fearers shall see me and rejoice; for in thy word have I hoped.* Compare Ps. v. 12 (11.) xxxiv. 3 (2.) They shall rejoice in my case, as a new proof that they who trust in God cannot be disappointed. The literal meaning of the last clause is, because for thy word I have waited, i. e. patiently and trustfully awaited its fulfilment.

75. *I know, Jehovah, that righteousness are thy judgments, and* (in) *faithfulness thou hast afflicted me* (or *made me suffer.*) *Thy judgments*, thy sovereign decisions and their execution, *are righteousness* itself, i. e. perfectly righteous. So in the next clause, for *in faithfulness* we may read *as faithfulness itself*, as one absolutely faithful to his promise and engagements. This confession would be untrue, if those who made it were not conscious of their guilt and ill-desert. Compare Deut. xxxii. 4.

76. *Oh that thy mercy might be for my comfort, according to thy saying to thy servant.* The optative expression, *oh that*, is here used to represent the Hebrew particle of entreaty (נָא), correctly paraphrased in the English Bible, *I pray thee. For my comfort*, literally, *to comfort* (or *console*) *me. Thy saying*, that which thou hast said or promised. *To thy servant*, to me as thy

servant, and as such in covenant with thee. This description is equally appropriate to the body and its members.

77. *Let thy compassions come unto me* (or *upon me*), *and I shall live, for thy law* (*is*) *my delights.* The construction in the first clause is like that in v. 41. *And I shall live,* or as we might express it, *that I may live.* See above, on v. 17. He pleads what he has received already as a ground for asking more. The plural (*delights*) expresses fulness and completeness, or perhaps implies that this joy is equal or superior to all others, or includes them all. The Hebrew noun is derived from the verb in vs. 16, 47, 70.

78. *Shamed be the proud, for falsely have they wronged me; I will muse of thy precepts. Falsely,* literally, *falsehood,* i. e. in or by it. *Wronged,* literally, bent, perverted. With the last clause compare vs. 27, 48.

79. *Let them return to me that fear thee and know thy testimonies.* Let thy servants who have looked upon me as abandoned by thee now restore to me their confidence. The various reading in the last clause (ידעי and וידעו) does not affect the meaning of the sentence, except that the reading in the text may be included in the wish, *and let them know thy testimonies,* i. e. let them learn from my experience to understand thy precepts better.

80. *Let my heart be perfect in thy statutes, to the end that I may not be shamed.* In thy statutes, in the knowledge and the practice of them, or as it is expressed in Ps. xix. 12 (11), *in keeping them. Shamed,* put to shame by the frustration of my highest hopes. See above, on v. 6. Two of the verses in this stanza begin with the same Hebrew word (יְהִי־).

---

81. *For thy salvation faints my soul; for thy word do I wait.* Both verbs are in the preterite, implying that it is so and has been so. *Faints*, is spent or wasted. This strong expression for intense desire is borrowed from Ps. lxxxiv. 3 (2.) With the last clause compare v. 74.

82. *My eyes fail for thy saying, so that I say, when wilt thou comfort me?* The first verb in Hebrew is the same with the first in the preceding verse. *Thy saying*, the fulfilment of thy promise. The Hebrew noun is derived from the following verb, *to say*, so as to say, so that I say. It might also be translated, but with less exactness, *while I say*.

83. *For I have been like a bottle in the smoke; thy statutes I have not forgotten.* The bottle meant is one of skin, still common in the east. The comparison is not entirely clear. Some suppose that the blackening and shrivelling effect of the smoke upon the skin is simply used as a figure for distress. Others understand the words as conveying the additional idea, that as wine-skins are not meant to be involved in smoke, so distress is not the normal or natural condition of God's people. Others, assuming that the skins were intentionally smoked by way of seasoning, suppose the principal idea to be that of painful but salutary discipline. There can be no doubt, that the clause relates, in some way, to the afflictions, either of the chosen people, or of individual believers, or of both. The meaning of the last clause is that, notwithstanding these afflictions, the sufferer has not forgotten God's commandments.

84. *How many (are) the days of thy servant? When wilt thou execute upon my persecutors judgment?* The shortness of life is indirectly urged as an argument for speedy action. See above,

on Ps. xxxix. 5, 14 (4, 13.) lxxviii. 39. lxxxix. 48, 49 (47, 48.) *Execute judgment*, or *do justice*, as in Ps. ix. 5 (4.)

85. *Proud (men) dig for me pits, which (are) not according to thy law.* The presumptuous sinners (vs. 51, 69, 78) who are his enemies use the most treacherous means for his destruction, without regard to the divine command or prohibition. See above, on Ps. vii. 16 (15.) lvii. 7 (6.)

86. *All thy commandments (are) faithfulness; falsely do they persecute me; help thou me.* The promises annexed to God's commandments are infallible. *Falsely*, as in v. 78, *falsehood*, i. e. in falsehood, without right or reason, or *with* (by means of) *falsehood*, as their instrument. The verb agrees with the remoter antecedent (*persecutors*) in v. 84.

87. *They almost consumed me in the land, and I did not forsake thy precepts.* The verb *consumed* or *destroyed* (כִּלּוּ) and the phrase *in the land* both occur in reference to the Canaanites, 2 Chr. viii. 8. The translation *in the earth* (v. 19) is admissible, but less significant, and less in keeping with the national import of the psalm. The second clause, as usual in such cases, declares that notwithstanding his afflictions, he still sought to know and do the will of God.

88. *According to thy mercy quicken me, and I will keep the testimony of thy mouth.* Restore me to life, or save me alive, as in vs. 25, 37, 40. *Of thy mouth*, as in vs. 11, 72. This closes the eleventh stanza and the first half of the psalm. Two of these eight verses begin with different forms of the verb (כלה) *to fail* or *faint*, and three (including v. 84) with the particle (כ) *as* or *like*

---

89. *To eternity, Jehovah, thy word is settled in heaven.* The

translation, *eternal* (art thou) *Lord*, is contrary to usage, which requires the pronoun, in that case, to be expressed. *Settled*, literally, made to stand, i. e. unalterably fixed. *In heaven*, beyond the reach of all disturbing causes. See above, Ps. lxxxix. 3 (2.)

90. *To generation and generation (is) thy faithfulness; thou hast fixed the earth and it stands.* Resolved into our idiom, the meaning of this verse is, that the truth of God's promises, or his fidelity to his engagements, is secured by the same divine perfection, which brought the world at first into existence, and has ever since preserved it. The verb translated *fixed* is not the one employed in v. 89, but that used in Ps. vii. 10 (9.) ix. 8 (7.) xl. 3 (2.) xlviii. 9 (8.) lxviii. 10 (9.) xc. 17. xcix. 4. cvii. 36. The sense *prepared* is rare and doubtful, and too feeble for this context.

91. *For thy judgments they stand to day, for all are thy servants.* The subject of the first verb, though obscure, is probably the heavens and the earth, mentioned in the two preceding verses. These stand, continue to exist, for the execution of God's judgments, with reference perhaps to the destruction wrought by fire from heaven, by the opening of the earth, etc. *All*, literally, *the whole*, τὸ πᾶν, the universe; but the construction of this with the plural *servants* would be harsh in English. The same expression is applied in Ps. xiv. 3 to all mankind, but here to the material universe. *Thy servants*, the instruments employed to execute thy will.

92. *Unless thy law were my delights, then should I perish in my affliction.* The verse admits also of the construction in the English Bible, which refers it to a remoter past, and represents the danger as escaped, whereas the first construction implies a continued state of suffering. The law of God, as usual in this psalm,

is here viewed, not as a body of mere requisitions, but as a covenant, a law accompanied by promises.

93. *To eternity I will not forget thy precepts, for in them hast thou quickened me.* *In them*, or *by them*, which is really included in the other, meaning in the practice of them and by means of them. *Quickened*, as in vs. 17, 25, 37, 40, 50.

94. *Thine am I—save me—for thy precepts I have sought.* The original form of the first clause is, *to thee (am) I.* *Sought*, as in vs. 2, 10, 45.

95. *For me have wicked* (*men*) *waited, to destroy me; thy testimonies will I understand.* With the first clause compare Ps. lvi. 7 (6.) *Consider*, though correct, is an inadequate translation of the last verb, which denotes a fixed and intelligent attention. The only effect of his enemies' malignant plots is a still more serious contemplation of God's precepts.

96. *To all perfection I have seen an end*, (but) *wide is thy command exceedingly.* By *end* we are not to understand the end of its existence, but the limit or boundary of its extent. To all other perfection (so called) I can see an end, but that required and embodied in thy law is boundless. All the verses of this stanza except one (v. 92) begin with the preposition (ל) *to* or *for*, as all those of the second do with (ב) *in.*

---

97. *How I love thy law! All the day it* (*is*) *my meditation*, i. e. the subject of my solitary musing. This continual representation of God's law, not as a mere rule, but as an object of affection and a subject of perpetual reflection, is characteristic of the Psalms, and appears at the very threshold of the whole collection See above, on Ps. i. 2.

98. (More) *than my enemies do thy commandments make me wise; for to eternity it is mine* (or *to me.*) This is the construction of the first clause preferred by the latest interpreters, although it requires a singular verb to be construed with a plural noun. But as the same irregularity exists in the construction of the pronoun in the second clause, however the first may be explained, it is best to explain both anomalies alike, i. e. partly by the relative position of the words, and partly by the aggregate sense in which *commandments* is here used as equivalent to *law*, and which, agreeably to general usage, may sufficiently account for its construction with a verb and pronoun in the singular. As analogous cases have been cited 2 Sam. xxii. 23—" (as for) his statutes, I depart not from it"—and 2 Kings xvii. 22—" the sins of Jeroboam which he did, they departed not from it." As the sins of Jeroboam were concentrated in one, so the statutes of Jehovah might be viewed as one great comprehensive precept. The meaning of the last clause is not merely, *it is ever with me*, but *it is forever to me*, i. e. mine, my inalienable indefeasible possession. See above, v. 94.

99. (More) *than all my teachers I act wisely, for thy testimonies (are) a meditation to me.* My teachers, my superiors in natural and worldly wisdom. As the Hebrew verb has always elsewhere an active meaning, it is better to retain it here, the rather as it indicates more clearly that the wisdom which he boasts was practical, experimental. See above, on Ps. ii. 10. xiv. 2. xxxii. 3 (7.) xli. 2 (1.) lxiv. 10 (9.) ci. 2. The essential meaning of the last clause is the same with that of v. 97, but the use of the expression (לִי) suggests the same idea of possession that is expressed in v. 98. Thy testimonies are mine, belong to me, as an object of incessant contemplation.

100. (More) *than old men I understand, because thy precepts I have kept.* The first verb is the same, and has the same sense

as in v. 95. The ambiguous Hebrew word (זְקֵנִים) cannot be expressed by any one in modern English, as it may mean either *old men* in the proper sense, whose greater experience entitled them to be considered wiser than their juniors; or the *ancients*, those of former generations, who are popularly looked upon as wiser than their children and successors. One of these senses suits the personal, the other the national design and application of the psalm. In either case, there is really no boast of superior intelligence, as a distinguishing endowment, but merely an assertion, in a striking form, that the highest wisdom is to do the will of God. See above, on Ps. cxi. 10.

101. *From every evil path I refrain my feet, to the intent that I may keep thy word.* Of the two ideas conveyed by *word*, that of command is here predominant, but not exclusive of the other. To keep God's word is primarily to obey his precept, but secondarily to verify his promise. This verse teaches clearly that the keeping of God's word is something incompatible with treading any evil path.

102. *From thy judgments I do not depart, because thou guidest me.* We have here another word of comprehensive meaning, in which sometimes one phase of the essential idea is presented prominently, sometimes another. The divine *judgments*, in this psalm, are always the external exhibitions of the divine righteousness, in word or deed, by precept or by punishment. Here of course the former are especially intended. The figure of a way, though not expressed, is still indicated by the verbs *depart* and *guide.* As to the latter, see above, on v. 33. From this verse it is doubly clear that he claims nothing as belonging to himself, or as accomplished in his own strength, but ascribes all to the power and grace of God. The preterite forms, in this and the preceding verse, merely make the past more prominent than the future, as an accessory idea to the present.

103. *How sweet to my palate are thy sayings, sweeter than honey to my mouth!* As the Hebrew verb occurs only here, it is better to follow the rabbinical tradition and the ancient versions, which make the idea to be that of sweetness, than the uncertain etymological deductions of the lexicons, which make it to be that of *smoothness.* The passive form may possibly denote that the psalmist's relish for God's word was not a native but acquired taste. Some interpreters unreasonably give to *word* the sense of law, excluding that of promise altogether, whereas both must unavoidably have been suggested to a Hebrew reader. The original word means neither more nor less than that which God has said. The figures of this verse are borrowed from Ps. xix. 11 (10.)

104. *From thy precepts I get understanding; therefore I hate every path of falsehood.* The common version of the first verb comes as near to the exact sense of the original as any other English word or phrase. The Hebrew verb is the same that occurs above, vs. 95, 100. As he knows no wisdom independent of the truth, he hates falsehood as the height of folly, and regulates his life accordingly. All the verses of this stanza begin either with the exclamation (מה) *how*, or with the preposition (מן) *from, than.*

---

105. *A lantern for my foot is thy word, and a light for my path.* To the figure of a path, so frequently presented in this psalm already, is now added that of a light, to make it plain amidst surrounding darkness. The parallelism is completed by adding the generic term, *light*, to the specific one, *lamp* or *lantern. For my foot*, i. e. to guide it. *For my path*, i. e. to show it.

106. *I have sworn, and will perform* (my oath), *to observe the judgments of thy righteousness.* The second verb occurs above,

v. 23, in its primary sense of raising up, or causing to stand upright. In the later books, particularly that of Esther, it occurs very often in the sense of ratifying or confirming, and might here be rendered, *I confirm* (my oath already made.) In either case, it merely strengthens the expression which precedes it. *Observe*, keep, or obey, as in vs. 4, 5, 8, etc. *Thy righteous judgments*, as in vs. 7, 62. Considered as the language of the whole church or nation, this verse may have reference to the covenant entered into at Mount Sinai and renewed in the plains of Moab, while as a personal profession, it has its counterpart in the experience of every true believer.

107. *I am afflicted even to extremity; Jehovah, quicken me according to thy word.* That the first clause does not relate merely to past sufferings (*I was afflicted*), seems to follow from the prayer in the last clause, which may, however, be understood as a petition for deliverance from the deadening effects of a calamity already past, such as the Babylonish exile, the enfeebling influence of which notwithstanding incidental benefits, continued to be felt for ages. The first verb in Hebrew, with the idea of suffering, always suggests that of humiliation. *Even to extremity*, the same words that occur above, in vs. 8, 43, 51. The meaning of the last clause is, bestow upon me that life which is promised in the Law to those who keep it. See Lev. xviii. 5. Deut. vi. 24.

108. *The free-will offerings of my mouth accept, I pray thee, oh Jehovah, and thy judgments teach me.* For the meaning of the first Hebrew word, see above, on Ps. cx. 3. It is here a figure for prayers and praises, as appears from the addition of *my mouth.* The verb *accept* is one continually used in the Law, with respect to sacrificial offerings. See above, on Ps. li. 18 (16), and compare Ps. l. 14. The recurrence of the prayer, *thy judgments teach me*, shows that the writer's object was to make everything

tend to this conclusion, and that however a sentence may begin, it cannot be complete without a repetition of this favourite idea.

109. *My soul is in my hand always, and* (yet) *thy law I have not forgotten.* The sense of the strong figure in the first clause is clear from Judg. xii. 13. 1 Sam. xix. 5. xxviii. 21, where he who risks or jeopards his own life, in war or otherwise, is said to put his soul into his hand, as if to have it ready to give up or throw away at any moment. The same expression reappears in Job xiii. 14. The meaning of the whole verse is, that even amidst the deadly perils which environed him, he still remembered the divine law, as an object of supreme affection.

110. *Wicked (men) have laid a snare for me, and* (yet) *from thy precepts I have not strayed. Laid for me*, literally, *given to me*, as we might speak of a snare as *presented* to a person, i. e set before him. The devices and temptations of the wicked were as powerless as all the other causes previously mentioned, in leading him away from the path of truth and safety.

111 *I inherit thy testimonies to eternity, for the joy of my heart (are) they.* The first verb means to take as a possession or inheritance, and is here used in allusion to those places of the Pentateuch where it is applied to the possession of the promised land. See for example Ex. xxiii. 30.

112. *I incline my heart to do thy statutes to eternity, (even to) the end.* The preterite form of the first verb represents the effort as already made but still continued. For the meaning of the last word, see above, on v. 33. This stanza, like the eighth, has a different initial word in every verse.

---

113. *Waverers I hate, and thy law I love.* The first word in

Hebrew occurs only here. According to the most probable etymology, it means men of divided and unstable minds. See above, on Ps. xii. 3 (2), and compare James i. 8.

114. *My hiding place and my shield (art) thou—for thy word I wait*, i. e. for the fulfilment of thy promise. See above, on v. 81. The first word in the verse means properly a secret or a secret place. See above, on Ps. xxvii. 5. xxxii. 7. lxi. 5 (4.) xci. 1. The shield is a favourite figure for protection See above, on Ps. iii. 4 (3.) vii. 11 (10.) xviii. 3, 31 (2, 30.)

115. *Depart from me, evil doers, and I will keep the commandments of God.* The first clause is borrowed from Ps. vi. 9 (8.) The meaning in both cases seems to be, that he has no fear of their enmity. The reason given in this case is, because he is resolved to do the will of God, and is therefore sure of his protection.

116. *Uphold me according to thy promise, and let me live, and let me not be ashamed of my hope.* Promise, literally, saying, that which thou hast said, as in v. 82. *Let me live* might also be translated *and I shall live*, or paraphrased *that I may live.* See above, on v. 17. *Of my hope*, literally *from my hope*, which some understand in a privative sense, *away from*, deprived of, without my hope, i. e. without having it fulfilled. *Ashamed of my hope* does not convey the sense so fully as *shamed in my hope*, frustrated, disappointed, in my expectations.

117. *Sustain me and I shall be saved, and I will look to thy statutes always.* The first verb is nearly synonymous with that at the beginning of v. 116, and the same that occurs above, Ps. xx. 3 (2.) xli. 4 (3.) xciv. 18. civ. 15. *I shall be saved*, or *let me be saved*, or *that I may be saved*, precisely as in the preceding verse. The strict future sense is here to be preferred, as the verb

is not both preceded and followed by a prayer, as in the other case. *Look to*, have respect to, regard, as the rule of my conduct. The construction of the verb and preposition is the same as in Ex. v. 9.

118. *Thou despisest all* (*those*) *straying from thy statutes, for a lie* (*is*) *their deceit.* They are objects not only of disapprobation but of scorn, because in attempting to deceive others they deceive themselves. Their deception of others is a lie to themselves.

119. *(As) dross hast thou made to cease all the wicked of the earth; therefore I love thy testimonies.* The purifying tendency of God's judgments is itself a reason for delighting in them. The verb in the first clause, which occurs in its primary sense in Ps. viii. 3 (2), is applied to the purging out of leaven at the passover (Ex. xii. 15) and to the extirpation of wild beasts (Lev. xxvi. 6.

120. *My flesh shudders from dread of thee, and of thy judgments I am afraid.* The first verb in Hebrew occurs only here, but is universally admitted to denote some bodily effect of fear, such as trembling, shuddering, or the instinctive creeping of the flesh. *Afraid of*, in the last clause, does not fully represent the Hebrew phrase, which denotes not mere apprehension of something still future or absent, but terror in view of something actually present. *Judgments* has its usual wide sense, but with special reference, in this case, to God's penal visitations. Here ends the fifteenth stanza, in which, as in the one before it, every verse has a distinct initial word.

---

121. *I do justice and righteousness; leave me not to my oppressors.* The first verb is in the past tense, I have done and I still do. *Do justice*, not in the restricted or forensic sense of redressing wrong judicially, but in the wide sense of executing justice or reducing it to practice.

122. *Be surety for thy servant for good; let not the proud oppress me.* The sense and construction of the first verb are precisely the same as in Gen. xliii. 9. xliv. 32. Compare Job xvii. 3, and see my note on Isai. xxxviii. 14. It means not merely take me under thy protection, but become answerable for me, stand between me and those who, under any pretext, even that of legal right, may seek to oppress me. *For good*, i. e. for my good, for my safety or deliverance. Compare Deut. vi. 24. x. 13. xxx. 9. This is noted in the masora as the only verse in which the word of God, or some equivalent expression, is not found.

123. *My eyes fail for thy salvation, and for the word of thy righteousness.* With the first clause compare v. 82. The word of thy righteousness, thy word of righteousness, thy righteous word, the promise of a righteous God who cannot lie.

124. *Deal with thy servant according to thy mercy, and thy statutes teach me.* The first words strictly mean *do with thy servant*, which may be an ellipsis for *do good to him*, or deal kindly with him, as in v. 65. See above, on Ps. cix. 21.

125. *Thy servant (am) I; make me understand and let me know thy testimonies.* That *thy servant* is not a mere periphrasis for *I* or *me* in v. 122 and elsewhere, appears from the first clause of the verse before us, where it constitutes the predicate of the proposition. In the second clause, we have the same choice of constructions as in vs. 116, 117. *Let me know*, or *(then) I shall know*, or *that I may know*, all implying one another, and amounting to the same thing.

126. (It is) *time for Jehovah to do—they break thy law.* The absolute use of *do*, without an object, or leaving it to be suggested by the context, is a peculiar Hebrew idiom. See above, on Ps. 22 (21.) We may here supply *justice* from v. 121 (compare

v. 84) ; or more indefinitely, whatever should be done ; or more indefinitely still, *it is time to do* (something), i. e. to act, which is substantially the meaning of the common version (*time to work.*) Retaining the order of the Hebrew words, the sense would seem to be, *it is time to do* (something) *for Jehovah*, i. e. for his people to do it. But the direct address to God in the last clause, and the whole tenor of the context, make it more probable, that God himself is here entreated to do something for the vindication of his broken law. The verb in the last clause is to be construed indefinitely ; *they*, i. e. men in general, or the wicked in particular. With this clause compare Isai. xxiv. 5.

127. *Therefore I love thy commandments* (*more*) *than gold and* (*more*) *than fine gold.* The first word refers not to the immediately preceding verse, but to the whole previous description of the excellence of God's commandments. The comparison in the last clause, like that in v. 103, is borrowed from Ps. xix. 11 (10.)

128. *Therefore all* (thy) *precepts* (as to) *all* (things) *I think right ; every way of falsehood do I hate.* The *therefore* is coordinate with that in the preceding verse, and to be explained in the same manner. Both were probably occasioned by the alphabetical arrangement here requiring an initial *ayin. Precepts* of course mean those of God, as *word* means his word in v. 49. The construction here is very foreign from our idiom, and by no means easily translated into it. The literal meaning of the words is, *all precepts of all*, which some understand to mean *of all kinds*, as in v. 14 and Ps. cxviii. 10. But others deny that *all* has this sense, even in the places cited, and explain it here to mean *concerning all*, on all subjects. The clause is then condemnatory of all partial distinctions between God's commandments, which may be the *way of falsehood* specially intended in the last clause. Compare Matt. v. 17—19. The verb in the first clause always elsewhere means to make straight, to go

straight, or to direct aright; but the best interpreters agree in making it here mean, to think right or approve. It is worthy of remark, that as to all these points, the true sense of this difficult clause seems to be given in the English Bible. With the last clause compare v. 104. In the sixteenth stanza, which here closes, two of the verses begin with (עַל־כֵּן) *therefore*, and two with different forms of the verb (עָשָׂה) *to do*.

---

129. *Wonderful (are) thy testimonies; therefore my soul keepeth them.* The first word in Hebrew is a plural form of that in Ps. lxxvii. 12, 15 (11, 14) lxxviii. 12. lxxxviii. 11 (10), and properly means *wonders*, i. e., miracles or prodigies of moral excellence. *My soul*, not merely I, but I with all my heart or soul.

130. *The opening of thy words enlightens, making the simple understand.* The common version of the first word (*entrance*) is inaccurate, and the one here given, though exact, is ambiguous. The clause does not refer to the mechanical opening of the book by the reader, but to the spiritual opening of its true sense, by divine illumination, to the mind which naturally cannot discern it. For the Scriptural usage of the word translated *simple*, see above, on Ps. xix. 8 (7.) cxvi. 6.

131. *My mouth I stretch and pant, because for thy commandments I long.* The first verb usually means to *gape* or *yawn*, but these verbs are intransitive in English, and cannot be construed with the noun directly. For the meaning of the next verb, see above, on Ps. lvi. 2, 3 (1, 2.) lvii. 4 (3.) Both are figurative expressions of the idea conveyed directly by the third verb, which occurs nowhere else, but differs only in a single letter from the verb of the same meaning used in vs. 40, 174, which also is peculiar to this psalm.

132. *Turn to me, and be gracious to me, as* (is) *due to the lovers*

of thy name. The first verb does not mean to *return* or come back, but to turn round to or towards an object from which the looks have been averted. See above, on Ps. cii. 18 (17.) *Be gracious* or *merciful*, show favour to or favour me. *As is due to*, or *according to the right of*, the lovers etc. The Hebrew word (מִשְׁפָּט) has here the meaning of the Latin *jus*, as in Ps. lxxxi. 5, (4.) For the meaning of *the lovers of thy name*, see above, on Ps. v. 12 (11.)

133. *My steps establish by thy word, and let not any iniquity rule over me.* Establish, i. e. make firm, cause me to walk safely. See above, on Ps. xl. 3 (2.) *By thy word* or *saying*, what thou hast said, i. e. by the fulfilment of thy promise. The last clause might seem to be a prayer against the power of his own corruption; but the frequent use of the Hebrew noun to denote the mutual injustice of men, together with the language of the next verse, seems to show that this too is a prayer against oppression. The verb in this clause is applied by Nehemiah (v. 15) to the oppression suffered by the restored Jews. The Arabic verb of the same form is the root of the royal title *Sultan*.

134. *Redeem me from the oppression of man, and I will keep thy precepts.* These two verses are peculiarly appropriate to the trials and temptations of the Jews at the time of the Restoration. The form of the last verb denotes strong desire and determination.

135. *Let thy face shine upon thy servant, and teach me thy statutes.* The prayer of the first clause is the same as that which forms the burden of Ps. lxxx. (4, 8, 20.) *Thy servant*, i. e. me who am thy servant; hence the first person is immediately resumed.

136. *Streams of water run down my eyes, for (that) they do*

not keep thy law. In the Hebrew of the first clause, *eye* is the subject, not the object, of the verb. See the same or similar idiomatic constructions, Jer. ix. 17. xiii. 17. Lam. i. 16. iii. 48. Ezek. vii. 17. The preposition in the last clause is to be construed with the relative understood, in the sense of *for that*, forasmuch as, because. The complete phrase occurs above, v. 49. *They do not*, i. e., men indefinitely, others. Here ends the seventeenth stanza, all the verses of which begin with different Hebrew words.

---

137. *Righteous (art) thou, oh Jehovah, and just thy judgments.* The English and the ancient versions make the second adjective agree with *judgments*, although different in number. This might be justified by making (יָשָׁר) *just* a neuter adjective or substantive, as in Ps. cxi. 8. It is much more simple and agreeable to usage to apply the epithet to God himself, as in Deut. xxxii. 4, and explain *thy judgments* as a kind of adverbial or qualifying phrase, very common in Hebrew, but in our idiom requiring the insertion of a preposition, *upright (in* or *as to) thy judgments.*

138. *Thou hast commanded righteousness thy testimonies, and faithfulness—exceedingly.* This is another elliptical construction, wholly foreign from our idiom. Some resolve it by supplying *to* or *to be:* thou hast commanded thy testimonies to (or to be) righteousness, i. e. hast made them righteous. It is simpler, however, and more like the syntax of the verse preceding, to supply *in* or *with:* thou hast commanded (in) righteousness thy testimonies, etc. The *very* or *exceedingly* may belong to *faithfulness* alone, or to the whole proposition. The mention of faithfulness shows that the idea of God's promise is included in his testimony. With this verse compare v. 86, and Ps. xciii. 5.

139 *My zeal consumes me, because my adversaries forget thy word.* The verbs strictly mean, *has consumed, have forgotten*, but

without excluding the present, as they might seem to do, if rendered literally into English. *Zeal*, jealous regard for God's authority and honour. See above, on Ps. lxix. 10, (9.) The first Hebrew verb occurs above, Ps. lxxxviii. 17 (16.) The last clause gives the reason or occasion of his jealousy. *Adversaries*, persecutors or oppressors. *Thy word* includes thy promise to me and thy command to them.

140. *Pure (is) thy word—exceedingly, and thy servant loves it.* Pure, literally, purged, tried, assayed, refined, like precious metal. See above, on Ps. xviii. 31 (30.) *Saying*, as elsewhere in this psalm, alternates with *word*, and has the same comprehensive meaning. *Thy servant*, I as thy servant, and because I am so. *Loves* and has long loved.

141. *Little (am) I and despised*, (but) *thy precepts do I not forget.* However proudly or however justly I may be despised, I can still lay claim to one distinction, that I have not, like my despisers, forgotten God's commandments. These words are peculiarly appropriate to Israel, as a body, at the Restoration.

142. *Thy righteousness (is) right forever, and thy law (is) truth.* *Right* is here used as a noun, in order to vary the expression in English as in Hebrew, where two cognate forms (צדקה and צדק) are employed. With the first clause compare Ps. ciii. 17. cxi. 3. The idea here is, that God's rectitude is not capricious or mutable, as might be inferred from the afflictions of his people, but unchangeable and *to eternity*. *Thy law*, both in its precepts and its promises, is true, is truth itself.

143. *Distress and anguish seize* (or *seized*) *me; thy commandments (are) my delight.* Even in the midst of suffering, thy commandments not only solace me but make me happy. *Seize*, liter-

ally *find*, as in Ps. cxvi. 3. *Delight*, literally, *delights*, a succedaneum for all other pleasures. See above, on v. 24.

144. *Right (are) thy testimonies to eternity; make me understand, and I shall live.* *Right*, righteousness, the second of the nouns used in v. 142. *Make me understand (them)*, i. e., these thy testimonies. *And (then) I shall live*, which includes *let me live* and *that I may live*. See above, on vs. 17, 116. Three of the verses in this stanza begin with derivatives of the root צדק.

---

145. *I invoke (thee) with a whole heart—answer me, Jehovah—thy statutes will I keep.* I have invoked thy favour with a heartfelt sense of its necessity; grant it to me, according to my prayer, and I am fully resolved to keep thy statutes.

146. *I invoke thee—save me—and I will observe thy testimonies.* The pronoun implied in the preceding verse is here expressed. The augmented form of the last verb is emphatic or intensive. *I* WILL observe thy testimonies, i. e. obey thy precepts and believe thy promises.

147. *I come before (thee) in the (morning) twilight, and I cry to (thee); for thy words do I wait.* The first verb has the same sense as in Ps. xcv. 2. Compare Ps. lxxxviii. 14 (13.) Early prayer implies importunate desire. The *twilight* meant is that of morning, as in 1 Sam. xxx. 17. Job vii. 4. The second verb means to cry for help. Its augmented form is common in verbs of speaking, and supposed by some grammarians to denote motion or direction towards the object of address, like the local or directive ה in nouns. See Judg. vi. 10. 1 Sam. xxviii. 15. Neh. v. 7. xiii. 11, 17, 21. Dan. ix. 4.

148. *My eyes anticipate the watches, to muse of thy promise.* Before the stated hours of vigil he is awake and ready for devout

meditation. *To muse*, that I may muse or meditate. See above, on v. 62, and compare Ps. lxiii. 7 (6). lxxvii. 5 (4.) Lam. ii. 19.

149. *My voice hear according to thy mercy, oh Jehovah, according to thy judgments quicken me.* According to the promises annexed to thy commandments.

150. *Near are those pursuing crime; from thy law they are far off. Pursuing*, eagerly devising and attempting. *Crime*, malicious mischief, as in Ps. xxvi. 10. In the last clause there is a kind of play upon the words *far* and *near*, as if he had said, the nearer they are to harming me, the further are they from obeying thee.

151. *Near (art) thou, Jehovah, and all thy commandments are truth.* The *lusus verborum* may be said to be continued. As they are near to injure, thou art near to save, and all thy promises to those who do thy will are true, are truth itself.

152. *Long have I known from thy testimonies* (themselves), *that thou unto eternity hast founded them.* The first word in Hebrew is a noun used adverbially, as in Ps. lv. 20 (19.) The precepts of the law describe themselves as everlasting. See Ex. xxvii. 21. xxviii. 43. xxxvi. 21. Lev. iii. 17. vi. 11. vii. 36. Num. x. 8. This concludes the nineteenth stanza, two of the initial words in which are derivatives of קרא, two of קרב, three of קדם.

---

153. *See my suffering and deliver me; for thy law I forget not.* The first petition, in the same words, occurs above, Ps. ix. 14 (13.) The first verb originally signifies to extricate or disembarrass. *I forget not*, and have not forgotten, both of which ideas would be necessarily suggested to a Hebrew reader.

154. *Strive my strife and redeem me; as to thy word, quicken me.* With the first clause compare Ps. xliii 1. lxix. 19 (18.)

As to, according to, in fulfilment of, *thy saying*, that which thou hast said, thy promise. See above, v. 41.

155. *Far from the wicked (is) salvation; because thy statutes they seek not.* The first word in Hebrew is a masculine adjective, and does not agree regularly with *salvation*, which is feminine, but is construed as a neuter, *something far*, as the first word in v. 72 means *a good thing*. *Seek not*, and have not sought, i. e. desired either to know or do thy will. See above, on v. 45.

156. *Many* (or *manifold are*) *thy compassions, oh Jehovah, according to thy judgments quicken me.* That the first word means *many*, not *great*, in this connection, seems clear from the next verse. *According to thy judgments*, as in v. 149.

157. *Many (are) my persecutors and oppressors; from thy testimonies I decline not.* The second noun is often rendered *adversaries*, as in v. 139, but it may here be taken in its primary sense, which is near akin to that of the preceding word. *I decline not*, and have not declined, deviated, swerved.

158. *I see traitors and am sickened—(those) who thy saying keep not.* The wicked are called traitors against God, their rightful sovereign, as in Ps. xxv. 8. The first verb is the reflexive form of that in Ps. xcv. 10, *I sicken* (or *disgust*) *myself*. The common version of the relative (*because*) conveys an idea not expressed but understood. There is no need of departing from the strict sense of the pronoun. *See* and have seen, *keep* and have kept.

159. *See how I love thy precepts, Jehovah; according to thy mercy, quicken me.* *See how*, literally *see that*, which is tantamount to saying, *thou seest that*.

160. *The head of thy word (is) truth, and to eternity (is) every*

judgment of thy righteousness. *Head* is by some explained as meaning the sum total, by others as synonymous with the cognate form (רֵאשִׁית) in Ps. cxi. 10. *Every judgment of thy righteousness*, every one of thy righteous judgments. Three verses of the twentieth stanza begin with some form of the verb (ראה) *to see.*

---

161. *Princes persecute me without cause—and at thy words my heart is awed.* Both Hebrew verbs are in the past tense. The first verb, like its representative, originally means to follow after, to pursue, but is commonly employed in a hostile sense. *Without cause* answers to a single Hebrew word (חִנָּם) an adverb related to the noun (חֵן) *favour*, as *gratis* is to *gratia* in Latin. So in modern English, the idea here might be expressed by the one word *gratuitously.* *At thy words*, literally, *from them*, i. e. because or on account of them. The last verb is not a passive in Hebrew, but a less usual synonyme of (יָרֵא) *to fear*, correctly paraphrased in the English versions (*standeth in awe.*) The masoretic reading is *thy word* in the singular, but, as in most other cases, the best critics now prefer the reading in the text.

162. *Rejoicing (am) I over thy saying, like (one) finding much spoil.* The participle indicates continued and habitual rejoicing. *Thy saying*, that which thou hast said, thy law with its attendant promises.

163. *Falsehood I hate and abhor; thy law I love.* Hate and have hated, love and have loved. *Falsehood* or *lying*, as in v. 29. The second verb has the same augmented and intensive form that occurs above, vs. 147, 158.

164. *Seven times in the day I praise thee, for the judgments of thy righteousness.* Seven times is a proverbial idiom for often or repeatedly. The use of this form of expression here is not the

effect but the occasion of the observance of canonical hours. See above, on Ps. lv. 18 (17.) *Praise thee*, and have been accustomed so to do. With the last clause compare v. 160.

165. (There is) *much peace to the lovers of thy law, and there is to them no stumbling block.* Peace, in opposition to the disquietude inseparable from a course of sin. A stumbling-block is a common scriptural figure for an occasion of unbelief or sin. The idea here is, that the best preservative against temptation is a love to God's commandments. The Prayer-Book version (*they are not offended at it*) and that in the text of the English Bible (*nothing shall offend them*) convey a very different meaning from the true one to a modern reader. The latter indeed seems directly contradictory to vs. 53, 158. The correct sense is intelligibly given in the margin of the common version.

166. *I hope for thy salvation, oh Jehovah, and thy commandments I do. I hope* and have hoped, *do* and have done. In the meantime, while expecting thy salvation, I am careful to perform thy will.

167. *My soul observes thy testimonies, and I love them greatly* (or *exceedingly.*) I observe them, pay particular regard to them, in regulating my behaviour, not with a mere external conformity, but from or with my soul, because I love them greatly.

168. *I observe thy precepts and thy testimonies, because all my ways are before thee.* He does not affect to be prompted by a love exclusive of all fear, but only of a slavish dread. He stands in awe of God's omniscience, and is influenced by dread of his disapprobation to obey his precepts, as well as by attachment to the law itself. *My ways*, my courses of conduct, mode of life, behaviour. *Before thee*, open to God's infallible inspection, and subjected to his judgment. Two of the verses in this stanza begin

with forms of the verb (שָׁמַר) *to observe* or *keep*. It is also worthy of remark that שׂ and שׁ are treated as one letter, three of the verses beginning with the former, namely, the two first and the sixth.

---

169. *Let my cry come near before thee, oh Jehovah; according to thy word, make me understand.* The first noun denotes an audible expression of strong feeling, whether sorrowful or joyful. See above, on Ps. xvii. 1. xxx. 6 (5.) *Come near before thee*, not only near enough to be heard, but into thy presence, so that he who utters it may be seen. *According to thy word*, thy commandment which requires, and thy promise which secures, the understanding of thy will. See above, vs. 25, 65, 107, and compare Deut. xxx. 6.

170. *Let my supplication come before thee; according to thy promise, free me* (or *deliver me.*) The first noun, according to its etymology, denotes a prayer for grace or favour. See above, Ps. vi. 10 (9.) lv. 2 (1.) In this and the preceding verse, the prayer for deliverance from outward troubles is subjoined, and as it were subordinated, to that for grace to do the will of God. The same connection may be traced in Ps. xc. 11—17.

171. *My lips shall pour forth praise; for thou wilt teach me thy statutes.* The first verb means to cause to gush or flow, and is the same with that in Ps. xix. 3 (2.) lxxviii. 2. It here denotes eager, abundant, and unceasing praise. The last clause expresses the confident expectation of the blessing so often and importunately asked throughout the psalm. As if he had said, Now shall my lips praise, for I am about to receive what I had prayed for; thou wilt indeed teach me thy statutes. The translation *when thou hast taught me* (or *shalt teach me*) is less exact, less forcible, and really included in the other.

172. *Let my tongue answer thy saying—that all thy commandments are right.* The verb which usually means to answer prayer

(see above, vs. 26, 145) is here used in the sense of responding to a precept or a promise by the language of praise and acquiescence. Compare v. 42. There is no need of treating the optative form of the verb as a poetic license. The strict sense agrees well with the prayer in the next verse. What is here asked is occasion thus to praise God. As the last clause seems to assign no pertinent reason for the prayer in the first, it may be regarded as the response itself. Let my tongue say in answer to all thy requisitions, that all thy commandments are right, or righteousness itself, as in vs. 142, 144.

173. *Let thy hand be* (near) *to help me; for thy precepts do I choose.* The word supplied in this translation is not necessary to the sense, but is introduced for the purpose of retaining the original construction, *be to help me*, i. e. be my help, or simply help me. The reason given in the last clause is, that as he voluntarily makes choice of God's will as his rule of conduct, he thereby renounces all other protection. The Hebrew verb is a preterite; *I choose*, and have already chosen.

174. *I long for thy salvation, oh Jehovah, and thy law (is) my delights.* I long and have longed. With the first clause compare vs. 40, 81, 131; with the second, vs. 24, 77, 92.

175. *Let my soul live and praise thee; and let thy judgments help me.* This verse sums up in conclusion the petitions of the whole psalm. Save me, and thereby give me cause to praise thee, for the blessings which I have derived from the promises and precepts of the law. *Let my soul live*, because it is that which is in danger. *Judgments*, as in vs. 149, 156.

176. *I wander like a lost sheep—seek thy servant—for thy commandments I do not forget.* The English versions of the first clause (*I have gone astray*), although they adhere strictly to the

form of the original, seem to make the primary idea that of sin, which is really included, but only as the cause of that which is directly intended, namely misery, represented by the wandering of a lost and helpless sheep. Compare Jer. l. 6. *Seek thy servant*, deliver from this wretched state one who is still thy servant, and as such remembers thy commandments, even in the midst of his worst sufferings. As the preceding verse sums up the petitions of the psalm, so this sums up its complaints in the first clause and its professions in the last, connected by the short prayer (*seek thy servant*) as by a single link. The predominant use of the past tense, even to the end, shows how deeply the entire psalm is founded upon actual and previous experience. In this last stanza, the only initial word repeated is (תְּהִי) the verb of existence.

PSALM CXX.

1. *A Song of the Ascents. To Jehovah, in my distress, I called, and he answered me.* This is the first of fifteen psalms (cxx—cxxxiv) all bearing the inscription, *song of ascents* or *upgoings*, i. e sung during the periodical journeys or pilgrimages to Jerusalem at the times of the great yearly festivals. On these occasions the people are said, even in historical prose, to *go up* to Jerusalem, in reference both to its physical and moral elevation. See Ex. xxxiv. 24. 1 Kings xii. 27, 28. The Hebrew verb (עָלָה) employed in such connections is the root of the noun (מַעֲלוֹת) *ascents* in these inscriptions. This explanation of the title is much more satisfactory than any other which has been proposed. A rabbinical tradition represents these psalms as having been sung by the

people, as they ascended the fifteen steps (in Hebrew מַעֲלוֹת), seven on one side and eight on the other, repeatedly mentioned by Ezekiel (xl. 6, 22, 26, 31, 34, 37.) But apart from the intrinsic improbability of this tradition, some psalms in the series were evidently not meant to be sung at the temple. No less improbable than this very ancient explanation is the modern one, that the inscription has reference to a peculiarity of structure, the repetition of a phrase or clause of one sentence in the next with an addition, forming a kind of climax or progression in the terms as well as the ideas. But even admitting that this peculiarity of form might be described by (מַעֲלוֹת) the Hebrew word in question, this word could not have been prefixed to each of the fifteen psalms, when the examples of the fact alleged are confined almost exclusively to one or two of them. Much nearer to the truth is the opinion, that these psalms were intended to be sung during the return from Babylon, which is called an *ascent* (מַעֲלָה) by Ezra (vii. 9.) But this can only be maintained by arbitrarily denying the genuineness of the titles, which ascribe four of the psalms (cxxii, cxxiv, cxxxi, cxxxiii) to David and one (cxxvii) to Solomon. The position assigned to these, and the difference of tone between them and the rest, are ingeniously accounted for by Hengstenberg's hypothesis, that these five ancient psalms, sung by the people, as they went up to Jerusalem, before the captivity, were made the basis of a whole series or system, designed for the same use by an inspired writer after the Restoration, who not only added ten psalms of his own, as appears from the identity of tone and diction, but joined them to the old ones in a studied and artificial manner, entirely inconsistent with the supposition of fortuitous or random combination. The one psalm by Solomon stands in the centre of the series or system and divides it into two equal parts, in each of which we find two psalms of David and five anonymous or new ones, the former being separated and surrounded by the latter, an additional and strong proof of intended adaptation to the times when the later psalms were written, to which Hengstenberg still further adds the number and distribution of the divine names in the whole series and its subdivisions. The psalm immediately before is anonymous, but its tone and diction mark it as belonging to the period of the Restoration. It begins with an acknowledgment of that great mercy, v. 1, followed by a prayer for deliverance from treacherous and spiteful enemies, v. 2, and a confident anticipation of their punishment, vs. 3, 4, but closes with a further lamentation and complaint of present suffering, vs. 5—7. In this, as in all the other psalms of the series, the ideal speaker is Israel or Judah, considered as the church or chosen people. This first verse, although general in its terms, is perfectly appropriate to the Captivity, as the *distress* out of which the sufferer cried to God, and to the Restoration, as the *answer* to his prayer. *In my distress*, literally, *in distress to me*, an expression like that in Ps. xviii. 7 (6.) The augmented form of the Hebrew noun is like that in Ps. iii. 3 (2.)

2. *Oh Jehovah, free my soul from lip of falsehood, from tongue of fraud.* The soul is particularly mentioned as usual when the life or the existence is in danger. The last two nouns in Hebrew are not in construction but in apposition, *a tongue* (*which is*) *fraud*, equivalent in meaning to the same English words in an inverted order, *fraud-tongue*. See a somewhat similar combination, Ps. xlv. 5 (4.) lx. 5 (4.) The terms of the description are too strong to be applied to mere delusive promises, and necessarily suggest the idea of calumnious falsehood, as in Ps. xxxi. 19 (18.) cxix. 69, 78. The reality answering to this description in the case of the restored Jews is the spiteful misrepresentation, by which the Samaritans retarded the rebuilding of the temple, as recorded in the fourth chapter of Ezra.

3. *What will he give to thee, and what will he add to thee, thou tongue of fraud?* Having complained to God of the false tongue, the ideal speaker turns to it as actually present and ad-

dresses it directly, speaking of God in the third person. The meaning of the question is, what recompense can you expect from an infinitely righteous God for these malignant calumnies? The peculiar form of the interrogation is derived from that of an ancient oath, *The Lord do so to me and more also*, literally, *and so add*, i. e. further do, or in addition to the thing in question. See 1 Sam. iii. 17. xiv. 44. As explained by this allusion, the words have a new force. What good or evil may be imprecated on thee, as the consequence of these malicious falsehoods?

4. *Arrows of a warrior sharpened*, (*together*) *with coals of juniper*. The general idea of severe and painful punishment is here expressed by the obvious and intelligible figures of keen arrows and hot coals. The *arrows of a mighty man*, warrior, or hero, are those used in battle, perhaps with an allusion to the fact, that one of the races mentioned in the next verse excelled in archery. See Isai. xxi. 17. The word which the rabbinical tradition explains to mean the juniper, is by modern lexicographers identified with the Arabic name of a species of broom-plant, which is thought, on account of its inflammatory quality, to make the best charcoal. See Robinson's Palestine, vol. i. p. 299. With the figures of the verse before us compare Ps. vii. 14 (13.) xviii. 13, 14 (12, 13.) cxl. 11 (10.)

5. *Alas for me, that I sojourn* (*with*) *Meshech* (and) *dwell near the tents of Kedar!* The first verb seems elsewhere, in the same construction, to denote the act of dwelling with one, Ps. v. 5 (4.) The Hebrew preposition in the last clause properly means *with* and denotes association and proximity. The English Bible, by twice employing our preposition *in*, obscures the meaning of both clauses, which is not that the people were in the power or even in the midst of the enemies here mentioned, but compelled to reside near them and to suffer from their neighbourhood. *Meshech* is the name given in Gen. x. 2 to the Moschi, a

barbarous people inhabiting the mountains between Colchis, Armenia, and Iberia. *Kedar* was one of the sons of Ishmael, (Gen. xxv. 13), whose name is sometimes used to designate an Arabian tribe (Isai. xxi. 16. xlii. 11), and in later Hebrew the Arabians generally. As these races, dwelling far off, in the north and south, were never in immediate or continued contact with the Israelites, they are probably named as types and representatives of warlike barbarism, just as the names Goths, Vandals, Huns, Turks, Tartars, Cossacks, have at different times been used proverbially in English, to describe those supposed to exhibit the same character, however unconnected or remote in genealogy and local habitation. A slight approach to the same usage was produced among ourselves by the revolutionary war, in reference to the national names, British and Hessian. In the case before us, it is evident from v. 6, that *Meshech* and *Kedar* are mere types and representatives of those who hate peace and delight in war. Compare Ezek. xxxviii. 2, where Meshech appears as a chief leader under Gog, the great prophetic representative of heathendom.

6. *My soul has dwelt too long for her with* (one) *hating peace.* The substitution of *my soul* for *I* implies the intimate conviction and the painful sense of what is here asserted. *Too long*, literally, *much* or *too much.* As to this peculiar idiom, see above, on Ps. lxv. 10 (9.) *For her* may be an idiomatic pleonasm, adding nothing to the meaning of the verb, with which it must be read in close connection; or it may have the meaning which the corresponding phrase would naturally seem to have in English, *for her good* or *for her interest.* See above on Ps. lviii. 8 (7.) *Hating peace* is clearly a collective or aggregate expression, comprehending all denoted by the Meshech and Kedar of the preceding verse, as an ideal individual.

7. *I am peace, and when I speak, they (go) to war.* The first

phrase resembles *I am prayer* in Ps. cix. 4, and seems to mean, I am all peace, nothing but peace, peace itself, i. e. entirely peaceful or pacific. *Speak* may be an ellipsis for *speak peace*, a phrase repeatedly occurring in the Psalms. See above, Ps. xxxv. 20. lxxxv. 9 (8), and below, Ps. cxxii. 8. The sense will then be, whenever I desire or propose peace. If the verb be absolutely understood, the sense is that every word he utters is made an occasion of attack or conflict. The double *for*, in the common version of this sentence, is as incorrect as the double *in* of v. 5, and more enfeebling to the sense. I am not only *for peace*, but am peace itself. They are not only *for war*, but arise, proceed, or address themselves to it.

PSALM CXXI.

1. *A Song for the Ascents. I raise my eyes to the mountains. Whence cometh my help?* The title differs from that of the preceding psalm only in the use of the preposition *for*, instead of the simple genitive construction. This variation, though without effect upon the sense, is favourable to the explanation which has been already given of these titles, as *a song for the ascents* or pilgrimages to Jerusalem is certainly more intelligible than *a song for the steps* of the temple, and still more so than *a song for the returns* from exile, while the modern theory of climacteric resumptions fails altogether to account for the expression here used. The whole psalm is a description of Jehovah as the guardian or protector of his people. The only material distinction of the parts is that arising from the alternate use of the first and second person, as in Ps. xci, which has led some to assume without ne-

cessity, that the psalm was intended to be sung by alternate or responsive choirs. The phrase to lift the eyes, though sometimes used to signify the mere act of directing them to an object, has its strict and full sense, when a higher object is particularly mentioned, such as hills or heavens. The mountains here meant are the heights on which Jerusalem is built. It is not improbable that this psalm was intended to be sung when the pilgrims came in sight of the Holy City. Some suppose moreover that it was meant to be an evening song and used when they halted for the last night's rest before they reached Jerusalem. The relative construction of the last clause yields a good sense, but is not in perfect keeping with the usage of the compound particle (מֵאַיִן) which is elsewhere always interrogative.

2. *My help is from Jehovah, Maker of heaven and earth.* The creative power of Jehovah is particularly mentioned, to demonstrate his ability to help his people. Compare Ps. cxv. 15.

3. *May he not suffer to be moved thy foot; may he not slumber —thy keeper.* This is the expression of a wish, the only sense consistent with the form of the original. *Let him not give up to moving thy foot.* See above, Ps. xxxviii. 17 (16.) lxvi. 9 (8.) The figure is peculiarly appropriate in the mouth of pilgrims, making their way among the hills and rocks of Palestine. The same thing is true of the figures in the subsequent verses.

4. *Lo, he shall not slumber, and he shall not sleep—the keeper of Israel.* What is desired in the third verse, is affirmed in this. The position of the subject at the end of the sentence, in both cases, is emphatic. Most interpreters assume a gradation in the meaning of the two verbs, as if one denoted lighter and the other deep sleep; but they differ on the question which is the stronger of the two expressions. The latest writers say the first See above, on Ps. iv. 9 (8.)

5. *Jehovah is thy keeper; Jehovah is thy shade upon thy right hand.* The keeper or protector of Israel, who had twice been mentioned by that title, is now named. A shade or shadow is a common figure for protector, and the right hand often mentioned as the place of a protector. See above, on Ps. cix. 6. cx. 5, and compare Num. xiv. 9

6. *By day the sun shall not smite thee, and the moon by night.* The last clause does not necessarily refer to injurious effects produced directly by the moon, but may be understood as a poetical description of all noxious influences operating in the night, over which the moon was constituted ruler at the time of its creation See Gen. i. 16. xxxi. 40. Jer. xxxvi. 30.

7. *Jehovah will keep thee from all evil; he will keep thy soul.* The protection which had been repeatedly promised to Israel on the part of God, is now described as extending to all evils and to the very life and soul.

8. *Jehovah will keep thy going out and thy coming in, from now even to eternity.* This is the third repetition of the phrase, *Jehovah will keep*, i. e. keep safe, protect, preserve, as if to silence the misgivings of a weak or tempted faith, by the reiterated declaration of this cheering truth. *Going out and coming in* is a proverbial Hebrew phrase for all the occupations and affairs of life See Deut. xxviii. 6. 1 Sam. xxix. 6. The original reference is to man's going out to labour in the morning and returning home to rest at night. See above, on Ps. civ. 23. With the last clause compare Ps. cxiii. 2. cxvi. 18. cxxv. 2. The promise of eternal preservation is addressed directly to the church as such; but that it involves the blessed immortality of individual believers, is admitted even by those least disposed to find allusions to the future state in the Book of Psalms.

PSALM CXXII.

1. *A Song of the Ascents. By David. I rejoice in* (those) *saying to me, To the house of Jehovah we will go.* This psalm, though so much older than the two before it, was probably placed third in the series, because it was intended to be sung, and was actually sung, at the entrance of the Holy City, whereas the others were used at the commencement of the march, and on coming in sight of Jerusalem. The ideal speaker represents the church or chosen people. After the introduction, vs. 1, 2, comes a panegyric on Jerusalem, as the royal and holy city, vs. 3—5, followed by a prayer for her prosperity as such, vs. 6—9. *The Ascents*, or upward journeys of the people to the sanctuary, as in Ps. cxx. 1. cxxi. 1. To *rejoice in those saying* is to rejoice because they say. On the last clause is founded Isai. ii. 3, where the gentiles are described as joining in the words here uttered by the Jews.

2. *Standing are our feet in thy gates, oh Jerusalem!* The common version (*shall stand*) is entirely ungrammatical. The past tense of the substantive verb with the participle means strictly *have been standing*, i. e. have begun to stand, or are already standing.

3. *Jerusalem, the* (*one*) *built like a city which is joined to itself together*. This seems to be a continuation of the address in the preceding verse. The unusual expressions in the last clause are intended to describe the city as substantially and strongly built. The sense is correctly given in the English Bible, *a city that is*

compact together. This seems to imply that Jerusalem had recently assumed this character, and may therefore help to determine the period in the reign of David, when the psalm was written. See 2 Sam. v. 9. The abbreviated relative (שֶׁחֻבְּרָה) has by some been made a proof of later date; but it no doubt belonged from the beginning to the dialect of common life, though not commonly employed in writing till a later date. It occurs in the song of Deborah, Judg. v. 7, and elsewhere in the Book of Judges (vi. 17. vii. 12. viii. 26.)

4. *Where the tribes go up, the tribes of Jah, (as) a testimony to Israel, to give thanks to the name of Jehovah.* There is obvious reference to the requisition in Ex. xxiii. 17. xxxiv. 23. Deut. xvi. 16, which is called a testimony, not merely as the law in general is (Ps. xciii. 5), but as a constant memorial of God's goodness to his people. The mention of the tribes seems to point to the period of the undivided monarchy.

5. *For there sit thrones for judgment, thrones for the house of David.* This means simply that Jerusalem was a civil as well as a religious capital. *There*, literally *thither*, implying that the singers were themselves in motion towards these thrones. *Sit*, or as we should say in English, *stand.* See below, Ps. cxxv. 1.

6. *Pray for the peace of Jerusalem; may they have peace that love thee!* Peace, in both clauses, includes all prosperity. There is obvious allusion to the meaning of the name *Jerusalem.* See above, on Ps. lxxvi. 3 (2.)

7. *Peace be within thy rampart, and repose within thy palaces.* Peace and repose from all distracting causes, of whatever nature. *Rampart*, breast-work, circumvallation. Rampart and palaces are put for the outer and inner masses of building. Compare Ps. xlviii. 14.

8. *For the sake of my brethren and my friends, let me speak, Peace (be) within thee.* By brethren and friends we are to understand the whole body of the chosen people. *For their sake* may include the sense of *in their behalf.* The last clause admits of a different construction, *Let me speak peace to thee*, literally *in thee.* See above, on Ps. lxxxv. 9 (8.) The optative meaning of the verb is determined by the particle (נָא) the use of which here seems to be imitated in Ps. cxv. 2. cxvi. 4.

9. *For the sake of the house of Jehovah our God, I will seek thy good.* The house of God is here the sanctuary and all the interests of which it was the local centre. *Jehovah our God*, our patron and protector, our peculiar covenant God. *Seek* includes every form of effort to promote it; but the prominent idea is that of intercession.

PSALM CXXIII.

1. *A Song of the Ascents. Unto thee do I raise my eyes, the (one) sitting in the heavens.* This psalm contains an expression of solicitous desire for divine help, v. 1, 2, a direct prayer for mercy, v. 3, and a statement of the circumstances which occasioned it. With the first clause compare Ps. cxxi. 1, with the second, Ps. ii. 4. xi. 4. ciii. 19. cxiii. 3, 5.

2. *Behold, as the eyes of servants* (are turned) *to the hand of their masters, as the eyes of a maid to the hand of her mistress, so our eyes* (are turned) *to Jehovah our God, until he have mercy upon us.* The *behold as*, at the beginning, is equivalent to *see how* in English. Some suppose the act of looking towards the hand of a

superior to denote desire of protection; others an appeal to his bounty, as in Ps. civ. 27, 28. cxlv. 15, 16; others an implied prayer that punishment may cease. Compare Gen. xvi. 6, 8, 9. Perhaps all these explanations err in being too specific, and the sense of the comparison is simply that they look with deference and trust to the superior power which controls them.

3. *Have mercy upon us, oh Jehovah, have mercy upon us; for greatly are we sated with contempt.* This petition forms the centre of the psalm, to which what goes before is introductory and what follows supplementary. The contempt is that of heathen neighbours, and especially that of the Samaritans, which is expressly mentioned in the history. See Neh. i. 3. ii. 19.

4. *Much sated in itself is our soul with the scorning of the secure, the contempt of the proud.* In itself, literally, *to* or *for itself*, as in Ps. cxxii. 3. *Secure* (*sinners*), those at ease, indifferent to the sufferings of others, and without apprehension of their own. Compare Ps. lxxiii. 12.

PSALM CXXIV.

1. *A Song of the Ascents. By David. If* (*it had*) *not* (*been*) *Jehovah who was for us—oh let Israel say.* This psalm consists of two parts, an acknowledgment of God as the deliverer of Israel, vs. 1—5, and a consequent determination to trust in him exclusively for future favours, v. 6—9. The verse before us propounds the theme of the whole composition, in a conditional and imperfect, but for that very reason a more striking form.

It is tantamount to saying, what if the Lord had not been for us?—leaving the answer to the imagination of the reader. *For us*, in our favour, on our side; or *to us*, belonging to us, ours, which really includes the other. See above, on Ps. lvi. 10 (9.) *Oh that* in the last clause represents (נָא) the particle of entreaty. The common version (*now*) conveys the very different idea, *at length*, after all that we have suffered, let Israel so say. The mistake is rendered more natural or rather unavoidable, to mere English readers, by the seeming antithesis between the *now* of this verse and the *then* of vs. 3, 4, 5, of which there is not the slightest trace in the original.

2. *If (it had) not (been) Jehovah who was for us, in the rising up of man against us*—What was left unfinished in the first verse, as a mere suggestion of the Psalmist's theme, is now repeated, for the purpose of being carried out. This is one of the rhetorical resumptions, which some modern critics hold to be the (מַעֲלוֹת) *degrees*, from which these fifteen psalms derived their common designation. With this verse compare Ps. lvi. 12 (11.)

3. *Then alive would they have swallowed us, in the kindling of their wrath against us.* With respect to the *then* at the beginning of this verse, there is danger of an error just the opposite of that already pointed out in reference to the *now* of v. 1. As the English reader would be almost sure to take that for a particle of time, which it is not, he would be equally certain to mistake this for a term of logic, meaning in that case, upon that supposition, or the like; whereas it really means *at that time*, the well remembered time of our extremity, when God so wonderfully interposed for our deliverance. The Hebrew particle occurs in this form only here, and is consequently no more a proof of recent than of early date. Another word liable to misconstruction in the English versions of this clause is *quick*, here used in its primary sense of *living* or *alive*, from which may be easily deduced its secondary

sense of *swift*, implying lively motion. The historical allusion, in this and other like passages, is no doubt to the fate of Korah and his company. Compare Num. xvi. 32, 33, where the same verb and adjective occur together. See above, on Ps. lv. 16 (15.) The plural pronoun *their* refers to the collective *man* in the preceding verse.

4. *Then the waters would have overwhelmed us* (and) *a stream passed over our soul.* The common version (*had overwhelmed us*) is entirely correct, and more poetical in form than that here given, but at the same time ambiguous, as the sentence, taken by itself, would seem to mean, that before the time signified by *then*, the waters had actually overwhelmed them, which was not the case. The figures are the same as in Ps. xviii. 5, 17 (4, 16.) cxliv. 7.

5. *Then had passed over our soul the waters, the proud* (*waters.*) The waters are so described, partly because of the ideas suggested by their swelling (Ps. lxxxix. 10), partly because they represent dangers arising from the selfish pride of human enemies. Some, without necessity, recur to the primary meaning of the root, and explain the adjective to mean boiling, effervescing.

6. *Blessed* (*be*) *Jehovah, who did not give us* (*as*) *prey to their teeth.* By one of those rhetorical transitions which are constantly occurring in the figurative diction of the psalms, the enemies and dangers, which had just been represented as an overwhelming flood or torrent, are suddenly transformed into devouring beasts. See above, on Ps. iii. 8 (7.) lviii. 7 (6.) With the benediction or doxology, *blessed* (*be*) *Jehovah*, compare Ps. xxviii. 6. xxxi. 22 (21.)

7. *Our soul is escaped, like a bird, from the snare of the fowlers; the snare is broken and we are escaped.* We have here a second transition and a third comparison, to wit, that of the enemies to fowlers, and of their devices to snares or traps used in catching

birds. In the second clause there is an obvious climax. Not only is the bird gone, but the snare is broken. This is peculiarly appropriate to the restoration of the Jews from Babylon, which was occasioned by the fall of Babylon itself. With the figures of this verse compare Ps. xviii. 5 (4.) xci. 3. The English phrase *is escaped*, denoting a change of state, and not, like *has escaped*, a single act, is well suited to represent the Hebrew verb, which, though active in meaning, has the passive form.

8. *Our help is in the name of Jehovah, maker of heaven and earth.* The conclusion drawn from the experience here recorded is, that he who had helped them must help them still. *Our help* for the future no less than the past. *In the name of Jehovah*, the manifested attributes, which constitute his *name*, in the peculiar dialect of Scripture, and especially of this book. See above, on Ps. v. 12 (11) xx. 2 (1.) With this verse compare also Ps xxxiii. 22. cxxi. 2.

PSALM CXXV.

1. *A Song of the Ascents. Those trusting in Jehovah* (*are*) *like Mount Zion,* (*which*) *is not moved* (*but*) *stands forever.* This psalm contains an expression of strong confidence in the divine protection, vs. 1, 2, especially against wicked enemies, v. 3, with a prayer that this confidence may not go unrewarded, v. 4, and a prophetic anticipation of the fate of the ungodly, v. 5. The condition of the chosen people, here described or pre-supposed, as suffering from the spite of heathen enemies, not in captivity or

exile, but at home in their own land, and internally divided into two great parties, the sincere and hypocritical, agrees exactly with the period of the Restoration, and especially that part of it in which the building of the temple was suspended, as known to us from history and prophecy. The psalm before us was well suited to alarm and warn the false Israel, as well as to encourage and support the true. According to Hengstenberg, it was intended, with the psalms before and after it, to form a trilogy, consisting of one ancient and two later compositions. *Those trusting in Jehovah* is a characteristic designation of the true church, the spiritual Israel, the chosen people. The meaning is not merely that they individually exercise this faith, but that collectively, or as a body, they are built upon it, and have no security except in the divine protection. *Mount Zion*, not as a figure for the church, which would then be compared with itself, but simply as a mountain, and like other mountains solid and enduring, here selected as a sample or an emblem of these qualities, because it had also a religious pre-eminence, as the earthly seat and centre of the true religion. It *is not* (and shall not be) *moved*, shaken from its firm position. See above on Ps. xlvi. 6 (5.) *Stands forever*, literally, *sits to eternity*, the Hebrew idiom using one of these postures as we use the other, or rather using both as we use only one, to denote the opposite of vacillation and prostration. See above, on Ps. cxxii. 5.

2. *Jerusalem* (has) *hills about her*, *and* (so) *Jehovah* (*is*) *about his people*, *from now even to eternity*. The site of Jerusalem, with its peculiar features, furnishes the psalmist with a striking image of the divine protection. As in v. 1, the permanent security of the church itself is likened to the firmness of Mount Zion on its base, so here the protecting care, which causes this security, is likened to the heights by which the city is surrounded upon all sides. The verb *has*, supplied in the translation of the first clause, is really a violation of the Hebrew

idiom, to which as well as to the kindred tongues the verb *to have* is utterly unknown. In our own idiom, however, it expresses the precise idea, and enables us to retain the Hebrew collocation, which assigns *Jerusalem* the first place in the sentence. The Hebrew corresponding to *about* is a compound phrase, consisting of a local adverb and a preposition, *around as to*. *His people*, meaning *those who trust him* (v. 1), to the exclusion of all hypocrites and unbelievers.

3. *For not to rest is the rod of wickedness over the lot of the righteous, to the intent that the righteous may not put forth to iniquity their hands.* This unusually long verse clearly shows the actual condition of the chosen people, here assumed or presupposed, as well known to the writer and original readers of the psalm. The present ascendency of wicked men is not inconsistent with the truth just stated, because it is to be brought to an end, lest the faith and patience of God's people should fail, and they should be tempted to renounce his service as unprofitable, nay as ruinous. Compare Ps. lxxiii. 13, 14. *To rest*, not merely to remain, but to continue undisturbed. The *rod* or *staff* is here a symbol of authority, and might be rendered *sceptre*, if the subject of discourse were kings. See above on Ps. ii. 9. xlv. 7 (6.) *The lot of the righteous*, their share of the inheritance of the chosen people, at first distributed by lot. *To the intent* indicates the reason why this undeserved superiority is not to last. The reason is founded not merely on the ill desert of the wicked, but on the interest and welfare of the righteous. *Put forth*, or stretch out, literally *send into*. See the same construction, Gen. xxxvii. 22. Ex. xxii. 7, 10 (8, 11.) To touch iniquity is here to meddle with it, not, as some suppose, in the shape of revenge merely, but in all its degrees and forms, by which the righteous can be tempted.

4. *Do good, Oh Jehovah, to the good, and to (those) upright in*

their hearts. These are additional descriptions of the true church or spiritual Israel, to whom alone the promise of divine favour and protection had been given. *Upright*, literally *straight*, straightforward, as opposed to all moral obliquity whatever. See above, on Ps. vii. 11 (10.) The prayer involves a prophetic declaration, that to such and such only, God will do good or act kindly in the highest sense. See above, on Ps. lxxiii. 1.

5. *And*, (as to) *those turning aside* (in) *their crooked* (ways), *Jehovah will let them go with the doers of iniquity. Peace* (be) *upon Israel!* The participle in the first clause is properly a transitive and means *causing to turn aside*, but has here the sense of *going aside*, or *turning* in the intransitive sense, the English verb having precisely the same double usage. This construction of the Hebrew verb, which occurs also in Isai. xxx. 11. Job. xxiii. 11, may be resolved into the usual one, by supposing an ellipsis of *their feet* or *steps.* The adjective translated *crooked* occurs only here and in Judg. v. 6, where the noun (*ways* or *paths*) is expressed. It denotes the bye-ways of corrupt inclination and transgression, by which men deviate from the straight and narrow highway of God's commandments. Compare Deut. ix. 16. Mal. ii. 8, 9. The *workers of iniquity* are not a different class from these wanderers, but that to which they belong, and the doom of which they would gladly escape ; but the Lord will let them go on still with those whom they resemble in character, and as they have been like them by the way, they shall be like them in the end. Compare Ps. xxvi. 9. xxviii. 3. Having thus excluded hypocritical pretenders from the object of the benediction, he concludes by wishing or invoking *peace upon* (the true or spiritual) *Israel.* Compare Isai. lvii. 19, 21.

PSALM CXXVI.

1. *A Song of the Ascents. In Jehovah's turning (to) the turning of Zion, we were like* (men) *dreaming.* The church acknowledges the good work of deliverance as joyfully begun, vs. 1—3, and prays that it may be completed, vs. 4—6. For the meaning and construction of the first verb see above, on Ps. xiv. 7. lxxxvi. 5 (4), and compare my note on Isai. lii. 8. Instead of the usual combination (שׁוּב שְׁבוּת) *return to the captivity*, we have here one resembling it in form (שׁוּב שִׁיבַת) but meaning to *return to the return* or meet those returning, as it were, half-way. Compare Deut. xxx. 2, 3. James iv. 8. The Hebrew noun denotes *conversion,* in its spiritual sense, and the verb God's gracious condescension in accepting or responding to it. The great historical example of this condescension, which the Psalmist had immediately in view, was the deliverance from Babylon; but the terms are so selected as to be appropriate to the most intimate personal experience of the same kind. *Zion* is here put for the church or chosen people, of which it was the local seat or centre. *Like the dreamers* or *those dreaming*, i. e. out of our ordinary normal state, and in an ecstasy or trance, arising from excess of joy. The idea of incredulity may be included, but must not be suffered to exclude all others.

2. *Then was filled with laughter our mouth, and our tongue with singing ; then said they among the nations, Jehovah hath done great things to these (people.)* The particle (אָז) *then* is followed by the future in the sense of the preterite, in prose as well as

poetry. See Ex. xv. 1. Deut. iv. 41. Josh. 10, 12. There is no need therefore of supposing that the writer simply retained the future forms of the passage from which this was copied, namely, Job viii. 21. *Laughter* and *singing*, both as signs of joy. *Done great things*, literally *magnified to do*, an idiomatic phrase borrowed from Joel ii. 21. *To these*, literally *with these*, i. e. in his associations and transactions with them.

3. *Jehovah has done great things to us. We are joyful.* This last is not a mere appendage to the first clause, we are glad that he has done great things for us, but an independent proposition, containing the proof of that by which it is preceded. He has indeed done much for us, for whereas we were lately wretched, we are now rejoicing, or more closely rendered, have become joyful.

4. *Turn, oh Jehovah, to our captivity, like the streams in the south.* The prayer is that God will return to or revisit his people in their bondage or distress, and by necessary implication set them free from it. See above on v. 1, where we have a studied variation of this favourite expression. According to the usual interpretation (*bring back our captivity*), this verse is either inconsistent with the first, or a proof that the restoration is not mentioned there as past already. *Like the streams in the south*, as the temporary torrents in the dry southern district of Palestine reappear in the rainy season, after having ceased to flow in the preceding drought.

5. *Those sowing with weeping with singing shall reap. Those sowing*, literally *the sowing*, i. e. the (same persons or the very persons) sowing. *With weeping*, or in tears; the Hebrew noun is a singular collective. See above, on Ps. vi. 7 (6.) xxxix. 13 (12.) lvi. 9 (8.) *Singing*, as a vocal expression of joy. See above, on v. 2. The figures are natural and common ones for means

and end, or for the beginning and the issue of any undertaking. They may have been suggested here by the mention of the parched and thirsty south, where the fears of the husbandman are often disappointed by abundant rains and the sudden reappearance of the vanished streams.

6. *He may go forth, he may go forth, and weep, bearing* (*his*) *load of seed. He shall come, he shall come with singing, bearing sheaves.* The emphatic combination of the finite tense with the infinitive is altogether foreign from our idiom, and very imperfectly represented, in the ancient and some modern versions, by the active participle (*venientes venient*, coming they shall come), which conveys neither the peculiar form nor the precise sense of the Hebrew phrase. The best approximation to the force of the original is Luther's repetition of the finite tense, *he shall come, he shall come*, because in all such cases the infinitive is really defined or determined by the term which follows, and in sense, though not in form, assimilated to it. *Load of seed*, literally *drawing* or *draught of seed*, an obscure phrase probably denoting that from which the sower draws forth seed to sow, or perhaps the seed itself thus drawn forth. The only analogous expression is in Am. ix. 13, where the sower is called (מֹשֵׁךְ הַזָּרַע) *a drawer* (*forth*) *of seed*. The common version (*precious seed*) has no foundation either in etymology or usage. The contrast so beautifully painted in this verse was realized in the experience of Israel, when " the priests and the levites, and the rest of the children of the captivity, kept the dedication of the house of God with joy" (Ezra vi. 16), " and kept the feast of unleavened bread seven days with joy, because the Lord had made them joyful, and turned the heart of the king of Assyria unto them, to strengthen their hands in the work of the house of God, the God of Israel" (Ezra vi. 22.) See also Nehemiah xii. 43.

PSALM CXXVII.

1. *A Song of the Ascents. By Solomon. If Jehovah will not build a house, in vain toil its builders in it, If Jehovah will not keep a city, in vain watches (its) keeper.* This is the central psalm of the series, having seven before and seven after it. This position it may owe to its being the only psalm of Solomon, whereas four are by David, and the remaining ten probably by one and the same author. See above, on Ps. cxx. 1. The admission of this psalm among the Songs of Pilgrimage was probably occasioned by its opening words, which, though admitting of a general application, were peculiarly appropriate to the building both of the first and second temple. It was perfectly natural, apart from all particular divine direction, that the rebuilders of the temple should rejoice to appropriate the words of Solomon, their great exemplar. The correctness of the title, which ascribes the psalm to him, is not only free from any plausible objection, but abundantly confirmed by its internal character, its allusions to a state of high prosperity, and its resemblance to the Book of Proverbs, where the sentiment here uttered is frequently reiterated. See for example Prov. x. 22. The general principle, that human care and toil are unavailing without God's blessing, is applied successively to several of the most familiar interests of real life. Beyond this the psalm admits of no subdivision. The first specification has respect to human dwellings, both on a small and on a large scale. The futures, *will not build*, *will not keep*, may also be explained as presents, *builds not*, *keeps not*. The phrase (בוֹ) *in it* or *on it* is to be connected with the verb and

not with *builders*. *Watches*, wakes, remains awake, but always with a view to the exercise of vigilance. See above on Ps. cii. 8, and compare Prov. viii. 34. The last word in Hebrew is properly the participle of the verb translated *keep*.

2. *It is in vain for you*, *rising up early*, *sitting down late*, *eating the bread of cares* (or *troubles*.) *So he giveth his beloved sleep*. The first phrase means, you labour in vain. *Rising up*, not merely from sleep, but to labour, addressing yourselves to work. *Sitting down*, to rest when the work is done. The contrast is sufficiently maintained by the common version, *sitting up late;* but it is objected that the Hebrews did not work in a sitting posture. Both these phrases are peculiar in their form—*making early* (or *hastening*) *to rise*—*making late* (or *delaying*) *to sit*. *Bread of cares* (or *troubles*) is bread earned by hard toil and consumed amidst it. There is obvious allusion to Gen. iii. 17, 19. The last clause is exceedingly obscure. Some understand it to mean that while others labour, God's beloved sleeps. But this is contradicted by notorious facts and inconsistent with the doctrine of the Bible, and especially the Book of Proverbs, with respect to idleness and diligence. See Prov. vi. 9, 10. xxxi. 27. Another possible interpretation is that God gives his beloved refreshing sleep after their labour, but this cannot be said of such exclusively. The latest writers understand the clause to mean, that what others hope to gain exclusively by labour, but in vain, the Lord bestows upon his people while they sleep, they know not how. According to this view of the passage, it must be translated, *so*, i. e. such, namely, what they thus seek, *he gives to his beloved one* (*in*) *sleep*. This, which is not a very obvious construction, derives some additional colour from the seeming allusion to Solomon's name Jedidiah (2 Sam. xii. 25), *the Beloved of the Lord*, and to the promise of prosperity communicated to him in a dream (1 Kings iii. 5, 15.)

3. *Lo, a heritage from Jehovah (are) children ; a reward (is) the fruit of the womb.* What is true of dwellings and the means of subsistence is no less true of those for whom these advantages are commonly provided. *An inheritance* or *heritage*, i. e. a valuable possession derived from a father. *Children*, literally *sons*, a term very often used indefinitely. *A reward* or *hire*, the expression used by Leah, in naming her son Issachar, Gen. xxx. 18. In the same chapter (Gen. xxx. 2) children are called the *fruit of the womb*, and represented as the gift of God. See also Deut. vii 13.

4. *As arrows in the hand of a warrior, so are the sons of youth.* The first clause describes them as defenders of their parents. *A warrior*, literally, *a strong* or *(mighty) one. Sons of youth*, i. e. born while their parents are still young. See Gen. xxxvii. 3. Isai. liv. 6. The allusion is not only to their vigour (Gen. xlix. 3), but to the value of their aid to the parent in declining age.

5. *Happy the man who has filled his quiver with them—they shall not be put to shame—they shall speak with adversaries in the gate.* The first clause carries out the figure of arrows in the verse preceding. The mention of the gate, in the last clause, as the place both of commercial and judicial business, seems to mark a transition from martial to forensic conflict, and to show that the enemies or adversaries here meant are adverse parties in litigation. See above, on Ps. lxix. 13 (12.) For a striking contrast to this picture, see Job v. 4. This last example, although perfectly in keeping with the views of the ancient Israelites in general, seems peculiarly natural and life-like in a psalm of Solomon.

PSALM CXXVIII.

1. *A Song of Ascents. Happy is every fearer of Jehovah, the (one) walking in his ways.* This psalm seems intended to assure the tempted and discouraged people of Judah, under the most adverse circumstances, that devotion to his service cannot lose its reward. As if he had said, however things may now seem to an eye of sense, it is still a certain truth, that the truly happy man is he who fears Jehovah, not in mere profession, but who testifies his fear of him by walking in his ways or doing his commandments.

2. *The labour of thy hands when thou shalt eat, happy thou and well with thee.* The promise implied is the opposite of the threatening in Deut. xxviii. 33. Lev. xxvi. 16. What the enemies of Israel are there described as doing, it is here said that Israel shall do himself. *Well with thee*, literally, *good for thee.* The conjunction (כִּי) in the first clause is not to be construed as in Ps. cxviii. 10, but as a particle of time. *Happy thou*, or oh thy *happinesses*, is an expression borrowed from Deut. xxxiii. 29.

3. *Thy wife, as a fruitful vine at the sides of thy house; thy sons, as olive-plants around thy table.* The word translated *sides* always means the edge or border, and, according to some, the innermost part. See above, on Ps. xlviii. 3 (2.) *Sons*, as usual, represent the children of both sexes. The olive-plants are emblems of luxuriance and fruitfulness. See above, on Ps. lii. 10

(8), and compare Jer. xi. 16. The Hebrew for *around* or *about* is the same as in Ps. cxxv. 2.

4. *See—for so shall be blessed the man fearing Jehovah.* The *lo* or *behold* at the beginning is equivalent to saying, Look upon this picture, for it represents the state of one who truly fears the Lord. Although such a connection between goodness and prosperity was far more uniform and constant under the Old Testament than now, it is not to be supposed that these promises were actually verified in the experience of every godly Israelite. This has led some of the most eminent interpreters to the conclusion, that the promises of this psalm are not personal at all, but addressed to an ideal person representing the whole class of true believers, the true Israel.

5. *Jehovah bless thee out of Zion, and look thou upon the welfare of Jerusalem.* The consecution of the future and imperative is the same as in Ps. cx. 2. The latter might therefore be translated as a promise, *the Lord shall bless thee*, but the optative meaning seems more natural in this connection. In either case, the imperative conveys substantially the same idea. See above, on Ps. xxxvii. 3, 4, 27. *From Zion*, as his earthly residence, the seat of the theocracy. See above, on Ps. xx. 3 (2.) *Look upon*, with joy and triumph. See above, on Ps. xxii. 18 (17.) xxxvii. 34. liv. 9 (8.) *Welfare*, literally *goodness*, not of character but of condition, good fortune. The Hebrew word occurs above, Ps. cxix. 66.

6. *And see thou sons to thy sons. Peace (be) upon Israel!* The first clause is a virtual promise of long life—*thou shalt see thy children's children.* An interesting parallel is furnished by Zech. viii. 4, the whole of which chapter is indeed a prophetic commentary on this psalm. For the meaning of the last clause, see above, on Ps. cxxv. 5.

PSALM CXXIX.

1. *A Song of the Ascents. Many (a time) have they distressed me from my youth—oh let Israel say!* On the recollection of deliverances in times past, vs. 1—4, rests the hope of others in time to come, vs. 5—8. The first word after the inscription properly means *much* or *too much.* See above, on Ps. cxx. 6. cxxiii. 4. But most interpreters agree in referring it to time, as in the English version, *many a time* or *often.* The *youth* of Israel, as a nation, was the period of his residence in Egypt. See Hos. ii. 17. Jer. ii. 2. xxii. 21. Ezek. xxiii. 3. For the optative meaning of the last clause, and the true sense of the Hebrew particle (נָא), see above, on Ps. cxviii. 2. cxxiv. 1. *Distressed*, persecuted or oppressed me. Compare the use of the participle in Ps. vi. 8 (7.) vii. 5 (4.) xxiii. 5.

2. *Many (a time) have they distressed me from my youth; yet have they not prevailed against me.* The statement in the first verse is repeated, for the sake of being joined with one of a more cheering character. *Yet*, literally, *also.* As if he had said: it is true that they have so done, but it is *also* true, etc. *Prevailed against me*, literally, *been able (as) to me*, i. e. able to accomplish their designs respecting me. See Gen. xxxii. 26 (25), and compare Ps. xiii. 5 (4.)

3. *Upon my back ploughed ploughers; they made long their furrows.* The expression *on my back* seems to show that the allusion

is to wounds produced by stripes. As if he had said, my back was furrowed by their whips or scourges. We have here then an example of the image of an image. The ploughing is a figure for scourging, and the scourging a figure for the manifold sufferings inflicted upon Israel by his cruel enemies.

4. *Jehovah (is) righteous; he cut the cord of the wicked.* He is righteous, and therefore faithful to his promise, and to his covenant engagements to his people. The *cord* (not *cords*) is that which fastened the ox to the plough. This continuation of the figure in v. 3 is much more natural than the assumption of a new one, that of confinement by the tying of the limbs, as in Ps. ii. 3. According to the first translation above given, the meaning of the clause is, that Jehovah put an end to their inflictions by a violent separation from their victim.

5. *Shamed and turned back are (*and shall be) *all haters of* Zion. What Jehovah has already done for Zion, as recorded in v. 4, creates and justifies the confident belief, that he will do still more. This language was peculiarly appropriate to Israel at the Restoration, when the main deliverance had already been accomplished, but others were still needed to complete the happy revolution. With the first clause compare Ps. vi. 11 (10.) xxxv. 4 (3.) xl. 14 (13.)

6. *They shall be like the grass of the house-tops, which, before one pulls (it), withers.* The flat roofs of the oriental houses being often covered with earth, grass and weeds readily spring up, but having no depth of root soon wither. Compare my note on Isai. xxxvii. 27, from which place the figure is here borrowed. The common version (*afore it groweth up*) is founded on Jerome's (*statim ut viruerit.*) The other is supported by the Septuagint and Vulgate (πρὸ τοῦ ἐκσπασθῆναι, *priusquam evellatur*),

and by the usage of the verb (שָׁלַף) in the sense of drawing (a sword), drawing off (a shoe) etc.

7. (With) *which the reaper fills not his hand and his bosom,* (when) *binding sheaves.* The ephemeral and worthless vegetation of the house-top is contrasted still further with the useful products of the earth, in order to contrast still more strongly the end of the righteous and the wicked. The last Hebrew word is translated above strictly as a participle of the verb (עמר) to bind or gather sheaves, and may agree with (קוצר) *reaper* in the first clause. Since the latter, however, is itself a participle used as a noun, most interpreters put the same construction on the other word, and suppose it to denote a different person from the reaper. *With which the reaper fills not his hand nor his bosom the sheaf-binder.* The word translated *bosom* is explained by lexicographers to mean the front fold of the oriental robe, in which things are carried. It might also be translated *lap.* Hengstenberg's version is *his arm.* Compare my note on Isai. xlix. 22.

8 *Nor do the passers by say, The blessing of Jehovah* (come) *unto you, we bless you in the name of Jehovah.* The negative description is still carried out, with unusual distinctness and particularity. This verse affords an interesting glimpse of ancient harvest usages, confirmed by the historical statement in Ruth ii. 4, from the analogy of which place it is altogether probable, although denied by some, that there is here allusion to the alternate or responsive salutations in common use among the people. We may then supply in thought before the last clause, *nor receive the customary answer.* As the Hebrew preposition before *you* does not mean *on* but *to* or *unto,* it seems better to supply *come* than *be.* With this verse compare Ps. cxviii. 26.

PSALM CXXX.

1. *A Song of Ascents. Out of the depths do I invoke thee, oh Jehovah!* This is the penitential psalm of the series, in which the guilt of the chosen people is distinctly acknowledged, as the cause of its calamities, but not as an occasion of despair. After an introductory petition to be heard, vs. 1, 2, comes the indirect confession of sin, vs. 3, 4, then an expression of strong confidence, vs. 5, 6, and an exhortation to Israel to indulge the same, vs. 7, 8. The distinction made in this last stanza, between Israel at large and the penitent who utters the previous confession, would seem to show, that the latter is to be conceived of as an individual, and not as representing the whole people. But the best interpreters are of opinion, that the distinction is entirely formal, and that the object of address in the last stanza is identical with the person speaking in the others. See above, on Ps. lxix. 3, 15 (2, 14), and compare Isai. li. 10, in all which places the word translated *depths* occurs, and in the same sense, as a figure for extreme dejection and distress. The figure itself is also used in Ps. xl. 3 (2.) Ezek. xxvii. 34.

2. *Lord, hearken to my voice; let thine ears be attentive to the voice of my supplications.* The first word in Hebrew is (אֲדֹנָי) the one strictly meaning *Lord*, and showing that the prayer is offered to a sovereign God. The common verb (שָׁמַע) *to hear* is here construed with a preposition (בְּ), thus resembling, in its syntax, our verbs *hearken, listen.* The adjective *attentive* is peculiar

to the later Hebrew, though its verbal root is of frequent occurrence in the psalms. *Supplications*, prayers for grace or mercy See above, on Ps. xxviii. 6. xxxi. 23 (22.)

3. *If iniquities thou mark, oh Jah—oh Lord, who shall stand?* This interrogation clearly implies consciousness of guilt, and is therefore an indirect confession of it. To *mark* is to note, take notice of, observe. The Hebrew verb is used in precisely the same manner, Job x. 14. xiv. 16. To *stand* is to stand one's ground, maintain one's innocence, and perhaps in this case, to endure one's sentence. See above, on Ps. i. 6, and compare Nah. i. 6. Mal. iii. 2. The question is equivalent to a strong negation, or an affirmation that none can stand.

4. *For with thee* (*there is*) *forgiveness, to the intent that thou mayest be feared.* The *for* has reference to a thought suppressed but easily supplied. Since none can stand, oh Lord, forgive, *for* with thee, etc. Or, since none can stand, our only hope is in free forgiveness, *for* with thee etc. *With thee*, belonging to thee, exercised by thee. The word rendered *forgiveness* is peculiar to the later Hebrew; its plural form occurs in Neh. ix. 17. *The forgiveness* that we need, *the* (*only*) *forgiveness* that is available or attainable. *To the intent*, for this very purpose, not merely *so that*, as an incidental consequence. *Fear* or godly reverence is here represented as one fruit and evidence of pardoned sin.

5. *I wait for Jehovah—my soul waits—and in his word do I hope.* The last verb also means *to wait for* his word, i. e the fulfilment of his promise, as in Ps. cxix. 74, 81, 82, 114, 147. *My soul waits*, I wait with all my soul or heart. My powers and affections are absorbed in this earnest expectation.

6. *My soul* (waits) *for the Lord more than* (those) *watching*

for the morning—watching for the morning. There is something beautiful and touching in this simple repetition, though it is not easy to account for its effect, which is sensibly impaired by the attempt made in the English version to relieve the baldness of the iteration, *I say more than they that watch for the morning.* The comparison suggested is between the impatience of nocturnal watchers for the break of day and that of sufferers for relief, or of convicted sinners for forgiveness.

7. *Hope thou, Israel, in Jehovah; for with Jehovah* (is) *mercy, and abundantly with him redemption.* The third person used in the English Bible (*let Israel hope in the Lord*) is an inaccuracy the more remarkable because not found in the Prayer Book Version (*Oh Israel, trust in the Lord.*) In Jehovah, literally to him, i. e. look to him with confident expectation, as in Isai. li. 5. The construction in the last clause is idiomatic and not susceptible of close translation. The word corresponding to *abundantly* is the infinitive of a verb meaning to increase or multiply, but is often used adverbially in the sense of much, greatly, or abundantly. See above, on Ps. li. 4 (2.) *Redemption*, deliverance, especially from bondage, that of Babylon in Ps. cxi. 9, that of sin or condemnation in the case before us.

8. *And He will redeem Israel from all his iniquities.* The pronoun is emphatic; only trust him for redemption, and he will himself redeem thee. As the first clause shows by whom Israel is to be redeemed, to wit, by God alone, so the second shows from what, to wit, from sin, as the cause of his sufferings. This is a very significant variation of the older passage, Ps. xxv. 22, where the sufferings alone are expressly mentioned.

PSALM CXXXI.

1. *A Song of Ascents. By David. Oh Jehovah, not haughty is my heart, and not lofty are my eyes, and I meddle not with great* (*things*) *and* (with things) *too wonderful for me.* This short psalm is perfectly in David's manner, as well as his spirit, displaying in a high degree that childlike royalty, in which he is resembled by no other even of the sacred writers. *Haughty*, literally *high*, but with particular reference to *hauteur* or loftiness of spirit. Lofty eyes are mentioned elsewhere by David himself as a sign of pride. See Ps. xviii. 28 (27.) ci. 5. The elation here described is elsewhere represented as the natural fruit of undisturbed prosperity. See Deut. xxxii. 15. 2 Chron. xxvi. 16. xxxii. 25. This confirms the Davidic origin of the psalm, and shows that it was only adapted by the later writer to his own purpose, when the original conception would have been almost impossible. *Meddle*, literally, *walk* or *walk about*, i. e. employ or (as the English versions have it) exercise myself. *Too wonderful for me*, wonderfully done (more) than I (can comprehend.) The great and wonderful things meant are God's secret purposes and sovereign means for their accomplishment, in which man is not called to co-operate but to acquiesce. As David practised this forbearance by his patient expectation of the kingdom, both before and after the death of Saul, so he here describes it as a characteristic of the chosen people.

2. (God knows) *if I have not soothed and quieted my soul, as a weaned* (child leans) *upon his mother; as a weaned* (child leans)

on me my soul. The first clause contains a strong asseveration, in the idiomatic form of an ancient oath, very feebly represented by our adverb *surely.* See above, on Ps. lxxxix. 36 (35.) The word translated *soothed* means rather *smoothed*, levelled, as in Isai. xxviii. 25. *Quieted*, stilled, hushed, reduced to silence. The repeated use of the preposition *on* in this connection is so marked and striking, that it seems to make it necessary to supply a verb with which it may be construed. This is certainly better than to give it a different meaning in the two clauses, or in both one which does not belong to it. In the version above given, the comparison suggested is between a weaned child, quietly reposing on its mother's breast, without desiring to be suckled as of old, and the soul of the Psalmist, by a bold conception represented as his child, and acting in like manner. Hengstenberg denies that there is any reference to the mother's milk, or that *weaned* has any other meaning here than that of infant or young child, as in Isai. xi. 8. xxviii. 9. The comparison is then coincident with that in Matth. xviii. 3, 4. But the use of the word *weaned*, which was here required by no parallelism as in Isaiah, and the singular aptness of the figure suggested by the word when strictly understood, have led most interpreters, and will probably lead most readers, to prefer the obvious and strict interpretation.

3. *Hope thou, Israel, in Jehovah, from now even to eternity.* This is the opposite of the feeling disavowed in the preceding verses. From the first clause that of Ps. cxxx. 7 was no doubt borrowed by the later writer, who prefixed that psalm to the one before us. With the last clause compare Ps. cxxi. 8.

PSALM CXXXII.

1. *A Song of Ascents Remember, oh Jehovah, for David, all his affliction.* This psalm contains a commemoration of David's zeal for the house of God, vs. 1—9, and a prayer that it may be rewarded by the fulfilment of the promise to him and to his house, vs. 10—18. The common version (*remember David and all his afflictions*) omits a preposition and inserts a conjunction, both without necessity. The same verb and preposition (זכר ל) are combined elsewhere, in the sense of remembering something in a person's favour, to his advantage, for his benefit. See above, on Ps. xcviii. 3. cvi. 45. cxix. 49. So here: remember, in behalf of David, how he was distressed. The common version of this last phrase (*all his afflictions*) supposes the Hebrew word (עֻנּוֹת) to be a plural noun, whereas it is the infinitive of the passive verb (עֻנָּה) to be afflicted or distressed (Ps. cxix. 71), and is therefore more correctly rendered in the Prayer Book (*all his trouble.*) The precise sense is, *his being afflicted.* The distress referred to is the great anxiety which David felt, first to reunite the ark and tabernacle, and then to build a more permanent sanctuary. This zeal for the house of God is one of the most characteristic features in the history of David, and for this he was rewarded, not only with a promise that his son should execute his favourite design, but also with a promise that God would build a house for him, by granting a perpetual succession in his family upon the throne of Judah. This promise seemed to be forgotten at the time of the Captivity, and even after the first Restoration, when the house of David was reduced so low, that its hereditary representative,

Zerubbabel, never even bore the royal title. The form of the petition in this verse is copied from that of Solomon, at the dedication of the temple, as recorded in 2 Chron. vi. 42.

2. *Who swore to Jehovah, vowed to the Mighty One of Jacob.* This last expression is borrowed, both here and in Isai. i. 24, from Jacob himself. See Gen. xlix. 24.

3. *If I go into the tent* (which is) *my house, if I go up on the bed* (which is) *my couch.* The elliptical form of swearing here used is equivalent to saying, *I will not go.* See above, on Ps. cxxxi. 2. *The tent my house, the couch my bed*, are mere poetical expressions for the house where I dwell, the couch where I lie. Instead of being in apposition, however, they may be in regimen, *the tent of my house, the couch of my bed*, i. e. the dwelling place of my house, the resting place of my bed.

4. *If I give sleep to my eyes, to my eyelids slumber.* This is a part of the sentence begun in v. 3 and completed in v. 5. The promise is, of course, not to be absolutely understood, but as meaning, that he would not sleep at ease, or abandon himself to undisturbed repose, till the condition was complied with.

5. *Until I find a place for Jehovah, dwellings for the Mighty One of Jacob.* The implication in the first clause, that Jehovah was without a place on earth, may remind us of Christ's memorable saying, Matt. viii. 20. Luke ix. 58. The word translated *dwellings* is peculiarly expressive, because, although strictly a generic term, it is specially applied in usage to the sanctuary with its enclosures and appendages. See above, on Ps. lxxxiv. 2 (1.)

6. *Lo, we heard it in Ephrathah; we found it in the fields of the wood.* These are most probably the words of David and his contemporaries, with respect to the recovery of the ark. *We*

heard it, or heard of it, i. e. of the ark, i nplying that they did not see it, that it was out of public view. *In Ephrathah* has been variously explained. Some suppose it to mean Ephraim, as *Ephrathi* means an Ephraimite, and apply the words to Shiloh, where the ark was long deposited. But *Ephrathah* itself is never so used elsewhere, and the ark, while at Shiloh, was as much in public view as at Jerusalem. Others, because *Bethlehem Ephrathah* and *Bethlehem Judah* are convertible expressions (1 Sam. xvii. 12. Mic. v. 1), make Ephrathah another name for Judah, which it never is, however, when it stands by itself. The only explanation, equally agreeable to usage and the context, is that which makes Ephrathah the ancient name of Bethlehem (Gen. xlviii. 7), here mentioned as the place where David spent his youth, and where he used to hear of the ark, although he never saw it till long afterwards, when he found it in the fields of the wood, or in the neighbourhood of *Kirjath-jearim*, which name means Forest-town or City of the Woods. Compare 1 Sam. vii. 1 with 2 Sam. vi. 3, 4.

7. *Let us come to his dwellings; let us bow down to his footstool.* Another step is here taken in reviewing the history of the sanctuary and of David's zeal for it. These are such words as might have been spoken at the public and solemn introduction of the ark into Jerusalem. As if it had been said: the ark of God has long been lost or out of sight, but now that a dwelling is provided for it on Mount Zion, let us come etc. Without any material change of sense, the future form may be retained, and the paragogic augment understood to express a strong determination. Now that the ark is established on Mount Zion, we will come etc. With respect to the representation of the ark as the footstool of Jehovah, and the act of bowing down to it, see above, on Ps xcix. 5.

8. *Arise, Jehovah, to thy resting-place, thou and the ark of thy*

strength. Here again the form of expression is borrowed from the words of Solomon at the dedication of the temple, as recorded in 2 Chr. vi. 41. This shows that the Psalmist regarded Solomon as merely carrying out his father's plan, or acting as the executor of his will, which is in fact the mutual relation of these personages as they appear in sacred history. A more remote allusion may be traced to Num. x. 35. See above, on Ps. lxviii. 2 (1.) The word translated *resting-place* has here its proper meaning as a local noun. The last clause shows the true import of the ark in the Mosaic system, as a pledge and token of Jehovah's presence, so that its solemn entrance into Zion was the entrance of the Lord himself, and to bow down to it was to worship him. *The ark of thy strength* is by some, in accordance with a common Hebrew idiom, resolved into *thy ark of strength*, and that into *thy strong* (or *mighty*) *ark.* It is simpler, however, and in this case yields a better meaning, to retain the original expression in its obvious sense, the ark which assures us of the presence and exertion of thy power for our protection.

9. *Let thy priests be clothed with righteousness, and let thy saints shout (or sing.)* This is the conclusion of the sentence quoted from 2 Chr. vi. 41. Instead of *righteousness* we there read *salvation*, which has led some to explain the two words as synonymous, while others understand by *righteousness* the practical justification which salvation carries with it. Another possible construction is to take the righteousness as that of God, which is displayed in the salvation of his people, and in which his priests, who officially declared it, might be said to clothe themselves. See the same figure in Job xxix. 14. *Saints*, gracious ones, or true believers. The parallel passage has, *rejoice in good* or *goodness.*

10. *For the sake of David thy servant, turn not away the face of thine Anointed.* The most obvious construction of this verse is that which makes it intercede, on the ground of the divine par-

tiality to David, for another person, supposed by some to be one or more of his successors in the kingly office, by others Israel at large. A comparison, however, of the place from which the words are borrowed (2 Chron. vi. 42) and of v. 17 below, makes it highly probable that both clauses relate to David himself. This may be rendered clearer and more natural by making the first clause an elliptical petition, entirely distinct from the second. *For the sake of David thy servant* (grant these requests which are really his); *turn not away* (his face which is) *the face of thine Anointed.* The frequency with which God is urged to hear and answer prayer *for David's sake* (1 Kings xi. 12, 13. xv. 4. 2 Kings viii. 19, etc.) is not to be explained by making *David* mean the promise to David, nor from the personal favour of which he was the object, but from his historical position, as the great theocratical model, in whom it pleased God that the old economy should reach its culminating point, and who is always held up as the type and representative of the Messiah, so that all the intervening kings are mere connecting links, and their reigns mere repetitions and continuations of the reign of David, with more or less resemblance as they happened to be good or bad. Hence the frequency with which his name appears in the later Scriptures, compared with even the best of his successors, and the otherwise inexplicable transfer of that name to the Messiah himself. It is in this unique character and office, as the Servant of the Lord, that David is here mentioned, first by his own name, and then as the Anointed King of Israel, whose face Jehovah is entreated not to turn away, a figure for refusing him an audience, or at least denying his petition, which we know to have been used in David's times. See the Hebrew of 1 Kings ii. 16, 17, 20.

11. *Sworn hath Jehovah to David* (in) *truth, he will not turn back from it: Of the fruit of thy body I will place on the throne for thee.* See above, on Ps. lxxxix. 4, 36 (3, 35), and compare 2 Sam. vii. 28. *Turn back*, recede from his engagement, or fail

to perform it. *Of the fruit*, from among thy posterity or offspring. *On the throne*, literally *to* or *for* it. See above, on Ps. ix. 5 (4.) *For thee*, in thy place, as thy representatives, or (*belonging*) *to thee*, i. e. thy throne.

12. *If thy sons will observe my covenant and my testimonies which I teach them*, (then) *likewise their sons unto perpetuity shall sit upon the throne for thee.* This is the condition of the promise, the breach of which accounts for the apparent violation of the promise itself. Such a suspension of the promise was not only just in itself, but foreseen and provided for (2 Sam. vii. 14, 15), as something perfectly consistent with the perpetuity of the engagement. *I teach you* refers not only to external legislation, but to spiritual guidance and illumination.

13. *For Jehovah has chosen Zion, has desired (it) for a dwelling for him.* Besides the oath and promise made directly to David, the petition of the psalm is here enforced by the divine choice of Zion, which was inseparably connected with the exaltation of the family of David. See the same thing asserted or implied, Ps. xliii. 2 (1.) lxv. 2 (1.) cxxv. 2. As in vs. 11, 12, the last words in Hebrew (לוֹ) may be also rendered *to him*, belonging to him, *his dwelling*.

14. *This is my resting-place to perpetuity; here will I dwell, because I have desired it.* These are the words of God, though not expressly so described. See above, on Ps. lxxxvii. 4. lxxxix. 4, 5 (3, 4.) The word translated *dwell* means originally to *sit*, and especially to sit enthroned, so that this idea would be necessarily suggested with the other to a Hebrew reader. See above, on Ps. xxix. 10. lv. 20 (19.) cii. 13 (12.) cxxiii. 1.

15. *Her provision I will bless, I will bless; her poor I will satisfy* (with) *bread.* The repetition of the verb may express

either certainty or fulness. *I will surely bless*, or *I will bless abundantly*. See above, on Ps. cxxvi. 6. The word translated *provision* is a cognate form to that in Ps. lxxviii. 25. *Satisfy*, amply or abundantly supply.

16. *And her priests I will clothe with salvation ; and her saints shall shout, shall shout* (for joy.) This is the promise corresponding to the prayer in v. 9. The word *salvation*, for which *righteousness* was substituted there, is here restored from the original passage, 2 Chron. vi. 41. The last verb in Hebrew means to express joy by shouting or singing. As to the emphatic repetition, see above, on v. 15.

17. *There will I make to bud a horn for David ; I have trimmed a lamp for mine Anointed.* These are common figures in the Scripture for strength and prosperity. See above, on Ps. xviii (10), 29 (28.) lxxxix. 18 (17.) xcii. 11, and compare 1 Sam. ii. 1. 2 Sam. xxi. 17. Ezek. xxix. 21. The last clause contains an allusion to the Law, which cannot be preserved in any version. The word translated *lamp* is used to designate the several burners of the golden candlestick (Ex. xxv. 37. xxxv. 14. xxxvii. 23. xxxix. 37), and the verb here joined with it is the one applied to the ordering or tending of the sacred lights by the priests (Ex. xxvii. 21. Lev. xxiv. 3.) The meaning of the whole verse is, that the promises of old made to David and to Zion should be yet fulfilled, however dark and inauspicious present appearances.

18. *His enemies I will clothe with shame, and on him shall bloom his crown.* The pronouns refer to David, as the Lord's Anointed, mentioned in v. 17. The figure in the first clause is the converse or counterpart of that in vs. 9, 16, and the same with that in Ps. xxxv. 26. cix. 29. With the last clause compare Ps. lxxxix. 40 (39.) The verb to *bloom* or *blossom* agrees well with the idea of a wreath or chaplet Compare the ἀμαράντινον στέφανον of

1 Pet. v. 4. Some prefer, however, to retain what they regard as the original meaning of the Hebrew verb; *on him shall his crown shine* (or glitter.) See above, on Ps. lxxii. 16.

PSALM CXXXIII.

1. *A Song of Ascents. By David. Behold, how good and how pleasant (is) the dwelling of brethren also together.* This psalm is an effusion of holy joy occasioned by the sight of the gathering of Israel as one great household at the yearly feasts. It is distinguished from the later compositions of this series by the absence of complaint or lamentation, while its freshness and vivacity and antique phraseology confirm the title which ascribes it to David. The idiomatic use of (גַּם) *also* in the last clause is not easily transferred to any other language. The meaning may be, that although the children of Israel were *brethren* even when divided and dispersed, it was only in these great convocations that besides being thus related to each other, they *also* actually dwelt together. There might likewise be allusion, in the first instance, to the previous jealousies and alienations in the family of Israel, which seemed to be exchanged for mutual concord and affection, on David's accession to the throne of the whole nation.

2. *Like the oil, the good (oil), on the head, running down upon the beard, the beard of Aaron, which runs down to the edge of his robes.* The joyous character of this great family meeting suggests the "oil of joy" (Isai. lxi. 3), the standing symbol of festivity, to which a more specific and religious character is then imparted by a beautiful transition to the *good oil* (i. e. sweet and costly), with

which Aaron was anointed (Ex. xxix. 7. xxx. 22. xl. 13), as a sign of consecration and of spiritual influences. See above, on Ps. ii. 2. As we read of the anointing of no subsequent High Priest, except prospectively (Lev. xxi. 10. Num. xxxv. 25), the reference here may be confined to Aaron himself. This is alleged to have differed from the unction of the other priests, by adding to the simple application of the oil to certain parts of the body, a copious affusion on the head, extending to the beard and even to the sacerdotal vestments. Some interpreters apply the last clause to the beard itself as reaching down to the mouth (פִּי) or opening at the neck of the official tunic. But the repetition of the verb (יֹרֵד), and the strong improbability that so much stress would have been laid upon the length of the beard, to which nothing is compared and which illustrates nothing, seem decisive in favour of the other explanation.

3. *Like the dew of Hermon, which comes down upon the mountains of Zion; for there has Jehovah commanded the blessing, even life for evermore.* The comparison with oil is now exchanged for one with dew, suggesting the idea of a refreshing, fertilizing influence. As the general comparison with *oil* is rendered more specific by the mention of the kind most highly valued, because made under the divine direction and applied to a most sacred use, so the general term *dew* is specified in like manner as the dew of Hermon, the dew falling on the lofty heights of Antilibanus. See above, on Ps. lxxxix. 13 (12.) How this dew could be said to fall upon the mountains of Zion, is a question which has much divided and perplexed interpreters. Some have assumed a peculiar theory or system of physics on the writer's part. Others suppose *dew of Hermon* to be merely descriptive of the quality, irrespective of the actual place of the deposit. Simpler and more natural than either of these, although not without difficulties of its own, is the interpretation which restricts the comparison itself to the first few words, and includes all that follows in the application. *Like the*

dew of Hermon (is the influence) *which descends upon the hills of Zion, for there, etc.* the last clause then explaining what this influence was. Whether this be the true solution of the question as to form or not, it is no doubt the essential meaning of the passage, upon any exegetical hypothesis whatever. The dew of Hermon was mere moisture, but the dew of Zion was the promise of eternal life, there made and verified. *Even life for evermore*, literally, *life even to eternity*

PSALM CXXXIV.

1. *A Song of Ascents. Behold! bless Jehovah, all ye servants of Jehovah, those standing in the house of Jehovah by night.* The whole series of pilgrimage songs closes, in the most appropriate manner, with a summons to bless the Lord, addressed by the people on arriving at the sanctuary to the priests there in attendance, vs. 1, 2, and indirectly answered by a priestly blessing on the worshippers themselves, v. 3. The *lo* or *behold* at the beginning is equivalent to saying, *See, we are here*, or *we are come.* To bless God, as in all other cases, is to praise him in a reverential and adoring manner. The *servants of the Lord* here meant are not his people indiscriminately, but his official servants, and most probably the priests, as will appear from v. 3 below. *The (ones) standing*, the appropriate posture of attendants, even in the courts of earthly monarchs. *By night*, literally, *in the nights*, which does not however necessarily mean *all night* (1 Chron. ix. 33), as appears from Ps. xcii. 3, where it stands opposed to *in the morning*, and may therefore denote simply *in the evening*, with

specific reference, as some suppose, to the *evening sacrifice*, with which the daily service of the priests concluded. We may then assume, although we cannot prove, that the pilgrims were accustomed to reach the sanctuary at that hour, singing this last "song of ascents."

2. *Raise your hands to the holy place, and bless Jehovah!* The gesture mentioned in the first clause symbolized the raising of the heart to God. See above, on Ps. xxviii. 2. lxiii. 5 (4.) The word for *holy place* or *sanctuary* is the same in form with that so frequently translated as an abstract, *holiness*. For its local meaning, see above, on Ps. xx. 3 (2.) It here denotes the temple or its site, as distinguished from the courts around it. As to the act of praying *to* or *towards* it, see above, on Ps. v. 8 (7.) xcix. 5.

3. *Jehovah bless thee out of Zion, Maker of heaven and earth.* As the priests were called upon to bless God in behalf of the people, so here they bless the people in behalf of God. Between the verses we may suppose the previous request to be complied with. The priests, having blessed God, turn and bless the people. The obvious allusion to the sacerdotal blessing, Num. vi. 23—27, favours the optative construction of this verse, which really includes a prediction (*the Lord will bless thee.*) *Out of Zion*, as in Ps. cxxviii. 5. *Maker of heaven and earth*, and therefore infinitely able to fulfil this prayer. See above, on Ps. cxv. 15. cxxi. 2. cxxiv. 8.

PSALM CXXXV.

The people of Jehovah are exhorted to praise him as their peculiar God, vs. 1—4, as the God of nature, vs. 5—7, as the deliverer of Israel from Egypt and in Canaan, vs. 8—12, as their hope also for the future, vs. 13—14, rendered more glorious by contrast with the impotence of idols, vs. 15—18, after which the psalm concludes as it began with an exhortation to praise God, vs. 19—21. According to Hengstenberg's arrangement and distribution, this is the first of a series of twelve psalms (135—146), sung at the completion of the second temple, and consisting of eight Davidic psalms (138—145), preceded by three (135—137) and followed by one (146) of later date. In this way he accounts for the omission of these ancient psalms in the former part of the collection, because they were no longer looked upon as independent compositions, but as inseparable parts of the series or systems into which they had been introduced.

1. *Hallelujah! Praise the name of Jehovah. Praise* (*it*), *ye servants of Jehovah!* The close of the Psalm shows that although the priests are included (v. 19) among the *servants of Jehovah*, they are not exclusively intended, as in Ps. cxxxiv. 1. Even there, however, the priests are representatives of Israel at large.

2. *Who* (*are*) *standing in the house of Jehovah, in the courts of the house of our God.* The participle indicates continued action. The mention of the courts confirms what has been already said, as to the objects of address in v. 1.

3. *Hallelujah* (praise ye Jah!) *for good (is) Jehovah. Make music to his name, for it is lovely.* The last words may also be translated, *he is lovely*, i. e. an object worthy of supreme attachment.

4. *For Jacob did Jah choose for himself, Israel for his own possession.* They are particularly bound to praise him, as his chosen and peculiar people. The last word in Hebrew means a possession of peculiar value, set apart and distinguished from all others. See Ex. xix. 5. Deut. vii. 6. xiv. 2. xxvi. 18.

5. *For I know that great is Jehovah, and our Lord (more) than all Gods.* However ignorant the world may be of his superiority, I, the representative of Israel and as such speaking in his name, know and am assured of the truth from my own observation and experience.

6. *All that Jehovah will he does in the heavens and in the earth, in the seas and all depths.* Compare Ps. cxv. 3. Ecc. viii. 3. Jon. i. 14. Isa. xlvi. 10, 11. It is not merely as their own peculiar God that they are bound to praise him, but as the universal sovereign. Heaven, earth, and sea, are put for the whole frame of nature, as in Ex. xx. 4.

7. *Causing vapours to ascend from the end of the earth—lightnings for the rain he makes—bringing out the wind from his treasures.* As certain portions of the world are specified in v. 6 to define the extent of his dominion, so here certain natural phenomena are mentioned as the product of his power. Compare Jer. x. 13. li. 16. *From the end of the earth*, i. e. from all parts of it, not excepting the most remote. See above, on Ps. lxi. 3 (2). The second clause is by some explained to mean, *turning lightnings into rain*, i. e. causing the thunder-cloud to dissolve in rain. But this is not so natural as the common version, *he maketh lightnings for the rain*, i. e. to accompany it, or according to the

paraphrase in the Prayer Book, *sendeth forth lightnings with the rain.* With the last clause compare Job xxxviii. 22.

8. *Who smote the first-born of Egypt, from man even to beast.* From the proofs of God's supremacy in nature, he now proceeds to those in history, and especially the history of his dealings with his people and their enemies. This is precisely the relation between Ps. civ and cv. The first example chosen here is the last and greatest of the plagues of Egypt. *From man to beast*, including both ; in other words, both man and beast.

9. *Sent signs and wonders into the midst of thee, oh Egypt, upon Pharaoh and on all his servants. Signs and wonders*, i. e. miracles, to wit, those which preceded and accompanied the exodus. See above, on Ps. lxxviii. 43. *In the midst of thee, oh Egypt*, an expression similar to that in Ps. cxvi. 19, *in the midst of thee, oh Jerusalem! Upon Pharaoh*, literally, in Pharaoh and in all his servants.

10. *Who smote many nations and slew mighty kings.* To the miracles of Egypt and the Exode are now added those of Canaan and the Conquest.

11. *Sihon king of the Amorites, and Og king of Bashan, and all the kingdoms of Canaan.* Each of these three particulars is preceded in Hebrew by the preposition (לְ) *to* or *for;* and that this is not an inadvertence or an accident, appears from its repetition in the next psalm (cxxxvi. 19, 20.) Though not in accordance with the usage of the verb (הָרַג) which is construed elsewhere with the verb directly, the particle must be regarded here as an objective sign, as in Ps. cxxix. 3, unless we suppose the sense to be, that what had just been said in general is true in particular *as to Sihon, as to Og*, and *as to the kingdoms* (here put for the kings) *of Canaan.*

12. *And gave their land (as) a heritage, a heritage to Israel his people.* The land of Canaan was an inheritance to Israel, not as the heirs of the Canaanites, but because it was to be transmitted from father to son, by hereditary right and succession. See above, on Ps. cv. 44. cxi. 6.

13. *Jehovah, thy name (is) to eternity. Jehovah, thy memory is to generation and generation. Name* and *memory* are here equivalent expressions, meaning that by which God is remembered or commemorated, namely, his perfections as exhibited in act. The perpetuity of this implies continued or repeated acts of goodness.

14. *For Jehovah will judge his people, and for the sake of his servants will repent.* He will fulfil the promise in Deut. xxxii. 36. *He will judge* (i. e. do justice to) his people. See above, on Ps. lxxii. 2. For the sense in which repentance is ascribed to God, see above, on Ps. xc. 13.

15. *The idols of the nations (are) silver and gold, works of the hands of man.* The divine perfection of the Lord is now exhibited in contrast with the impotence and nullity of idols. The terms of the comparison are borrowed, with several variations, from Ps. cxv. 4—8.

16. (There is) *a mouth to them, and* (yet) *they speak not;* (there are) *eyes to them, and* (yet) *they see not.* See above, on Ps. cxv. 5, which agrees exactly with the verse before us.

17. (There are) *ears to them, and* (yet) *they hear not; likewise there is no breath in their mouth.* See above, on Ps. cxv. 6. This verse contains the most considerable variation of the passages. The second clause in both begins with the same Hebrew word (אַף); but in the one case it is a noun, meaning the *nose*, in the other an adverb, meaning *likewise.* This kind of variation.

in which the form is retained but with a change of meaning, is perfectly agreeable to Hebrew usage.

18. *Like them shall be those making them, every one who (is) trusting in them.* See above, on Ps. cxv. 8, with which this verse agrees exactly. If the meaning had been simply, those who make them *are* like them, Hebrew usage would have required the verb to be suppressed. Its insertion, therefore, in the future form (יִהְיוּ) requires it to be rendered strictly *shall be*, i. e. in fate as well as character. Idolaters shall perish with their perishable idols. Compare Isai. i. 31.

19. *Oh house of Israel, bless Jehovah! Oh house of Aaron, bless Jehovah!* Having shown what God is, in himself and in comparison with idols, he repeats the exhortation which this description was intended to explain and justify. With this and the next verse compare Ps. cxv. 9—11. cxviii. 2—4. Instead of *trust* we have here *bless*, as at the beginning of the Psalm. Compare Ps. cxxxiv. 1.

20. *Oh house of Levi, bless Jehovah! Fearers of Jehovah, bless Jehovah!* The Levites are not particularly mentioned in the parallel passages.

21. *Blessed (be) Jehovah from Zion—inhabiting Jerusalem—Hallelujah!* There is here an allusion to Ps. cxxxiv. 3. As Jehovah blesses out of Zion, so also he is blessed out of Zion, by the diffusion of his praise, as from a radiating centre. This is said to be the only place in which Jerusalem is put for Zion, as the earthly residence of God. But see above, on Ps. lxxvi. 3 (2), and compare Ps. cxxv. 1, 2.

PSALM CXXXVI.

In theme and structure, this psalm resembles that before it, a resemblance rendered still more striking by particular coincidences of expression. In this case also, the people are invited to praise Jehovah, vs. 1—3, as the God of nature, vs. 4—9, as the deliverer of Israel from Egypt, vs. 10—15, his guide in the wilderness, v. 16, the conqueror of his enemies, vs. 17—24, the provider of all creatures, v. 25, and the God of heaven, to whom, in conclusion, praise is again declared to be due, v. 26. The grand peculiarity of form in this psalm, by which it is distinguished from all others, is the regular recurrence, at the close of every verse, of a burden or *refrain*, like the responses in the Litany, but carried through with still more perfect uniformity. The text or theme, which thus forms the second clause of every verse, is one which has repeatedly occurred already, in Ps. cvi. 1. cvii. 1. cxviii. 1—4,29. Compare 1 Chron. xvii. 34. It has been a favourite idea with interpreters that such repetitions necessarily imply alternate or responsive choirs. But the other indications of this usage in the Psalter are extremely doubtful, and every exegetical condition may be satisfied by simply supposing that the singers, in some cases, answered their own questions, and that in others, as in that before us, the people united in the burden or chorus, as they were wont to do in the Amen. See above, on Ps. cvi. 48.

1. *Give thanks unto Jehovah—for unto eternity (is) his mercy.* This introductory sentence is identical with those already cited from Ps. cvi, cvii, cxviii.

2. *Give thanks unto the God of Gods—for unto eternity (is) his mercy.* The divine title or description, both in this verse and the next, is borrowed from Deut. x. 17. *Gods* does not here mean false gods, but is a superlative plural qualifying that before it. See above, on Ps. lxxvii. 14 (13.) cxxxv. 5.

3. *Give thanks unto the Lord of Lords—for unto eternity (is) his mercy.* The *Lord of Lords*, i. e. the supreme Lord, the Lord by way of excellence, as in the English phrase *heart of hearts* for inmost heart.

4. *To (him) doing wondrous (things), great (things), alone—for unto eternity (is) his mercy.* Compare the expression *doing wonders*, Ex. xv. 11. *Alone*, not merely more than others, but to their exclusion. The *for*, in this and the following verses, has reference, not to what immediately precedes, but to the verb *give thanks*, to be supplied at the beginning of the sentence.

5. *To him that made the heavens in wisdom—for unto eternity (is) his mercy.* *That made*, literally *making*, perhaps in reference to the continued exercise of God's creative power. *In wisdom*, or with *understanding*. See above, on Ps. civ. 24, and compare Prov. iii. 19.

6. *To him that spread the earth above the waters—for unto eternity (is) his mercy.* *That spread*, literally *spreading*, as in v. 5. *Above* (not upon, but higher than) *the waters.* See above, on Ps. xxiv. 2.

7 *To him that made great lights—for unto eternity (is) his mercy.* The plural *lights* (אוֹרִים) occurs only here, but is cognate and synonymous with the one used in Gen. i. 14, 16.

8. *The sun to rule by day—for unto eternity (is) his mercy.*

The musical design of the composition is especially observable where the burden or chorus is interposed between inseparable parts of the same sentence, as in this one, the substance of which is borrowed from Gen. i. 16, but with some change both in the words and the construction.

9. *The moon and stars to rule by night—for unto eternity* (*is*) *his mercy.* *To rule*, literally, *for rules* or *dominions*, perhaps because the stars are here made sharers with the moon in the dominion of the night.

10. *To him that smote Egypt in their first born—for unto eternity* (*is*) *his mercy.* We have here the transition from nature to history, as in Ps. cxxxv. 8. *Him that smote* (or *the smiter of*) *Egypt*, i. e. the Egyptians. Hence the plural pronoun, *their first born.*

11. *And brought out Israel from the midst of them—for unto eternity (is) his mercy.* Here for the first time we have a finite tense (the future conversive), interrupting the long series of participles, all agreeing with *Jehovah* understood.

12. *With a high hand and with an arm outstretched—for unto eternity is his mercy.* These are favourite Mosaic figures for the active and energetic exercise of power. See Ex. iii. 19. vi. 1, 6 xiii. 9. xv 12. Deut. iv. 34. v. 15. vii. 19. xi. 2. xxvi. 8.

13. *To him that parted the Red Sea into parts—for unto eternity* (*is*) *his mercy.* *Parted* and *parts* have the same relation to each other as the Hebrew verb and noun.

14. *And made Israel to pass through the midst of it—for unto eternity* (*is*) *his mercy.* Here again we have a finite tense, not the conversive future, as in v. 11, but the preterite. *Through*

the midst of it, between the parts into which it was divided. Some suppose an allusion to the covenant transaction in Gen. xv. 17, where the word translated *parts* is the one used in v. 13 above.

15. *And cast Pharaoh and his host into the Red Sea—for unto eternity (is) his mercy.* The first verb strictly means *knocked off* or *shook off*, and is borrowed from Ex. xiv. 27. A passive form of it occurs above, Ps. cix. 23.

16. *To him that led his people in the wilderness—for unto eternity (is) his mercy.* Led, literally, caused to go. See above, Ps. cxxv. 5. The participial construction is again resumed.

17. *To him that smote great kings—for unto eternity (is) his mercy.* Compare the parallel passage, Ps. cxxxv. 10, which is here divided by the theme or chorus. See above, on v. 8.

18. *And slew mighty kings—for unto eternity (is) his mercy.* The first clause answers to the latter half of Ps. cxxxv. 10, with the substitution of another Hebrew word for *mighty*.

19. *Sihon king of the Amorite—for unto eternity (is) his mercy.* Literally, *to*, *for*, or *as to* Sihon, etc. See above, on Ps. cxxxv. 11.

20. *And Og king of Bashan—for unto eternity (is) his mercy.* To, for, or as to, Og king of Bashan.

21. *And gave their land as a heritage—for unto eternity (is) his mercy.* As a heritage, literally, for it. See above, on Ps. cxxxv. 12.

22. *A heritage to Israel his servant—for unto eternity (is) his mercy.* This is the latter half of Ps. cxxxv. 12, divided from the first half by the theme or chorus.

23. *Who in our low estate remembered us—for unto eternity (is) his mercy.* In our low estate, in our humiliation, in our being humbled or reduced. Remembered us, or for us, for our benefit, as in Ps. cxxxii. 1. From the analogy of Ps. cvii. 16, 18, 26. cxv. 12, we learn that this relates to the captivity in Babylon, which is also the subject of the next psalm.

24. *And snatched us from our adversaries—for unto eternity (is) his mercy.* The first verb always denotes violent action. See above, on Ps. vii. 3 (2.) It here means to snatch or tear away, as in Lam. v. 8, and has reference to the great catastrophe by which the Babylonian power was broken and the Jews set free.

25. *Giving bread to all flesh—for unto eternity (is) his mercy.* Here the description passes suddenly from God's acts of mercy towards his people to his general beneficence towards all that lives, perhaps with a design to intimate that he who thus cares for men in general and even for the lower animals, will not and cannot let his people perish. See Matth. vi. 30.

26. *Give thanks unto the God of heaven, for unto eternity (is) his mercy.* The God of heaven is a new description as to form, but substantially equivalent to that in Ps. vii. 8 (7.) xi. 4. xiv. 2. xxxiii. 13, 14.

PSALM CXXXVII.

This is the most direct and striking reminiscence of the Babylonish Exile in the whole collection, and could scarcely have been written but by one who had partaken of its trials. The first part of the psalm recalls the treatment of the Jews in Babylonia, vs, 1—6 ; the second anticipates the punishment of Edom and of Babylon, as persecuting enemies of Israel, vs. 7—9.

1. *By the rivers of Babylon, there we sat down, yea we wept, when we remembered Zion.* The first word sometimes means *along*, and especially along the course of streams, as in Ps. xxiii. 2. *Babel* or *Babylon* is here put for the whole country which we call Babylonia. Its rivers are the Tigris, the Euphrates, the Chaboras, and the Ulai, with their tributary branches. Various explanations have been given of the exiles being represented as sitting by the rivers ; but none of them are so satisfactory as the obvious and simple supposition, that the rivers are mentioned as a characteristic feature of the country, just as we might speak of the mountains of Switzerland or the plains of Tartary, meaning Switzerland or Tartary itself *There* is emphatic ; there, even in that distant heathen country. *Sat* or *sat down*, if significant at all, may mean that they sat upon the ground as mourners. *Yea*, literally *also* ; we not only sat but *also wept*. *When we remembered*, literally, in our remembering, i. e. at the time, and as the effect, of our so doing. *Zion*, not merely as the mother-country or its capital, but as the seat of the theocracy and earthly centre of the true religion.

2. *On willows in the midst of it we hung our harps.* It has been objected that the willow is unknown in the region once called Babylonia, which is said to produce nothing but the palm-tree. Some avoid this difficulty by explaining the whole verse as metaphorical, hanging up the harps being a figure for renouncing music, and willows being suggested by the mention of streams, perhaps with some allusion to associations connected with this particular tree. It may also be observed that extraordinary changes have taken place in the vegetable products, and especially the trees, of certain countries. Thus the palm-tree, so frequently referred to

in the scriptures, and so common once that cities were called after it, is now almost unknown in Palestine.

3. *For there our captors asked of us the words of a song, and our spoilers mirth,* (saying) *Sing to us from a song of Zion. Words of a song* may either be an idiomatic pleonasm meaning simply song itself, or denote, as in English, the words sung as distinguished from the music. *Our spoilers* is by some taken in a passive sense, our spoiled or plundered ones; but the usual explanation is favoured by tradition and analogy. *One of the songs* can hardly be the meaning of the Hebrew phrase, in which the noun is singular. The literal translation above given yields a perfectly good sense. *A song of Zion* is a psalm, a religious lyric, such as many of the heathen knew to be employed in the temple worship at Jerusalem. Many interpreters suppose the object of this request to be contempt or ridicule; but the words themselves necessarily suggest nothing more than curiosity.

4. *How shall we sing the song of Jehovah on a foreign soil?* These are the words with which the invitation was or might have been rejected at the time. The question implies a moral impossibility. The idea is not, that the psalms themselves would be profaned by being sung there, but that the expression of religious joy would be misplaced and incongruous, implying an oblivion of the sanctuary and its forfeited advantages. *A foreign soil,* a ground or land of strangeness. See above, on Ps. xviii. 45, 46 (44, 45.)

5. *If I forget thee, oh Jerusalem, let my right hand forget (its skill.)* This is a disavowal of the forgetfulness which would have been implied in yielding to the wishes of their captors. *Jerusalem* is here used precisely as *Zion* is in vs. 1, 3. The object of the verb in the last clause is supposed by some to be *me;* let my right hand forget me, i. e. let me be forgotten by myself. But most

interpreters concur in the correctness of the common version, in which *cunning* has its old English sense of *skill*. The only question then is, whether this is to be understood indefinitely of all that the right hand can do, and is wont to do, for the convenience of the person, or whether it is to be understood specifically of its use in playing on an instrument. The former is the more comprehensive meaning, but the latter is more pointed and better suited to this context. The sense will then be: if I so far forget thee as to strike the harp while in this condition, let my right hand lose the power so to do.

6. *Let my tongue cleave to my palate if I do not remember thee, if I do not raise Jerusalem above the head of my rejoicing.* What he had first wished as to his power of instrumental performance, he now wishes with respect to his vocal organs. If I forget thee, let my hand forever cease to strike the harp, and my tongue to utter sound! The most natural meaning of the last clause is the one paraphrastically given in the English version, *if I prefer not Jerusalem above my chief joy.*

7. *Remember, oh Jehovah, against the sons of Edom, the day of Jerusalem,* (against) *those saying, Make bare, make bare, to the very foundation in it.* Most interpreters regard this as a kind of comment by the Psalmist on the preceding recollection of the Captivity. But the transition then seems too abrupt and unaccountable. The best explanation is, that these are still the real or supposed words of the captives, in reply to the request of their oppressors, far from granting which they break forth in a prayer for the destruction of those who had destroyed Jerusalem. As if they had said: No, instead of singing psalms to gratify your idle or malignant curiosity, we will rather pray God to avenge the insults offered to his holy city. This interpretation is moreover recommended by its rendering the strong terms that follow more natural than if uttered in cold blood and in calm

deliberation at a later period. *Remember against*, literally *for* or *with respect to*. See above, on Ps. cxxxii. 1. cxxxvi. 23, where the same idiomatic phrase is used in a favourable sense. The *day of Jerusalem* is the day of its calamity or great catastrophe. Compare Obad. 11—13, where the same crime is charged upon Edom, namely that of concurring and rejoicing in the downfal of his kinsman Israel. See also Jer. xlix. 7—22. Lam. iv. 21, 22. Ezek. xxv. 12—14.

8. *Daughter of Babylon, the desolated! Happy (he) who shall repay to thee thy treatment wherewith thou hast treated us.* The daughter of Babylon (or virgin Babylon) is the people or kingdom of Babylonia, personified as a woman. See above, on Ps. ix. 14 (13.) *The wasted* or *desolated* is the epithet belonging to her by way of eminence in prophecy and history. There is no need therefore of distinguishing between a partial and total desolation, or between that of the city and the kingdom at large. The last clause may mean nothing more than that such a revolution is at hand that he will be esteemed a fortunate man who treats thee as thou hast treated us. For the true sense of the last verb, see above, on Ps. xiii. 6 (5, 6.)

9. *Happy he (who) shall seize and dash thy little ones against the stones.* This revolting act was not uncommon in ancient warfare. See 2 Kings viii. 12. Hos. xiv. 1. Nah. iii. 10. Isai. xiii. 16, 18. The more revolting, the stronger the description of the change awaiting Babylon. The day is coming when he shall be deemed fortunate who, according to the usages of war, requites thy own sanguinary cruelties. The word translated *dash* means really to dash in pieces, as in Ps. ii. 9. The act here meant is commonly expressed by (רטש) a different Hebrew verb. *Taketh and dasheth* is equivocal, the first of these verbs being used in familiar English as a kind of auxiliary, whereas the corresponding verb in Hebrew denotes a distinct and independent act.

PSALM CXXXVIII.

This is the first of a series of eight psalms (cxxxviii—cxlv), probably the last composed by David, a kind of commentary on the great Messianic promise in 2 Sam. vii. They are found in this part of the Psalter, in consequence of having been made the basis, or rather the body, of a system or series (cxxxv—cxlvi) by a later writer. See above, on Ps. cxxxv. 1. The psalm before us contains an acknowledgment of God's goodness as experienced already, vs. 1—3, an anticipation of his universal recognition by the nations, vs. 4, 5, and in the mean time of additional favours to the Psalmist, or to the church of which he was the temporary head, vs. 6—8. Such a psalm was of course well suited to sustain the faith and revive the hopes of a later generation.

1. *By David. I will thank thee with all my heart; before gods I will praise thee.* The Davidic style and tone of composition are acknowledged even by the skeptical interpreters. *With all my heart* implies the greatness of the gift to be acknowledged, which was no doubt the promise of Messiah contained in 2 Sam. vii. See above, on Ps. ix. 2 (1.) *Before gods*, i. e. in the presence, to the face, and in contempt of all imaginary rival deities. The translation *before God* is grammatical, but confounds the second and third person in a single clause. The Septuagint and Vulgate have *before angels*, which is inconsistent with the usage of the Hebrew word. *Thank thee*, in the strict sense of praising

for benefits received; or in a wider sense, *acknowledge thee* as God. *Praise thee*, make music, sing and play to thee. With this verse compare Ps. vii. 18 (17.) xviii. 50 (49.) liv. 8 (7.) lvii. 10 (9.) ci. 1.

2. *I will bow down to thy holy temple, and will thank thy name, for thy mercy and for thy truth ; for thou hast made great, above all thy name, thy promise.* With the first clause compare Ps. v. 8 (7.) *Bow down*, or prostrate myself, as an act of worship. *Mercy* in promising, *truth* in performing. See above, on Ps. xxv. 10. *Above all thy name*, i. e. all the previous manifestations of thy nature. *Thy word*, literally, *thy saying*, that which thou hast said, but applied specifically to the divine promise. See above, on Ps. xviii. 31 (30.) cxix. 38, 50, 103, 140. The transcendant promise here referred to is that of the Messiah in 2 Sam. vii. which is there described as unique by David himself, and which forms the basis of many psalms, but especially of Ps. xviii, xxi, lxi, ci, cii, ciii, and the one before us.

3. *In the day I called and thou didst answer me, thou makest me brave in my soul (with) strength.* This may be connected with what goes before, thou didst magnify thy word in the day when I called etc. The promise in 2 Sam. vii was an answer to his prayer for a perpetual succession. See above, on Ps. xxi. 3, 5 (2, 4.) lxi. 6 (5.) The common version of the last clause *(strengthenedst me with strength in my soul)* contains a paronomasia not in the original, where the verb and noun have not even a letter in common. The verb is by some translated *made me proud*, i. e. elated me, not with a vain or selfish pride, but with a lofty and exhilarating hope. *In my soul*, as opposed to a mere outward influence. *Strength*, i. e. strength of faith and confidence in God.

4. *Jehovah, all kings of the earth shall acknowledge thee, when*

they have heard the sayings of thy mouth. Not merely one king, though that king be David, shall acknowledge, thank, and praise thee, but all others who receive the true religion, when they know what thou hast promised, and especially when they compare the promise and fulfilment, with particular reference to the promise of Messiah, which is described in Scripture as a grand means for the conversion of the nations and the chiefs which represent them. See above, on Ps. lxviii. 30, 32 (29, 31.) cii. 16 (15.)

5. *And they shall sing in the ways of Jehovah, for great* (shall be) *the glory of Jehovah.* The kings of the earth, representing its nations, shall join in the praise of the true God, walking in his ways, i. e. as converts to the true religion. Compare Mic. iv. 2. Isai. iv. 3. Instead of *for* we may read *when*, as in v. 4; when the glory of Jehovah has been duly exalted and diffused by the extension of the true religion. Some make this clause the theme or subject of the praise—they shall sing that the glory of Jehovah is great—a less natural construction, but one which yields an equally good sense.

6. *For lofty is Jehovah—and the low he sees—and the haughty from afar he knows.* The first two clauses may be in antithesis, *and yet he looks upon the low*, or simply co-ordinate, *and therefore he looks upon the low*, i. e. the lowly, who shall be exalted, while the opposite end of the proud is implied in the concluding declaration. Even from afar, from the distant heaven where he seems to behold nothing, he knows precisely what the proud man is, what he deserves, and what is actually to befall him. See above, on Ps. i. 1.

7. *If I go through the midst of distress, thou wilt save* (or *make*) *me alive; upon the wrath of my enemies thou wilt stretch forth thy hand, and save me (with) thy right hand.* The first clause resembles that of Ps. xxiii. 4. *Go through* or *walk in the midst of*

trouble. To *quicken* or *revive*, as in Ps. xxx. 4 (3.) lxxi. 20. *Upon the wrath*, implying motion from above, which is more significant and graphic than *against*. The common version of the last words *(and thy right hand shall save me)* is equally grammatical and found in all the ancient versions ; but the other is recommended by its ascribing the deliverance directly to God, and by the analogy of Ps. lx. 7 (5), where *hand* is adverbially construed with the same verb. See also Ps. xvii. 14.

8. *Jehovah will complete for me* (what he has begun) *Jehovah, thy mercy (is) forever ; the works of thy hands do not forsake.* The work begun and yet to be completed was the whole series of God's gracious dispensations towards David and his seed, beginning with the first choice of the former and ending in the Messiah. With the first clause compare Ps. lvii. 3 (2.) Phil. i. 6. The second member of the sentence might be read, *let thy mercy be forever* or *unto eternity*. But it is more probably an affirmation, similar to that in Ps. ciii. 17, and the clause contains an appeal to the promise of eternal favour, 2 Sam. vii. 13, 26, or perhaps to the eternity of God's compassions, as a reason why he should not and could not abandon what had been so graciously begun.

PSALM CXXXIX.

THE Psalmist describes God's omnipresence and omniscience, vs. 1—12, as attributes necessarily belonging to him as the Creator, vs. 13—18, and appeals to them in attestation of his own aversion to the wicked, vs. 19—24. From its collocation it is probable that this psalm records David's exercises under the powerful impressions of the great Messianic promises in 2 Sam. vii, and is therefore to be regarded as a confession and profession made not merely for himself but for his successors on the throne of Israel, and intended both to warn them and console them by this grand view of Jehovah's constant and infallible inspection.

1. *To the Chief Musician. By David. A Psalm. Jehovah, thou hast searched me and knowest.* As a later writer could have no motive for prefixing the title *to the Chief Musician*, it affords an incidental proof of antiquity and genuineness. *Thou hast searched me* or continually *searchest me.* The Hebrew verb originally means to *dig* and is applied to the search for precious metals (Job xxviii. 3), but metaphorically to a moral inquisition into guilt. See above, on Ps. xliv. 22 (21), and compare Job xiii. 9. It is here used in the intermediate sense of full investigation. *Thou hast known* or *knowest* all that can result from such a scrutiny, not only my corruptions and infirmities but my cares and sorrows. The object is not expressed in this verse, which is a summary of the whole psalm, because the very object of what follows is to state it in detail.

2. *Thou knowest my sitting and my rising ; thou understandest as to my thought from afar.* Sitting and rising or standing represent rest and motion, or all the various conditions of the living, waking man. See above, on Ps. i. 1. xxvii. 2. In every posture, state, and occupation, thou knowest me. The next phrase does not merely signify, thou perceivest the meaning of my thought, but thou knowest all about it, its origin, its tendency, its moral quality; *thou understandest* (every thing) *respecting it. From afar*, unimpeded by local distance, by which men are prone to imagine the divine omniscience to be circumscribed. See Job xxii. 12—14, and compare with this verse Ps. cxxxviii. 6. Jer. xxiii. 23.

3. *My path and my lair thou siftest, and with all my ways art acquainted.* Path is here put for going, lair for lying, and these, like the terms of the preceding verse, for motion and rest, or the active and passive parts of human life. The poetical word *lair* is used to represent a Hebrew one, occurring only here, but the verbal root of which is used by Moses, Lev. xviii. 23. xx. 16. The last verb means to be accustomed (Num. xxii. 30), and then by a natural association, acquainted or familiar (Job xxii. 21.) *My ways*, my condition and my conduct, what I do and what I suffer.

4. *For there is not a word in my tongue*, (but) *lo*, *Jehovah, thou knowest all of it.* The relation of the clauses may be also expressed thus in English, *which, oh Lord, thou knowest not, all of it* (or *altogether.*) *In my tongue*, in its power, or, as it were, in its possession. This verse merely applies to his words specifically what was said before of all his actions. The *lo* or *behold* is equivalent to *see there*, or to the act of pointing at the words as objects of sight and as actually present.

5. *Behind and before thou dost beset me, and layest upon me thy hand.* There is here an insensible transition from God's omniscience to his omnipresence, out of which the Scriptures represent it as arising. *Behind and before*, i. e. on all sides. The idea of *above* and *below* is suggested by the last clause. *Beset*, besiege, hem in, or closely surround. *Thy hand*, or the palm of thy hand, as the Hebrew word strictly denotes.

6. *Such knowledge is too wonderful for me; it is exalted, I cannot* (attain) *to it.* The literal meaning of the Hebrew word is, *wonderful knowledge away from me*, or *more than I* (can comprehend); *it is exalted, I cannot* (do any thing) *as to it.* With the word *wonderful* compare the use of the cognate verb, Deut. xxx. 11. Prov. xxx. 18. The knowledge meant is man's finite knowledge of the infinite.

7. *Whither shall I go from thy Spirit, and whither from thy face shall I flee?* The interrogation involves a denial of all possible escape from God's inspection, when a guilty conscience prompts to seek one. Compare Am. ix. 2.

8. *If I scale the heavens, there* (art) *thou; and if I spread the grave, lo thou* (art there.) The word *scale* is used to represent a Hebrew verb occurring only here, and no doubt belonging to the dialect of poetry. The verb translated *spread* means specifically to spread a couch or make a bed. *If I make sheol my bed*, i. e. lie down in the grave or hell, in the wide old English sense. See above, on Ps. vi. 6 (5.)

9. *I will raise the wings of day-break. I will dwell in the end of the sea.* By supplying *if*, although the sense is not materially changed, the form of expression becomes much less striking. The conditional construction is forbidden also, or at least rendered highly improbable, by the form of the second verb, expressing strong desire and resolution. The truth is that we have here a bold transition. After speaking of guilty flight from God himself, the Psalmist now speaks of anxious flight from other enemies, and as if visibly surrounded by them, here resolves to escape from them. This, which is Hengstenberg's interpretation, is strongly favoured by the unconditional construction, although he himself retains the other. The same writer objects to the translation *raise the wings*, that before one can raise wings he must have them. But for that very reason the possession of them may be presupposed, or considered as implied in the act expressed. The same combination is employed by Ezekiel (x. 16, 19), in a way that admits of only one translation. The Hebrew word (שַׁחַר) is not the common one for morning, but one denoting day-break or the dawn See above, on Ps. lvii. 9 (8.) The point of comparison appears to be the incalculable velocity of light. The *extremity* (or *end*) *of*

the sea is added to heaven and hell, in order to convey the idea of the most remote points.

10. *Even there thy hand guides me, and thy right hand holds me.* From the use of similar expressions to denote a friendly guidance and support, in Ps. xviii. 17 (16.) lv. 7—9 (6—8.) v. 9 (8.) xxiii. 3. xxvii. 11. lxxiii. 24, and other places, Hengstenberg infers that this must mean, when I fly to the ends of the earth before my enemies, thou art still there to protect me, and that the psalm was therefore meant not merely to alarm but to console.

11. *And I say, only darkness overwhelms me, night is the light become around me.* The ideal situation is the same as in v. 9, one of danger and terror, in which he is constrained to say, nothing but darkness comes upon me, smites me, and the very light is turned to darkness round about me. According to this view of the passage, darkness, as in many other places, is a figure for calamity and danger. See Isai. l. 10. Ps. cxxxviii. 7. According to the usual interpretation it denotes concealment from the eye of God.

12. *Even darkness does not make (it) dark to him, and night like day shines; as the darkness, so the light.* The interpretation given of the foregoing verse does not necessarily affect the sense of this, which still means that nothing can prevent God's seeing either sin or suffering, either the danger of his people or the malice of their enemies. *Make dark*, as in Ps. cv. 28. *To thee*, literally, *from thee*, i. e. so as to conceal from thee.

13. *For thou possessest my reins; thou coverest me in my mother's womb.* The meaning of the first clause seems to be: thou hast in thy power and at thy control the very seat of my strongest sensibilities, my pains and pleasures; and this subjection is coeval with my being, for even before birth I was under

thy protection and command, as I am now. The sense of *weaving*, which is given to the last verb by some modern writers rests on a mere etymological deduction and has no foundation either in tradition or in usage. The *for* at the beginning of this verse marks the transition from the fact of God's omniscience to its origin or reason in his creative character and rights. As a logical particle, the *for* relates, not to the immediately preceding verse, but to the whole preceding context. God is omnipresent and omniscient, *for* he is the maker of the universe.

14. *I thank thee because fearfully I am distinguished; wonderful (are) thy works, and (that) my soul knoweth right (well.)* He makes it a subject of grateful acknowledgment, that God has distinguished him or made him to differ from inferior creatures, both in constitution and in destiny. *Because* is in Hebrew a compound particle (עַל כִּי) like *for that, forasmuch as. Fearfully*, literally *fearful (things)*, but used adverbially, as in Ps. lxv. 6 *(5.)* It might here be rendered *(by) fearful (things.)* The words corresponding to *distinguished* and *wonderful* are in Hebrew passive forms from cognate roots *(*פלה and פלא*)*. The particular statement of the first clause is resolved by the last into the general one, of which it is a mere specification. The concluding words express a strong and, as it were, experimental conviction of the truth.

15. *Not hid was my frame from thee, when I was made in secret, embroidered in depths of the earth.* The *not hid* is a meiosis, implying that God saw it clearly and fully understood it, inasmuch as he himself created it. *Frame*, literally *strength*, as in Deut. viii. 17, but applied to the bones and sinews as the strength or frame-work of the body. See above, on Ps. vi. 3 (2), and compare Job x. 11. The common Hebrew word for *bone* differs only in the pointing. The word translated *when* is (אֲשֶׁר) the relative pronoun, and may here retain its proper meaning

although then not easily translated, as its antecedent is latent in the phrase *my frame*, which may be thus resolved, *the frame of me who was made*, etc. *In secret*, i. e. in the womb. *Embroidered*, which is the invariable meaning of the Hebrew verb, is a bold but beautiful expression for the complicated tissue of the human frame, in which so many and such various threads are curiously interwoven. *Depths of the earth* can only be explained as a comparative expression, corresponding to *in secret* and denoting the same thing, which it describes as no less dark and hidden from the view of men than subterraneous caverns, or as some suppose *sheol*, the invisible world. See above, on Ps. lxiii. 10 (9), and compare Job i. 21, where the figure is inverted, and the grave is confounded with the womb.

16. *My unformed substance did thine eyes see, and in thy book all of them are written, days are formed, and there is not one among them.* This is one of the most obscure and doubtful verses in the book of Psalms. Its difficulty to our own translators may be gathered from the fact, that *substance yet being unperfect* answers to a single Hebrew word, and that *my members* is a gratuitous addition to the text. The first word in Hebrew occurs only here, but is clearly derived from a verb which means to *roll* or *roll up* (2 Kings ii. 8), and may therefore be supposed itself to signify something rolled up or rolled together, and from this may be deduced the sense of something shapeless or unformed, or more specifically that of an embryo or fœtus. The next difficulty lies in the expression *all of them*, evaded in the English Bible by changing it to *all my members* and then making this the subject of the plurals following. The best interpreters are now disposed to construe *all of them* with *days* by a grammatical prolepsis. In thy book all of them are written, namely, all my days, as they were planned, projected, or decreed, before as yet one of them had really existed. *Written* and *formed* are then parallel expressions. *All of them are written, days are de-*

lineated or *depicted*. By *days* (translated in our Bible *in continuance*) we are then to understand not merely the length but the events and vicissitudes of life. See Job xiv. 5. Ps. lvi. 9 (8.) This is one of those cases in which the difficulty lies in the particular expressions, while the general import of the passage is clearly determined by the context. Instead of (לא) *not*, the keri or marginal reading in the Hebrew Bible has (לו) *to him*, a variation to which no one has succeeded in attaching a coherent sense. Precisely the same difference of text exists in Ps. c. 3.

17. *And to me how precious are thy thoughts, oh God! How great is the sum of them!* Having presented this impressive view of God's omniscience, he now tells how he is himself affected by it. So far from thinking it a hardship to be subject to this scrutiny, he counts it a most valuable privilege. However others may regard this truth, *to me*, my judgment and my feelings, *how costly*, valuable, *are thy thoughts*, i. e. thy perpetual attention to me. For the true sense of *precious*, see above, on Ps. xxxvi. 8 (7.) xlv. 10 (9.) *Great is the sum*, literally, *strong* (or *many*) *are their sums*, an expression which can hardly be retained in our idiom.

18. *I will count them*—(but no)—*more than sand they are many*—*I awake and still I (am) with thee.* The first clause is equivalent to a conditional proposition, *if I would count them* etc. but far more striking and poetical in form. See above, on Ps. xl. 6 (5.) *I am still with thee* has the same essential meaning with the similar expression in Ps. lxxiii. 23, namely, I am still in thy society or company. But there the reference is chiefly to divine protection, here to meditation on the divine attributes. Thou art still before me as an object of adoring wonder, not by day only, but by night; not merely in the *watches* of the night, but even in my sleep. See above, on Ps. i. 2. xvi. 7. lxiii. 7 (6.)

19. *If thou wilt slay, oh God, the wicked (man)! And ye men of blood, depart from me!* The first clause is in fact, though not in form, the expression of a wish. If thou wouldst but slay! In form, there is an aposiopesis, which may be variously supplied by adding, I will praise thee, I will rejoice, it will be just, or the like. *Men of bloods*, murderers or murderous men. See above, on Ps. v. 7 (6.) xxvi. 9. lv. 24 (23.) *Depart from me* is the same expression as in Ps. vi. 9 (8.) cxix. 15, but the main idea here is that of disavowal or repudiation. Oh that God would slay them, and until he does, I desire to have no communion with them. Compare Job xxi. 14. Matth. vii. 23.

20. *Who speak of thee for wickedness and take in vain—thy foes!* Speak of thee, or name thee, use thy name, for the accomplishment of wicked ends. The other clause will then be strictly parallel, *and take* (thy name) *in vain*, as in Ex. xx. 7. For the meaning of this difficult expression, see above, on Ps. xxiv. 4. The subject of the proposition is placed emphatically at the end.

21. *Thy haters, oh Jehovah, shall not I hate, and with thine assailants be disgusted?* The simple future in the first clause comprehends several distinct shades of meaning. Do I not, may I not, must I not, hate those hating thee? Hate them, not as man hates, but as God hates. See above, on Ps. v. 6 (5.) The construction of the verb and preposition in the last clause is the same in Hebrew and in English. *Be disgusted*, literally, sicken or disgust myself, abhor, or loathe. *Thine assailants*, those rising up against thee, as rebellious enemies. The Hebrew word is a noun formed from the participle used above, Ps. xvii. 7. lix. 2 (1.)

22. *(With) perfection of hatred do I hate them; as enemies they are to me.* Literally, *they are for enemies*, i. e. I so esteem them. As enemies of God, they must be mine.

23. *Search me, God, and know my heart; try me, and know my thoughts.* The last expression is emphatic, meaning even my most anxious and disturbed thoughts, into which corruption might most easily find entrance. See above, on Ps. xciv. 19, the only other place where the Hebrew word occurs. In this verse, he again appeals to the divine omniscience for the purity of his intentions, and thus comes back to the point from which he started.

24. *And see if a way of pain be in me, and guide me in a way of eternity.* In the first clause some translate, *the way of an idol*, an idolatrous way. But the meaning *idol* is not justified by usage. A way of pain is one that leads to suffering and misery hereafter. The opposite of this is *a way of eternity*, by which some understand an everlasting way, as distinguished from the perishable way of sinners, Ps. i. 6. Others, more probably, the way that leads to everlasting life. Usage, however, is in favour of a third and very different interpretation, which gives the Hebrew phrase (דֶּרֶךְ עוֹלָם) the same sense with a kindred one (נְתִיבוֹת עוֹלָם) used by Jeremiah (vi. 16), to wit, that of *old* or *ancient way*, the one pursued by prophets, patriarchs, and saints of old. Similar expressions are found in Jer. xviii. 15. Job xxii. 15, applied, in a bad sense, to the course pursued by ancient sinners. The prayer, however, still amounts to the same thing, to wit, that God would lead him in the good old way, which is itself the way to everlasting life.

PSALM CXL.

1. *To the Chief Musician. A Psalm. By David.* We find ourselves, in this psalm, carried back not only to the times of

David, but to those of the Sauline persecution, from which the images are evidently borrowed. Besides the warlike tone, the vigorous conciseness, the verbal agreements with Davidic psalms combined with eminent originality, the very structure is Davidic, and exhibits the familiar sequence of complaint, vs. 2—6 (1—5), prayer, vs. 7—9 (6—8), and confident anticipation, vs. 10—14 (9—13.) So clearly do these features of the composition mark its origin, even independently of the inscription, that nothing can account for its position here but the hypothesis already stated, that these ancient psalms were incorporated into a series of later date, and placed in the collection, not according to their individual antiquity, but according to the date of the whole set or system, into which they had been made to enter. Like the psalms immediately preceding, this was probably composed by David after the reception of the great Messianic promise, and with immediate reference to it.

2 (1.) *Deliver me, Jehovah, from the bad man; from the man of violences thou wilt preserve me.* This is one of those pictures so abundant in the genuine Davidic Psalms, of which Saul seems to have furnished the original. Compare Ps. lii. The first *man* is the generic term (אָדָם), the other the individual designation (אִישׁ), which seem, however, to be used here as equivalents. The insensible transition from direct prayer to confident anticipation is characteristic of the psalms of David. *Man of violence* is another favourite expression. See above, on Ps. xviii. 49 (48), and compare the parallel passage, 2 Sam. xxii. 49, where the plural form (*violences*) is used, as in the verse before us.

3 (2.) *Who imagine evils in (their) heart; all the day they gather (for) battles.* That the preceding verse, notwithstanding the reference to Saul, is the description of a whole class, is clear from the plural forms in this verse. *Think*, meditate, devise, imagine. *Evils*, particularly such as are inflicted on others, well expressed

in the common version, *mischiefs.* Another construction of the last clause, preferred by some interpreters, is, *all the day they dwell with wars* (or *in wars*), i. e. are constantly involved in them and busied with them. This use of the verb (גּוּר) is justified by Ps. v. 5 (4.) cv. 23. cxxv. 5. But the analogy of Ps. lvi. 7 (6.) lix. 4 (3) is decisive in favour of the other explanation. Compare Ps. xxxi. 14 (13.) xxxv. 15. Isai. liv. 15.

4 (3.) *They sharpen their tongue as a serpent; the poison of an adder (is) under their lips, Selah.* Not *as a serpent (does)*, but (spiteful or venomous) *as a serpent.* See above, on Ps. lxiv. 4 (3.) With the last clause compare Ps. x. 7. lviii. 5 (4.) The word for *asp* or *adder* occurs only here. The only point of exegetical importance is, that it means a poisonous serpent, and is thus a specification of the general expression in the other clause.

5 (4.) *Keep me, Jehovah, from the hands of the wicked (man); from the man of violences thou wilt preserve me, who have thought to subvert my steps.* A varied repetition of the prayer in v. 1. With the last clause compare Ps. xxxv. 5. xxxvi. 13 (12.) lvi. 14 (13.) cxviii. 13.

6 (5.) *High (ones) have hid a snare for me, and cords—they have spread out a net by the side of the road—traps have they laid for me, Selah.* This is little more than an accumulation of the various terms in which David elsewhere clothes one of his favourite figures, as if he saw his own perils reappearing in the future. *High ones*, i. e. proud or haughty men. *By the side*, literally, *the hand*, as we say on either hand. The word translated *road*, according to its etymology, denotes a wagon-road, a track worn by wheels.

7 (6.) *I have said to Jehovah, My God (art) thou; give ear, Jehovah, (to) the voice of my supplications.* All the component

parts of this verse are of constant occurrence in the psalms of David. With the first clause compare Ps. xvi. 2. xxxi. 15 (14.) With the second, Ps. v. 2, 3 (1, 2.) xvii. 1. xxviii. 2, 6 (1, 5.) xxxi. 23 (22.) xxxix. 13 (12.) liii. 4 (3.)

8 (7.) *Jehovah, Lord, the strength of my salvation; thou hast covered my head in the day of battle.* My covenant God and sovereign, whose power saves me. *Head* is preceded by a preposition (לְ), *thou hast been a covering* (or *afforded shelter*) *to* (or *for*) *my head.* The day of battle, literally, of armour or of weapons, i. e. the day when they are used. With this verse compare Ps. v. 12 (11.) lx. 9 (7.) lxii. 2, 12 (1, 11.) cxxxix. 13. 1 Sam. xxviii. 2.

9 (8.) *Grant not, Jehovah, the desires of the wicked man—his device succeed not—they will be exalted.* Succeed not, suffer not to prosper; literally, draw not out, i. e. to a successful issue. The last clause states what would be the effect of their success; they would be elated, or exalt themselves. With this verse compare Ps. xxvii. 12. xxxi. 14 (13.) xxxvii. 12. lxvi. 7 (6.) Deut. xxxii. 27.

10 (9.) *The head of those surrounding me—the mischief of their lips shall cover them.* The nominative absolute refers back to the covering of the Psalmist's head in v. 8 (7.) While my head is covered by the divine protection, the head of those by whom I am beset shall be covered with the consequences or the punishment of the mischief occasioned by their calumnies and insults. Or the trouble, which their lips have caused to others, shall return upon themselves. Compare Ps. vii. 17 (16.) *Those surrounding me*, or, as a noun, *my surroundings*, as in 2 Kings xxiii. 5. The participle would, according to analogy and usage, mean *causing me to turn back* or *retreat* (Jer. xxi. 4), which yields a good sense here. The head of those who once drove me back shall be covered, etc.

11 (10.) *Coals shall be cast upon them; into the fire he shall make them fall, and into deep waters,* (whence) *they shall not rise.* The first noun in Hebrew always means burning or live coals. See above, on Ps. xviii. 13, 14 (12, 13.) *Shall be cast* is the keri or marginal reading, no doubt intended to relieve the harshness and obscurity of the reading in the text, *they shall cast* or *shake*, an indefinite or impersonal construction, really equivalent in meaning to the passive. In the second member of the sentence the action is ascribed to God himself. *Deep waters* answers to a single Hebrew word occurring only here, and by some supposed to mean *deep pits* or excavations. The first sense above given is founded on an Arabic analogy.

12 (11). *A man of tongue shall not be established in the land,* (nor) *a man of violence, a bad* (man)—*he shall hunt him to destruction.* A man of a calumnious unbridled tongue (James i. 26) shall not be permanently seated in a prosperous condition. See above, on Ps. ci. 7. cii. 29 (28.) The next words may be variously construed; *a man of wicked violence*, or, disregarding the accents, *a man of violence, evil shall hunt him*, etc. According to the other constructions, God is the subject of the verb, as of the second in v. 11 (10.) *To destructions*, the plural form denoting fulness and completeness. Others render it *by strokes*, i. e. successive strokes; others again, *in haste*, which agrees well with the usage of the verbal root. See 2 Chr. xxvi. 20. Esth. iii. 15. vi. 12. viii. 14.

13 (12.) *I know that Jehovah will do justice to the sufferer, and judgment for the poor.* Compare Ps. ix. 5, 17 (4, 16.) Literally, *the right of the sufferer, the judgment of the poor.*

14 (13.) *Only the righteous shall give thanks unto thy name, the upright shall sit in thy presence.* Only the righteous shall have occasion for thanksgiving. There is no need therefore of depart-

ing from the proper sense of (אַךְ) the Hebrew particle. See above, on Ps. lxxiii. 1. *Sit in thy presence*, as thy friends or guests or favoured servants. Perhaps it may mean *sit (enthroned) before thee.* Compare Matth. xix. 28. Some understand the sense to be, *shall dwell* (in the land) *before thee*, i. e. under thy protection and inspection. Compare Ps. xxi. 7 (6.) xli. 13 (12.) lvi. 14 (13.)

PSALM CXLI.

AFTER an introductory petition for a favourable hearing, vs. 1, 2, the Psalmist prays to be delivered from the power of temptation, vs. 3, 4, comforts himself under his afflictions as paternal chastisements, vs. 5, 6, anticipates the ruin of his enemies, v. 7, and prays for deliverance from them in the mean time, vs. 8—10. This psalm, like the one before it, is distinguished by a pregnant brevity and the use of rare expressions, while at the same time it is full of verbal and real coincidences with the psalms of David. These indications are so clear and undeniable, that a skeptical critic of great eminence (De Wette) pronounces it one of the oldest psalms in the collection. With respect to its position in the Psalter, see the prefatory notes to Ps. cxxxv, cxl.

1. *A Psalm. By David. Jehovah, I invoke thee; hasten to me; give ear to my voice in my calling to thee.* This verse is entirely made up of phrases frequently occurring in the psalms of David. *I invoke thee*, Ps. xvii. 6. *Hasten to me*, Ps. xxii. 20 (19.) lxx. 2 (1.) lxxi. 12. *Hear my voice*, Ps. cxl. 7 (6.) *In my calling*, Ps. iv. 2 (1.)

2. *Let my prayer continue (as) incense before thee, the offering of my hands (as) the evening oblation.* *Continue*, literally, *be established*, as in Ps. cxl. 12 (11.) He prays not only for acceptance, but for constant or perpetual acceptance, as the offerings referred to were the stated daily services of the Mosaic ritual. *Incense* is in scripture the symbol of prayer. In the books posterior to the Pentateuch it is commonly mentioned as an evening oblation (1 Kings xviii. 29, 36. 2 Kings xvi. 15. Dan. ix. 21. Ezra ix. 4, 5), perhaps because in the evening it was reckoned the main offering, whereas in the morning it was merely an appendage to the animal sacrifice. *Lifting up* is not the meaning of the Hebrew word (משאת) in any other place, whereas it often means a gift, and especially a portion of food (Gen. xliii. 34. 2 Sam. xi. 8), in which sense it might naturally be applied to the vegetable offerings of the Law.

3. *Set, oh Jehovah, a guard at my mouth; watch over the door of my lips.* The prayer, for which he had bespoken audience and acceptance, was a prayer against the power of temptation, and first with reference to sins of speech. See above, on Ps. xxxix. 2 (1.) The words translated *watch* and *door* are forms occurring only here, but etymologically near akin to others which are in common use.

4. *Incline not my heart to an evil word, to practise practices in wickedness with men* (who are) *workers of iniquity, and let me not eat of their dainties.* An *evil word* may be strictly understood, as referring still to sins of the tongue, or be taken in the idiomatic sense of an *evil matter*, which last is preferred by most interpreters. The assonance in *practise practices* is copied from the Hebrew, where the cognate verb and noun are combined in the same manner. *Practices in wickedness* or wicked practices. The last words seem to be a prayer, that he may not be tempted.

by the luxurious prosperity of wicked men, to follow their example. See above, on Ps. lxxiii. 3—7, 12.

5. *Let the righteous smite me (in) mercy and chasten me—oil for the head let not my head refuse—for* (it is) *still* (to come)—*and my prayer* (must still ascend) *in their injuries.* This verse is so obscure as to be almost unintelligible. According to the English versions, it expresses his willingness to be rebuked by good men for his benefit. But this sense is not only hard to be extracted from the words, but foreign from the context. Of the many contradictory interpretations which have been proposed the most probable is that which makes the sentence mean, that the sufferings endured by the good man, even at the hand of the wicked, are chastisements inflicted by a righteous God in justice and in mercy, and as such may be likened to a festive ointment, which the head of the sufferer should not refuse, as he will still have need of consolation and occasion to invoke God, in the midst of trials and of mischiefs yet to be experienced.

6. *Thrown down among the rocks are their judges; and* (then) *they hear my words, for they are sweet.* When the judgments in reserve for the leaders of my enemies shall come upon them, they will perceive too late how reasonable are my words, and wish that they had hearkened to them sooner. *Thrown down*, originally *let go*, here used as in 2 Kings ix. 33. *Among the rocks*, literally *in* (or *into*) *the hands of the rock.* Some understand this to mean *into its power* (see v. 9 below); others, *against its sides* (see Ps. cxl. 6); but the simplest explanation is that which supposes the rock to be personified and represented as standing below and holding out its hands to catch the person or thing falling. Some in the last clause read, *that they are sweet.* Then, when it is too late, they shall perceive how sweet my words are.

7. *Like (one) ploughing and cleaving the earth—scattered are*

our bones at the grave's mouth (or *the mouth of hell.*) There are only two plausible interpretations of this obscure comparison. As the first Hebrew verb (פלח), in its derivative forms, has the general sense of *cleaving*, and the second (בקע) is expressly used (Ecc. x. 9) in that of *splitting wood*, some interpreters give both verbs that specific meaning here, and suppose the verse to be simply a description of mortality or carnage, the effect of which is, that human bones lie about the opening of the grave, or the devouring jaws of hell (Isai. v. 14), as numerous and as little heeded as so many logs or sticks of wood. To this it is objected, that the phrase *in* (or *on*) *the earth* is then unmeaning, or at least superfluous, and that the verse, if thus explained, does not cohere with the ensuing context, which supposes the contents of this verse to be cheering and consolatory. The other interpretation avoids these objections, by explaining the first clause not of cleaving wood but ploughing, to which the first verb is applied in Arabic. *Like (one) ploughing and cleaving* (making furrows) *in the earth*, not for the sake of mangling its surface, but to make it fruitful and productive, (so) *our bones are scattered at the mouth of hell*, as the necessary means of a glorious resurrection.

8. *For unto thee, Jehovah, Lord, (are) my eyes—in thee have I confided—pour not out my soul.* The *for* refers to the consolatory import of the verse preceding. The one before us contains several favourite Davidic phrases. *My eyes are unto thee*, Ps. xxv. 15. *In thee have I confided* (or *sought refuge*), Ps. ii. 12. xxxi. 2 (1.) In the last clause the soul or life is confounded with its vehicle. See Gen. ix. 4. Lev. xvii. 11, 14. The same remarkable expression is applied by Isaiah (liii. 12) to the voluntary death of the Messiah. That the verb literally means to *pour out*, is clear from Gen. xxiv. 20. Isai. xxxii. 15. This verse resembles Ps. cxl. 8 (7), in two points, the combination *Jehovah Adhonai*, and the supernumerary ה in סַכּוֹתָה and בְּכָה.

9. *Keep me from the hands of the snare which they have netted for me, and the nets of the doers of iniquity.* The word *hands* is entirely omitted both in the English Bible and the Prayer Book version. It is put, by a favourite personification, for power or possession. The use of the expression here was probably occasioned by its previous use in Ps. cxl. 4. The verb *netted* is here employed to represent the cognate verb and noun in Hebrew.

10. *Let the wicked fall into their own traps, while I at the same time escape.* Compare Ps. vii. 16 (15.) The combination of the singular and plural in the first clause—*wicked (men)* and *his snares*—shows that the singular denotes not a real but ideal person, representing a whole class. The best construction of the last clause is that given in the English Bible and retained above, with the single change of *withal* to the synonymous but less ambiguous expression, *at the same time.* The transpositions of this clause are unusual, even in Hebrew—*at the same time I until* (or *while) I pass*, i. e. pass by uninjured or escape.

PSALM CXLII.

1. *Maschil. By David, when he was in the cave. A Prayer.* It is called a *maschil* or didactic psalm because it might otherwise have seemed to contain matter wholly personal to David. See above, on Ps. xxxii. 1. *When he was*, literally, *in his being*, which does not refer exclusively to time, but suggests the occasion or exciting cause. The reference may be either to the cave of Adullam (1 Sam. xxii. 1), or to that of Engedi (1 Sam. xxiv. 3), or to that period and mode of life in general, when David was

obliged to seek refuge in caves, and which he might expect to see reproduced, under other forms, in the experience of his successors, for whose guidance and encouragement this psalm was written. See above, on Ps. lvii. 1. It is called a *prayer*, because the complaint or description of the danger, vs. 2—5 (1—4), is merely introductory to the petition for deliverance, vs. 6—8 (5—7.) See above, on Ps. xvii. 1. lxxxvi. 1. xc. 1. cii. 1.

2 (1.) (*With*) *my voice to Jehovah I cry; (with) my voice to Jehovah I make supplication.* With the first clause compare Ps. iii. 5 (4); with the second, Ps. xxx. 9 (8.) There are also coincidences of expression with Ps. xxii. 6 (5.) lxxvii. 2 (1.) cxl. 7 (6.) cxli. 1. *With my voice*, i. e. audibly, aloud, as opposed to a mere mental prayer. The word translated *supplication* means, according to its etymology, a prayer for grace or mercy.

3 (2.) *I pour out before him my care; my trouble before him I tell.* With the first clause compare Ps. xlii. 5 (4.) lxii. 9 (8.) 1 Sam. i. 15. Lam. ii. 19. The word translated *care* means properly reflection, meditation, musing, especially such as is anxious and sad. See above, on Ps. lxiv. 2 (1.)

4 (3.) *Because my spirit is overwhelmed within me—and thou knowest my path—in the way that I go, they have hid a snare for me.* The literal translation of the first words is, *in my spirit's being overwhelmed*, which may indicate either the time or the cause of his distress. See above, on v. 1. Some adopt this construction: when my spirit is overwhelmed (then) thou knowest my path. Others suppose two reasons to be given for his calling upon God, his distress and his trust in the divine omniscience. Because my spirit is overwhelmed, and (because) thou knowest my path. But as the form of the two phrases is entirely different in Hebrew, the simplest and safest construction is to treat the second clause as parenthetical. *Within me*, literally *upon me*; see above, on Ps.

xlii. 5—7 (4—6.) *In the way that I go*, i. e. along my path. See above, on Ps. cxl. 5 (4.) The words may mean, however, as in Ps. cxliii. 8, *in the way that I should go*, i. e. in the path of duty. Without my fault they hid a snare for me. With the first clause of this verse compare Ps. xlii. 5 (4.) lxi. 3 (2.) lxxvii. 4 (3), and with the last Ps. cxl. 6 (5.) cxli. 9. cxliii. 8.

5 (4.) *Look to the right and see—and there is no one knowing me—refuge has failed me—there is no one caring for my soul.* The first two verbs must be translated as imperatives, as in the margin of the English Bible. The right hand is mentioned as the post of a protector. See above, on Ps. cix. 6. cx. 5. cxxi. 5 The *and* at the beginning of the second clause is foreign from our idiom, which would seem to require *that* or *for*. We might however say, look to the right and see, and (you will find that) there is no one etc. *Knowing*, recognizing, willing to acknowledge, much less to defend. *There is none to me*, i. e. I have none. Far from having a protector at my right hand, I have not even one who will acknowledge that he knows me. *Caring*, literally, *seeking*, asking, or inquiring after it, in order to assist or save it. Nearly the same form of speech is used to express the very opposite idea, that of *seeking one's soul* to destroy it. See above, on Ps. xxxv. 4.

6 (5.) *I have cried unto thee, Jehovah. I have said, Thou (art) my refuge, my portion in the land of life.* I have cried and still cry; I have said and still say. With this last expression compare Ps. xxxi. 15 (14.) xli. 5 (4.) *Thou (art) my refuge*, as in Ps. lxii. 8 (7.) lxxi. 7. *My portion*, as in Ps. xvi. 5. lxxiii. 26. cxix. 57. *Land of life* (or *of the living)*, as in Ps. xxvii. 13. lii. 7 (5.)

7. (6.) *Hearken to my cry, for I am reduced greatly ; free me from my persecutors, for they are mightier than I.* All these are

favourite Davidic phrases. *Hearken to my cry*, as in Ps. xvii. 1. lxi. 2 (1.) *I am reduced* (or *weakened) greatly*, as in Ps. lxxix. 8 (7.) cxvi. 6. Compare Judges vi. 6. *Free me from my persecutors*, as in Ps. vii. 2 (1.) *They are mightier than I*, as in Ps. xviii. 18 (17.)

8. *Bring out from prison my soul, to thank thy name. Me shall the righteous surround when thou shalt bestow on me* (favour.) With the first clause compare Ps. xxv. 17. cvii. 10. cxliii. 11. Some suppose an allusion to Joseph's imprisonment and liberation. See above, on Ps. cv. 17—20. *To thank* (or *praise*) *thy name*, although an exact translation, is restricted by the English idiom to the person mentioned just before, and can only mean in accordance with our usage, *that I may thank thy name;* whereas the Hebrew infinitive knows no such limitation and in this case simply means, that some one (without defining who) may praise thy name; or, exchanging the active for the passive form, *that thy name may be praised;* or, retaining the indefiniteness of the original expression, *for the praising of thy name.* The agents here intended are probably *the righteous*, who are mentioned in the next clause. The verb *surround*, which has a hostile sense in Ps. xxii. 13. Hab. i. 4, here means to gather round one with a friendly curiosity and eagerness, which some suppose to be suggested by the construction with the preposition (בְּ), which cannot be expressed in English. This sympathy of the righteous in his joys and sorrows is a favourite idea with David. See above, on Ps. xxxv. 27. xl. 17 (16.) For the meaning and construction of the last verb, see above, on Ps. xiii. 6. ciii. 10. cxvi. 7.

PSALM CXLIII.

This psalm may be divided into two equal parts, separated by the Selah in v. 6. The first contains a complaint, vs. 1—6 ; the second a prayer for mercy, vs. 7—12. It resembles the preceding psalm, not only in this relation of its parts, but in its whole tone and diction, its Davidic phraseology combined with an originality never exhibited by the mere imitator or compiler.

1. *A Psalm. By David. Jehovah, hear my prayer, give ear unto my cries for mercy ; in thy faithfulness answer me (and) in thy righteousness.* The combination of faithfulness and righteousness is like that in Ps. xxxvi. 6, 7 (5, 6.) They can hardly be regarded as distinct grounds of argument, but rather as modified statements of the same. The faithfulness of God has direct reference to his promise or covenant engagements; his righteousness has reference to the claims of his own people, but claims which owe their existence to those same covenant engagements.

2. *And enter not into judgment with thy servant, for just before thee is no one living.* To enter into judgment is a forensic phrase meaning to go to law, to prosecute, to sue. See Job ix. 32. xxii. 4. The verb in the last clause is not a passive meaning to be justified, but a neuter meaning to be just or innocent, to be in the right or on the right side of the controverted question. The acknowledgment in this verse has caused the psalm to be reckoned among the penitential psalms. The verse is often imitated or

referred to elsewhere. See Job ix. 2. xiv. 3. xv. 14. Rom. iii. 20, etc.

3. *For the enemy persecutes my soul, crushes to the earth my life, makes me dwell in dark places like the dead of old.* This verse assigns a reason for the preceding prayers, a connection indicated by the *for*. He prays that God will deal with him in mercy, not in justice, by abandoning him to the fate here described. Compare Ps. vii. 6 (5), but especially Ps. lxxxviii. 4—7 (3—6.) See also Lam. iii. 6. The last words some understand to mean *forever dead.*

4. *And overwhelmed within me is my spirit; in the midst of me desolated is my heart.* With the first clause compare Ps. cxlii. 4 (3); with the second Ps. xl. 16 (15.)

5. *I remember the days of old; I meditate of all thy doing; of the work of thy hands I muse.* He recalls and ponders them, not as a source of comfort, as in Ps. xliv. 2—4 (1—3), but of sorrow, from their painful contrast with his actual condition. See above, on Ps. xxii. 4—6 (3—5.) lxxvii. 6 (5), and with the last clause compare Ps. xcii. 5

6. *I spread my hands unto thee; my soul is like a weary land to thee*, i. e. thirsts or longs for thee, as a dry or thirsty land for rain. See above, on Ps. lxiii. 2 (1.) A *weary land* is an unusual expression, and one of the peculiar features of this psalm. With the first clause compare Ps. xliv. 21 (20.) The close of the complaint or lamentation, and the strength of the feeling with which it is uttered, are both indicated by the *Selah.*

7. *Hasten, answer me, Jehovah—my spirit fails—hide not thy face from me—or I shall be confounded with (those) going down (to) the pit.* The meaning of the first clause is, hasten to grant

my petition. *Fails*, is spent or exhausted. See above, on Ps. xxviii. 1. xxxix. 11 (10.) lxix. 18 (17.) cii. 3 (2.) That he is in extremity, is urged as a reason why God cannot fail to hear and answer him. This verse begins the main prayer of the psalm, that in vs. 1, 2, being merely introductory to the complaint in vs. 3—6, which is itself introductory to the prayer that follows.

8. *Let me hear in the morning thy mercy ; let me know the way that I must go, for unto thee I raise my soul.* All these are familiar thoughts and terms to the readers of the psalms of David, and may be severally found in Ps. xxv. 1—4. li. 10 (8.) lix. 17 (16.) *The way that I must go*, not merely to be right, but to be safe and happy ; the way of safety as well as that of duty. See above, on Ps. cxlii. 7 (6.)

9. *Free me from my enemies, Jehovah, with thee I hide myself.* With the first clause compare Ps. lix. 12 (11.) cxlii. 7 ; with the second, Ps. xxvii. 5. xxxi. 21 (20.) The form of expression here, however, is peculiar and original. The literal meaning is *to thee I cover*, i. e. cover myself, the reflexive use of the Hebrew verb being clear from Gen. xxxviii. 14. Deut. xxii. 12. Jon. iii. 6. The force of the pregnant construction is well though freely given in the English version, *I flee unto thee to hide me.*

10. *Teach me to do thy will, for thou (art) my God. Thy spirit (is) good ; let it guide me in level ground.* This is a prayer for external safety, and at the same time for that spiritual guidance, without which it is unattainable. Compare Ps. v. 9 (8.) xxvi. 12. xxvii. 11. xl. 9 (8.) cxxxix. 10, 24. Some make but two clauses, and instead of the short proposition in the middle, read, *let thy good spirit guide me etc.* or *let thy spirit,* (which is) *good guide me etc.* *Level ground*, literally *earth (or land) of evenness (or straightness.)* See above, on Ps. xxvi. 12.

11. *For thy name's sake, Jehovah, thou wilt quicken me; in thy righteousness thou wilt bring out of distress my soul.* Here again we have an accumulation of Davidic ideas and expressions. *For thy name's sake*, as in Ps. xxiii. 3. xxv. 11. xxxi. 4. cix. 21. *Thou wilt quicken me*, as in Ps. cxxxviii. 7. *In thy righteousness*, as in Ps. xxxi. 2. *Bring my soul out of trouble*, as in Ps. xxv. 15. xxxiv. 18 (17.) cxlii. 8 (7.)

12. *And in thy mercy thou wilt destroy my enemies and cause to perish all that vex my soul; for I (am) thy servant.* With the first clause compare Ps. xxxi. 17 (16.) xviii. 41 (40.) Some find here an allusion to the promise in Deut. vii. 24. *Vexers*, adversaries, persecutors, of my soul. *Thy servant*, not merely a believer but a chosen instrument, not merely one of thy people but their chief and representative, and as such entitled to deliverance, both for their sake and my own. In these two verses, the form of direct petition is insensibly exchanged for that of confident anticipation.

PSALM CXLIV.

This is a kind of supplement or counterpart to Ps. xviii, in which the view there taken of David's personal experience is applied to the anticipated case of his successors. The design thus assumed accounts for the position of the psalm in the collection. That its being placed precisely here is not fortuitous, may be inferred from its furnishing a kind of link between the urgent entreaties of the preceding psalms and the triumphant praise of those which follow. The Davidic origin of this psalm is as marked as that of any in the Psalter. The accumulation of Davidic phrases is confined to the first part, while the last is independent and original, a fact entirely inconsistent with the supposition of a later compilation. The Psalmist thanks God for his protection of himself and of mankind in general, vs. 1—4, prays for deliverance from present dangers, vs. 5—8, expresses his confident anticipation of a favourable answer, vs. 9—10, renews his prayer, not only for himself but for the chosen people, vs. 11—14, and felicitates them that they are such, v. 15.

1. *By David. Blessed be Jehovah, my Rock, the (one) training my hands for fight, my fingers for war.* See above, on Ps. xviii. 35, 47 (34, 46), where most of these expressions have already been explained. *Fight* and *war* are both verbs and nouns in English, but the Hebrew words are nouns with the article prefixed. David here begins by referring all the successes of himself and his successors to Jehovah.

2. *My mercy and my fortress, my high place, and a deliverer for me, my shield and (he) in whom I trust, the (one) subduing my people.* No less than five of these descriptive epithets are taken from a single verse of Ps. xviii, viz. v. 3 (2.) Peculiar to the place before us is *my mercy*, i. e. my God of mercy. See above, on Ps. lix. 18 (17.) The benefit of these relations to Jehovah David claims not merely for himself but for his royal race, which was closed and yet perpetuated in the Messiah. *He in whom I trust*, literally, *and in him I trust. My people*, in its widest sense, including Israel and the Gentiles who were to be added to the kingdom of David under the reign of the Messiah. Compare Ps. xviii. 44, 48 (43, 47) with the parallel passages in 2 Samuel.

3. *Jehovah, what (is) man, that thou shouldst know him, the son of man, that thou shouldst think of him?* The greatness of God's goodness is enhanced by a view of man's insignificance and

unworthiness. The original construction seems to be, *what is man?* (nothing), *and* (yet) *thou knowest him* etc. To know is here to recognise as being in existence, to take notice of. The first *man* is the generic term, the second one denoting weakness. See above, on Ps. viii. 5 (4), and compare 2 Sam vii. 18.

4. *Man to vanity is like; his days (are) as a passing shadow.* He cannot therefore be a worthy object, in himself, of the divine regard and favour. With the first clause compare Ps. xxxix. 6, 7 (5, 6), lxii. 10 (9); with the second, Ps. cii. 12 (11.) ciii. 15.

5. *Jehovah, bow thy heavens and come down; touch the mountains and let them smoke.* With the first clause compare Ps. xviii. 10 (9.) What God is there described as doing, he is here besought to do again. With the last clause compare Ps. civ. 32 *Mountains*, in all such connections, would necessarily suggest the idea of states and kingdoms. See above, on Ps. xlvi. 3, 4 (2, 3.)

6. *Lighten lightning and scatter them; send out thy arrows and confound them.* The first word in Hebrew is a verb occurring nowhere else, and composed of the same radicals with the common word for *lightning* which immediately follows. For the meaning of the other terms, see above, on Ps. xviii. 15 (14), and compare the parallel passage, 2 Sam. xxii. 15 (14), with which the writer of the psalm before us was certainly acquainted, as appears from his occasional use of its peculiar readings.

7. *Send thy hands from on high; rid me and free me from* (the) *many waters, from the hand of aliens.* With the first clause compare Ps. xviii. 17 (16.) For *hand* we have here the plural *hands*, and for the two verbs there used two substantially equivalent, the first of which has the sense here given to it only in this place and the cognate languages, and is therefore well represented by the less usual English word *rid.* With the last clause, compare

Ps. xviii. 45, 46 (44, 45), where the phrase *sons of strangeness* (or *of foreign parts*) has been explained already.

8. *Whose mouth speaks fraud, and their right hand (is) a right hand of falsehood.* The word translated *fraud* is properly a negative meaning vanity or emptiness, but applied to the want of moral goodness and especially of truth. See above, on Ps. xxiv. 4. The right hand is mentioned in allusion either to the practice of swearing with uplifted hand (Ps. cvi. 26), or to that of striking hands in bargains (2 Kings x. 15.) There seems to be reference, in this verse, to the feigned obedience of the enemy, Ps. xviii. 45 (44.)

9. *Oh God, a new song I will sing to thee; with a lyre of ten* (strings) *I will play* (or *make music*) *to thee.* See above, on Ps. xxxiii. 2, 3, where David exhorts others to do what he here resolves and vows to do himself. The new song still implies a new occasion for it, so that he here begins to anticipate the answer to his foregoing prayers.

10. *The (one) giving salvation to kings; the (one) ridding David his servant from an evil sword.* This mode of connecting sentences, by a participle agreeing with a noun in the foregoing context, is a characteristic feature of Ps. xviii. See vol. i. pp. 144, 145. The *kings* particularly meant are the theocratical sovereigns, the royal family of David. *Ridding*, the participle of the verb so rendered in v. 7. *David (as) his servant*, because he is his servant, in the sense repeatedly explained already. See above, on Ps. cxliii. 2, 12. David speaks of himself by name, not only here but in Ps. xviii. 51 (50.) lxi. 7 (6.) lxiii. 12 (11.) 2 Sam. vii. 26. *An evil sword*, not only dangerous but wicked. Compare Ps. xxii. 21 (20.)

11. *Rid me and free me from the hand of aliens, whose mouth*

speaks fraud, and whose right hand (is) a right hand of falsehood In resuming the language of direct petition, the terms of vs. 7, 8, are studiously repeated, as if to show that this prayer is parallel to that, and not an addition to it.

12. *So that our sons* (may be) *as plants grown large in their youth, our daughters as corner-stones hewn* (for) *the building of the temple.* The reminiscences or imitations of Ps. xviii suddenly cease here, and are followed by a series of original, peculiar, and for the most part no doubt antique expressions. On the supposition that the title is correct in making David the author, this is natural enough. On any other supposition it is unaccountable, unless by the gratuitous assumption, that this is a fragment of an older composition, a mode of reasoning by which any thing may be either proved or disproved. The first word in Hebrew is the relative pronoun, and the literal meaning of the clause is, *(by) which* (or *in consequence of which)* our sons, etc. The *which* refers to the deliverance prayed for in the preceding verse. *Grown large*, literally *magnified* or *made great.* The common version *(grown up in their youth)* has a paradoxical appearance, arising from the ambiguity of our phrase *grown up*, which is applied (like the Greek ἡλικία) both to age and stature. The word translated *corner-stones* has the same sense in Zech. ix. 15. The corner-stones are mentioned as those which were hewn and polished with peculiar care. *Likeness* or *model* would agree better with the usage of the Hebrew word (תַּבְנִית), but its primary sense, as a derivative of the verb (בָּנָה) *to build*, is here still more appropriate. Most interpreters give the last word the vague sense of *a palace*, considered as a splendid building. There is something, however, far more striking in the translation *temple*, found in the Prayer-Book and the ancient versions. The omission of the article is a poetic license of perpetual occurrence. The temple was the great architectural model and standard of comparison, and particularly remarkable for the great size and skilful elaboration of its

foundation-stones, some of which, there is reason to believe, have remained undisturbed since the time of Solomon. See Robinson's Palestine, vol. i, pp. 422—426.

13. *Our garners full, affording from kind to kind ; our flocks bearing thousands, multiplied by myriads, in our streets.* From kind to kind seems to denote not only variety but regular succession, as expressed in Hengstenberg's version, *one kind after another*. Compare Ps. lxxxiv. 8 (7.) The participles in the next clause are highly idiomatic and scarcely reproducible in any other language. A somewhat similar example occurs above, Ps. lxix. 32 (31.) But there both forms are active, whereas here we have one active and one passive participle, formed directly from the Hebrew words denoting a thousand and a myriad, the last of which is a derivative of the verb *to increase* or *multiply*, and would therefore necessarily suggest that idea. See above, on Ps. iii. 7 (6.) lxviii. 18 (17.) *Streets*, though not incorrect, is an inadequate translation of the Hebrew word (חוּצוֹת), which means external spaces, streets as opposed to the inside of houses, fields or country as opposed to a whole town. Here it includes not only roads but fields.

14. *Our oxen loaded—no damage and no loss—and no complaint in our streets.* The first particular implies abundance. For the use of oxen as beasts of burden, see 1 Chr. xii. 40. *Damage* and *loss*, literally, *breach* and *going forth*. *Complaint*, literally, *cry*, but especially for loss of the fruits of the earth. See Isai. xxiv. 11. Some give the sentence an entirely different meaning, by supposing the word translated *oxen* to mean *princes*, as it does in Zech. ix. 7. xii. 5, 6, and giving the participle joined with it the Chaldee sense of *raised erect* or *upright*. *Going out* then means going out to war, as in Am. v. 3, *breach* the incursion of an enemy, and *cry* a war-cry. But the first Hebrew word in question (אַלּוּף) is applied only to the chiefs of Edom (Gen. xxxvi. 15), except in the latest

books of the Old Testament, such as Zechariah; and we naturally look for oxen after sheep, as in Ps. viii. 8 (7.)

15. *Happy the people (with) whom (it is) thus! Happy the people whose God (is) Jehovah!* The clauses are not antithetical but equivalent. *The people* means *the (chosen) people*, Israel, with whom, in prosperous times, it was thus, and was thus for the very reason that Jehovah was their God.

PSALM CXLV.

This has been happily characterized as the "new song" promised in Ps. cxliv. 9. In other words, it is the song of praise, corresponding to the didactic, penitential, and supplicatory psalms of this series. In form it is an alphabetical psalm, and like others of that class (see vol. i. p. 206) admits of no analysis, being made up of variations on a single theme, the righteousness and goodness of the Lord to men in general, to his own people in particular, and more especially to those who suffer. The letter *nun* is wanting, being omitted, as some suppose, for the sake of having three equal stanzas, each containing seven verses. The Septuagint supplies the omission, in a very inartificial manner, by anticipating v. 17 before v. 15, with a simple change of *righteous* (צַדִּיק) to *faithful* (נֶאֱמָן), as in Ps. cxi. 7.

1. *Praise. By David. I will exalt thee, my God, the King and will bless thy name to eternity and perpetuity.* This is the only case in which the word *Praise* stands alone as the designation or description of a psalm. It evidently bears an antithetical relation to the title *Prayer* in Ps. cxlii. 1, the rather as the Hebrew

words (תְּפִלָּה and תְּהִלָּה) are still more alike than their English equivalents, differing only in a single letter. *I will exalt thee*, as in Ps. xxx. 2 (1), where the reason is expressed that is here implied, to wit, that God had exalted him. *The king*, the only true king, the king of kings, by whom they are put up and down, protected and punished. See above, on Ps. cxliv. 10, and compare Ps. v. 3 (2.) xx. 10 (9.) xxiv. 8, 10. xxix. 10. xciii. 1. xcv. 3. xcvi. 10. xcix. 1. The regal honours paid to himself by others David here transfers as due to God alone. *Bless thy name*, i. e. reverently praise it. See above, on Ps. v. 12 (11.) xxxiv. 2 (1.) ciii. 1. *Forever and ever*, in reference not merely to himself but to his royal race, which is to live forever. See above, on Ps. cxxxviii. 8.

2. *Every day will I bless thee and praise thy name to eternity and perpetuity.* Compare Ps. lxviii. 20 (19.) lxix. 31 (30.) xcii. 2, 3. *Every day* denotes constancy and regularity.

3. *Great (is) Jehovah and to be praised exceedingly, and to his greatness there is no search*, i. e. it is unsearchable. The first clause is quoted in Ps. xlviii. 2 (1.) *Greatly to be praised*, as in Ps. xviii. 4 (3.) xcvi. 4. cxiii. 3. *His greatness*, as displayed in act, his great performance or performances. See above, on Ps. lxxi. 21. With the last words of the verse compare Ps. xl. 6 (5.)

4. *Generation to generation lauds thy deeds, and thy mighty doings they declare.* With the first clause compare Ps. xix. 3 (2.) The verbs are of the future form, lauds and will laud, declare and will declare. The first verb is the one used in Ps. lxiii. 4 (3.) cxvii. 1. *Mighty doings*, literally, *mights* or *powers*, but always used, like *greatness*, in an active not an abstract sense. See above, on Ps. xx. 7 (6.) cvi. 2. *They declare* may agree with

men indefinitely, or with the double *generation* in the first clause, which, however, is there construed with a verb in the singular.

5. *(Of) the beauty of the honour of thy majesty, and the words of thy wonders, I will muse* (or *meditate.)* The accumulation of synonymous expressions in the first clause has been falsely represented as a proof of later date and a corrupted taste, whereas it only proves intensity of admiration. For examples of the same thing in undisputed psalms of David, see above, Ps. xviii. 3 (2.) lxii. 8 (7). *Beauty* and *majesty*, as in Ps. xlv. 4 (3.) *Honour* or *glory*, as in Ps. xix. 1. *Words of thy wonders* are the wonders or wondrous deeds themselves, considered as subjects of discourse or celebration. See above, on Ps. lxv. 4 (3.) cv. 27. *I will muse*, as in Ps. lxxvii. 13 (12.) cxix. 15, 23, 27, 48, 78, 148.

6. *And the force of thy dread (deeds) they utter—and (as to) thy greatness, I will recount it. Dread*, literally, *feared*, and then *to be feared*, as *praised* means *to be praised* in v. 3 above. *Utter*, literally *say*, precisely as in Ps. xl. 11 (10.) *Greatness*, or according to the reading in the text of the Hebrew Bible, *greatnesses*, i. e. great deeds, as *mights* means *mighty deeds* in v. 5.

7. *The memory of thy great goodness they pour forth, and (of) thy righteousness they sing* (or *shout.)* Memory, as in Ps. vi. 6 (5.) *Great goodness* is the order of the words not only in English but in Hebrew, where it is unusual. See above, on Ps. lxxxix. 51 (50.) *Pour forth*, as in Ps. xix. 3 (2.) lxxviii. 2. Compare Ps. lix. 8 (7.) *Thy righteousness*, as in Ps. xxxi. 2 (1.) li. 16 (14.) cxliii. 1. *Sing* or *shout* for joy. The construction is like that in Ps. li. 16 (14.) lix. 17 (16.)

8. *Gracious and compassionate (is) Jehovah, slow to anger and great (in) mercy.* Compare Ps. lxxxvi. 15 (14.) ciii. 8. cxi. 4.

Instead of the usual expression (רַב) *much* or *abundant*, we have here *great*, in allusion to its previous use in vs. 3, 6.

9. *Good (is) Jehovah to all, and his compassions (are) over all his works.* *All*, literally, *the all*, the whole universe. See above, on Ps. cxix. 91. *Over* or *upon*, the first suggesting the idea of a covering, the second that of a descent from above. *His works*, the things which he has made, his creatures. See above, on Ps. ciii. 22. The argument implied is, how much more to his own people, the creatures of his grace. See above, on Ps. cxxxviii. 8.

10. *All thy creatures, oh Jehovah, praise* (or *thank*) *thee, and thy saints bless thee.* The future forms, as usual, denote that it is so and will be so. The superfluous ה in the last word is an orthographical peculiarity like that in Ps. cxxxix. 3. cxl. 8. cxli. 8. As *saints* (or *gracious ones)* are more than *creatures*, so to *bless* is more than to *praise.* See above, on v. 1.

11. *The glory of thy reign they utter, and thy might they speak.* Compare Ps. ciii. 19. *Thy reign* or *kingdom*, which is universal. The whole phrase may mean *thy royal dignity* or honour.

12. *To make known to the sons of man his mighty deeds, and the glory of the majesty of his reign* (or *kingdom.*) Some give the infinitive the force of a gerund, *by making known ;* but the true sense seems to be, *so as to* (or *so that they) make known.* See above, on Ps. lxxviii. 18.

13. *Thy reign is a reign of all eternities, and thy dominion in generation and generation.* These words are also found in Dan. iii. 33. iv. 31. The meaning of the last clause is, thy dominion still exists and shall exist in every successive generation.

14. *An upholder (is) Jehovah for all the falling, a lifter up for all the bowed down.* The first word in each clause is properly a participle, here used as a noun, and therefore followed by the preposition *to* or *for*. Translated in either way, the words necessarily suggest the idea of habitual action. With the first clause compare Ps. xxxvii. 17, 24. liv. 6 (4.) cxix. 116.

15. *The eyes of all unto thee* (look and) *wait, and thou givest them their food in its season.* The verb in the first clause means to wait, expect, or hope, but is here construed with the preposition *to* or *towards*, which implies the act of turning or looking to the object confided in. *Givest*, literally *giving*, i. e. *(art habitually) giving*. See above, on Ps. civ. 27, where these words are quoted.

16. *Opening thy hand and satisfying to every living* (thing its) *desire*, or the desire of every living thing. Another construction, preferred by some interpreters, is, satisfying (giving satisfaction) to every living thing (in its) desire, viz. that which it desires. See the imitation of this verse in Ps. civ. 28, and compare Ps. ciii. 5. Acts xiv. 17. The words *satisfy* and *will* (or *desire*) are combined, as here, in Deut xxxiii. 23.

17. *Righteous (is) Jehovah in all his ways and merciful in all his works.* Justice and mercy are not mentioned here as opposites, but rather as equivalents, the goodness of God being really included in the rectitude so frequently ascribed to him.

18. *Near (is) Jehovah to all calling upon him, to all calling upon him in truth*, i. e. sincerely, with importunate desire and strong confidence. With this verse compare Ps. xxxiv. 7, 19.

19. *The will of his fearers he will do, and their cry he will hear, and will save them.* He will do what they desire, or grant

their prayer, especially their prayer for help in time of danger and distress, as intimated in the last clause. Compare Ps. xxxiv. 10, 16 (9, 15.) xxxvii. 40.

20. *Jehovah keeps all that love him, and all the wicked will he destroy.* The *fearers* of v. 19 and the *lovers* of this verse are identical, which shows that godly fear and love are not incompatible. *Keeps*, literally *keeping*, as in v. 15, from all danger and distress, preserving.

21. *The praise of Jehovah shall my mouth speak, and all flesh shall bless his holy name forever*, or retaining the idiomatic form of the original, *all flesh shall bless the name of his holiness* (or *his name of holiness) to eternity and perpetuity.* The use of the word *praise* connects this verse with the title or inscription in v. 1, which is thereby justified or proved to be correct. *All flesh*, as in Ps. lxv. 3 (2.) *His holy name*, as in Ps. xxxiii. 21.

PSALM CXLVI.

This psalm may be divided into two equal parts, the first of which describes the happiness of those who trust in God and not in man, vs. 1—5, while the second gives the reason, drawn from the divine perfections, vs. 6—10. The psalm is distinguished from the Davidic series which precedes it (cxxxviii—cxlv) by its whole internal character. At the same time its coincidences of expression with the one immediately before it show that it was meant to be used in connection with it, and may therefore be regarded as the closing psalm of the whole series beginning with

Ps. cxxxv, and belonging to the time of Haggai and Zechariah, to which the psalm before us is expressly referred in the Septuagint Version.

1. *Hallelujah! Praise, oh my soul, Jehovah!* See above, Ps. ciii. 1, 22. civ. 1, 35. The *Hallelujah* never appears in any psalm which bears the name of David, and is indeed as characteristic of the later psalms as the *Selah* is of the more ancient.

2. *I will praise Jehovah while I live; I will make music to my God while I still* (exist.) For the literal meaning of these words, see above, on Ps. civ. 33, from which they are borrowed, with the unimportant change of *sing* to *praise.*

3. *Trust ye not in princes, in the son of man, to whom there is no salvation*, who cannot save either himself or others, but is wholly dependent upon God. Compare Ps. xl. 5 (4.) lxxv. 7, 8 (6, 7.) cviii. 13. cxvi. 11. cxliv. 10. This may be regarded as an exhortation to men in general from Israel, an exhortation founded on his own experience.

4. *Forth goes his spirit, he returns to his earth; in that very day his thoughts perish.* For the meaning of the first clause, see above, on Ps. civ. 29. The primary idea of *breath* and the secondary one of *spirit* run into each other in the usage of the Hebrew word (רוּחַ), so that either may be expressed in the translation, without entirely excluding the other. *His thoughts*, his vain notions or ambitious schemes.

5. *Happy he whose help is the God of Jacob*, (and) *his reliance on Jehovah his God. Whose help*, literally, *in whose help*, i. e engaged, employed in it, or more probably, *among whose helpers.* Compare Ps. xlv. 10 (9.) liv. 6 (4.) xcix. 6. cxviii. 7. The divine name (אֵל) here used suggests the idea of almighty power, as

opposed to that of human weakness. *Reliance*, literally, *expectation*, *hope*; but the first idea is necessarily suggested by the preposition *on*.

6. *Who made heaven and earth, the sea, and all that (is) in them—the (one) keeping truth forever.* Two reasons are here given for thus relying upon God; his almighty power, as exercised and proved in the creation of the world, and his unchangeable fidelity. See above, Ps. xxv. 5. *Who made*, literally, *making*, with the usual reference to God's creative power as still exerted in the sustentation of the universe. See above, on Ps. lxv. 7 (6.) cxxi. 2. cxliv. 2.

7. *Doing justice to the oppressed—giving bread to the hungry—Jehovah, freeing* (or *the liberator of*) *the bound.* He is not only able but accustomed to relieve those in distress, of whom several distinct classes are here specified as samples. Compare Ps. xxxvii. 19. lxviii. 6, 7 (5, 6.) cvii. 5, 9, 10. cxlv. 14. Hunger and captivity are both familiar figures for spiritual evils, as well as literal designations of external ones, both which may here be considered as included.

8. *Jehovah opens (the eyes of) the blind; Jehovah raises up the bowed down; Jehovah loves the righteous.* The ellipsis in the first clause is not so harsh in Hebrew as in English, because the verb (פָּקַח) is almost confined, in usage, to the eyes, and would at once suggest them to a Hebrew reader. All the verbs are of the participial form, *opening*, *raising*, *loving*, i. e. continually doing so. The first clause is applicable both to bodily and mental blindness. Compare Deut. xxviii. 29. Isai. lix. 10. Job xii. 25. The second clause is borrowed from Ps. cxlv. 14.

9. *Jehovah preserves strangers; orphan and widow he relieves; and the way of wicked men makes crooked.* The stranger, the or-

phan, and the widow are constantly presented in the Law as objects of compassion and beneficence. See above, on Ps. lxviii. 6, 7 (5, 6.) *Relieves*, restores, raises up from their low condition. As a straight path is an emblem of prosperity, to render one's path crooked is to involve him in calamity. The same verb is applied, in a moral sense, to the perverse conduct of the wicked, Ps. cxix. 78.

10. *Jehovah* (reigns and) *shall reign to eternity; thy God, oh Zion, to generation and generation. Hallelujah* (praise ye Jah)! The Psalm closes with a grand sentence from the Song of Moses, Ex. xv. 18, to which a parallel clause is added, and a concluding *Hallelujah*, winding up the whole series of psalms, supposed to have been sung at the completion of the second temple.

PSALM CXLVII.

A song of praise to Jehovah on account of his goodness to his creatures generally, and to his church or chosen people in particular. Both these themes run through the psalm; but one is predominant in the first part, vs. 1—11; the other in the second, vs. 12—20. The four remaining psalms (cxlvii—cl), connected together, and distinguished from what goes before, by the *Hallelujah* with which they all begin and end; by their joyous tone, unmixed with lamentation or complaint; by their frequent allusions to some great deliverance recently experienced; and by the peculiar way in which they bring together the exhibitions of God's glory in the works of nature and in his dealings with the church; have not improbably been represented as a series, intended to commemorate the completion of the walls of Jerusalem by Nehemiah, an event described in the history itself, as putting an end to the reproach of Israel, and restoring the Holy City to its proper rank. See Neh. i. 3. ii. 5, 17. vi. 6, 7, 15, 16. vii. 4. ix. 6, 13, 14. x. 29. xii. 27, 35, 41, 43.

1. *Hallelujah* (praise ye Jah), *for it is good to celebrate our God, for it is sweet (and) praise becoming.* This is made up of the beginnings of three other psalms. See above, Ps. xcii. 2 (1.) cxxxv. 3. xxxiii. 1. *Celebrate*, make music to, with voice and instrument. See above, on Ps. vii. 18 (17.) Instead of *it is sweet* some read *he is lovely*, i. e. a worthy object of supreme affection, as in Ps. cxxxv. 3. But even there the construction is a doubtful one, and here the first proposed above is recommended by the fact that the epithets before and after relate not to God himself but to his praise.

2. *Building Jerusalem (is) Jehovah; the outcasts of Israel he gathers.* The rebuilding of the walls in the days of Nehemiah, may be said to have completed the fulfilment of the promise in Isai. xi. 12. lvi. 8. Compare Ps. cvii. 3.

3. *The (one) healing the broken-hearted and binding up their wounds.* This was true as a general description, and specially exemplified in the deliverance which Israel had experienced. See above, on Ps. xxxiv. 19 (18.) ciii. 3, and compare Isai. lxi. 1.

4. *Telling the number of the stars—to all of them names he calls.* The God who thus provides for Israel is the God of nature no less than of grace. *Telling*, counting, reckoning, estimating. Not determining beforehand, but simply doing what man cannot. See Gen. xv. 5, and compare Gen. xiii. 16, Num. xxiii. 10. Isai. lxv. 12. He not only counts but names them, *calling them all by name.* The verse is borrowed from Isai. xl. 26, where as here

God's knowledge and control of nature is presented as a source of consolation to his people.

5. *Great is our Lord and of much power; to his understanding there is no number*, i. e. it is incalculable and immense. Compare Isai. xl. 26, 28. *Of much power*, or abundant in strength.

6. *Raising up the humble (is) Jehovah, casting down the wicked to the very earth.* See above, Ps. cxlvi. 8, 9. *To the very earth*, literally, even to the earth.

7. *Respond to Jehovah with thanksgiving; make music to our God with a harp.* The first verb has its proper sense of answering or responding, as in Ps. cxix. 172. It may be doubted whether it ever has that of simply singing. *Respond*, i. e. to his manifold favours.

8. *The* (one) *covering the heavens with clouds—the* (one) *providing for the earth rain—the* (one) *causing the mountains to put forth grass.* The grass as produced by means of the rain, and the rain by means of the clouds. See above, on Ps. civ. 13.

9. *Giving to the cattle its food—to the young ravens which cry.* The first noun may also be translated *beast*, but still with reference to domestic animals, with which is contrasted in the other clause the raven, as a wild bird, unconnected with mankind, and as some suppose with allusion to its harsh and piercing cry. See above, on Ps. civ. 21. cxlv. 15, and compare Job xxxviii. 41. *Young ravens*, literally, *sons of the raven.*

10. *Not in the strength of a horse does he delight; not with the legs of a man is he pleased.* The best explanation of the singular expressions in the last clause is, that the whole verse was

intended to describe horse and foot, or cavalry and infantry, as forming the military strength of armies. It is not to those who trust in these that God is disposed to extend favour, nor do these advantages at all attract him.

11. *Pleased (is) Jehovah with those fearing him, with those hoping for his mercy.* This implies the want of secular advantages, or at least an absence of reliance on them, and a sense of dependence upon God alone.

12. *Laud, oh Jerusalem, Jehovah! Praise thy God, oh Zion!* Here begins the second division of the psalm, in which the goodness of God to his people is the theme, and the people itself the object of address.

13. *For he hath strengthened the bars of thy gates; he hath blessed thy sons in the midst of thee.* Although the first clause admits of a general figurative application, it seems to contain an evident allusion to the historical occasion of the psalm, or at least to favour the opinion, that it was designed to celebrate the renewed fortifications of the Holy City.

14. *(It is) he that makes thy border peace,* (and with) *the fat of wheat he satisfies thee. He that makes,* literally, *the (one) placing. Border* is put for all that it contains or bounds, thy territory or domain. To make it peace is to make it peaceful or to give it peace. See Isai. liv. 12. With the last clause compare Ps. lxxxi. 17. Deut. xxxii. 14.

15. *He that sendeth his commandment (upon) earth—very swiftly runs his word.* The construction is like that in the preceding verse. *He that sendeth,* the (one) sending. *Commandment,* literally, *saying,* what he says. *Very swiftly,* literally, *even to swiftness.* The authoritative word of God is here personified as

his messenger or agent, whose swift running signifies the prompt execution of the divine will.

16. *He that gives snow like wool, hoar-frost like ashes sprinkles.* As easily as a man scatters wool or ashes, does God cover the earth with snow or frost. The selection of phenomena peculiar to winter may have reference to the season when the psalm was written or originally sung. At the same time they were probably designed to serve as emblems of the long distress, to which the Restoration put an end, as spring does to winter. The comparisons in this verse are less striking to us than to the people of countries where snow and frost are less familiar.

17. *He that sendeth his ice like crumbs. Before his cold who can stand?* The second noun means scraps or morsels, but in usage is specially applied to food. See Gen. xviii. 5. Judg. xix. 5. This seems to be descriptive of hail, which God sends upon the earth as easily and freely as man scatters crumbs or throws away the refuse of his food. The allusion to the feeding of domesticated animals, which some assume, is needless though admissible.

18. *He sends his word and melts them—he makes his wind blow—waters flow. Sends his word,* utters his command. The plural pronoun *(them)* refers to snow, frost, and ice, in vs. 16, 17. The winds meant are the warm winds of the spring, attended by a general thaw.

19. *Declaring his word to Jacob, his statutes and his judgments to Israel.* The God of Nature is the God of Revelation. He who thus controls the elements and seasons is the God of Israel, and will work spiritual changes corresponding to these natural phenomena, for the benefit of the people whom he has entrusted with the revelation of his will.

20. *He has not done so to every nation—and* (as for) *judgments, they know nothing of them.* This revelation to Israel is peculiar and exclusive. *Every nation*, and by implication, *any one.* This is indeed the only form in which that idea could be expressed in Hebrew. The last clause declares the other nations ignorant not only of *his laws* or *judgments*, but of any that deserve the name.

PSALM CXLVIII.

The universe, in all its parts, is summoned to praise God as its maker, and as infinitely worthy of its adoration. The invitation is addressed, in the first instance, to heaven and its inhabitants, exhorting them to praise God as their maker and preserver, vs. 1—6. It is then addressed to the earth and its inhabitants, exhorting them to praise him for his infinite perfection, as displayed in his works, but especially in his dealings with his chosen people, vs. 7—14. Even the most skeptical critics are constrained to acknowledge that this psalm and the two which follow are admirably suited to their purpose.

1. *Hallelujah! Praise ye Jehovah from the heavens! Praise him in the heights!* This verse designates the place, or part of the creation, from which the praise is to proceed. *Heights*, or high-places, is a simple equivalent to *heavens*, the plural form of which it takes by assimilation. Compare the singular in Ps. xviii. 17 (16.) The preposition *from* denotes the direction of the sound, the preposition *in* the place where it is uttered.

2. *Praise ye him, all his angels! Praise ye him, all his hosts!*

As this last expression is applied both to the angels and the heavenly bodies, it here affords a natural transition from the one to the other. See above, on Ps. xxiv. 10. xxix. 1. ciii. 21.

3. *Praise ye him, sun and moon! Praise him, all ye stars of light!* This is a specification of the general term, *his hosts*, in v. 2. *Stars of light* is a beautiful poetical expression for bright or shining stars.

4. *Praise him, ye heavens of heavens, and ye waters which are above the heavens!* The object of address in the first clause is the highest heaven, the heaven of that which is heaven to us. See above, on Ps. lxviii. 34 (33), and compare Deut. x. 14. 1 Kings viii. 27. 2 Cor. xii. 2. The *waters* meant are the watery clouds above the lower heavens, as in Gen. i. 7. See above, on Ps. civ. 3.

5. *Let them praise the name of Jehovah, for he commanded and they were created.* The direct invitation to the heavens is followed by a statement of the reason why they should comply with it, expressed in the third person, as if addressed to others. The pronoun *he* is emphatic. (It was) *he* (that) *commanded* (and no other.) See above, on Ps. xxxiii. 9, and compare Gen. i. 3.

6. *And made them stand to perpetuity and eternity; a limit he gave (them) and they cannot pass (it.)* The immutability ascribed to the frame of nature, Ps. lxxii. 5. lxxxix. 3, 37 (2, 36), is not absolute but relative to the will of the creator. All that is required by the context in such cases is, that they cannot change in opposition to his will or independently of it. See Ps. cii. 27. The first word in the second clause is here used in its primary sense of a definite boundary or limit, from which may be readily deduced the usual one of statute or permanent enactment. See above, on Ps. ii. 7. As the last verb is in the singular number,

the most obvious construction is the one given in the English Bible, *a decree which shall not pass.* Compare Matth. v. 18. But the highest authorities appear to be agreed that the analogy of Job xiv. 5. Ps. civ. 9. Jer. v. 22, requires the verb to be taken in the sense of transcending or transgressing, and construed with the aggregate of the heavenly bodies.

7. *Praise Jehovah from the earth, ye dragons and all depths!* Here begins the second part, in which the address is to the earth and its inhabitants. *From the earth* is in antithesis to *from the heavens* in v. 1. *Earth* here includes land and water; hence the last clause makes exclusive mention of the latter, as the word translated dragons is applied to huge aquatic animals, (Ps. lxxiv. 13), and the one translated *depths* to large bodies of water (Ps. xxxiii. 7.) As the first, however, sometimes means serpents (Ps. xci. 13), it may here be the connecting link between land and water.

8. *Fire and hail, snow and vapour, stormy wind doing his word.* The address here passes to the inanimate and unconscious agencies of nature. *Fire and hail*, as in Ps. cv. 32. The fire meant is commonly supposed to be lightning; but according to Hengstenberg the word is to be taken in its ordinary sense and is separated from its natural attendant *smoke* (for such is the meaning of the Hebrew word elsewhere, e. g. Ps. cxix. 83) only for the purpose of contrasting hot and cold, white and black, which seems a little fanciful and far-fetched. The *storm-wind* (or *stormy wind*) is mentioned as a natural agent the least likely to be under control, and it is expressly described as doing God's word, i. e. executing his command. See above, on Ps. ciii. 20. civ. 4.

9. *The mountains and all hills, fruit-trees and all cedars.* Not *fruitful* trees, as distinguished from barren trees, but *fruit-trees*

(literally, *tree of fruit*), as distinguished from forest-trees, here represented by the cedar, which is usually spoken of in scripture as the noblest species, and therefore called the *cedar of God*, Ps. lxxx. 11 (10.)

10. *The wild (beast) and all cattle, creeping thing and flying fowl.* The contrast in the first clause is analogous to that between fruit-trees and cedars in v. 9. The Hebrew word (רֶמֶשׂ) translated *creeping thing* has no exact equivalent in English. It seems strictly to denote animal or vital motion, or as a concrete term whatever so moves, and is even applied to aquatic animals, Ps. civ. 25. But when used distinctively, it denotes the smaller classes of terrestrial animals, including insects, reptiles, and the smallest quadrupeds. It is here added simply to complete the expression of the general idea, all animals whatever. *Flying fowl*, literally, *bird of wing*. The first of the Hebrew words is specially applied to the smaller birds, and sometimes specifically to the sparrow. See above, on Ps. xi. 1. lxxxiv. 4 (3.) civ. 17. cxxiv. 7. This and the preceding item in the catalogue, suggesting the idea of the smallest animals, may possibly have been used to denote the universality of the call here made upon all creatures, from the greatest to the smallest, to praise God their maker.

11. *Kings of the earth and all nations, chiefs and all judges of the earth.* He here passes from the lower animals to man. *Kings* and the nations whom they represent. *Princes* is not an exact translation of the Hebrew (שָׂרִים), which is especially, though not exclusively, applied to military leaders of various rank, and may therefore best be represented by the English *chiefs* or *chieftains*.

12. *Young men and also maidens, old men with children.* The obvious meaning of this verse is, all men, without distinction of sex or age. There is no need, therefore, of refining on the several particulars, or undertaking to explain why old men and

young men are both mentioned, since neither of them could have been omitted without failing to accomplish the design of the enumeration. For the etymology and primary meaning of the first word in Hebrew, see above, on Ps. lxxviii. 63, where it stands in precisely the same combination. The two nouns in the last clause may be considered as of common gender.

13. *Let* (all these) *praise the name of Jehovah, for exalted is his name alone, his glory is above earth and heaven.* The mention of earth and heaven shows that the first verb relates not merely to that which immediately precedes, but to the whole enumeration of God's creatures with which the psalm is occupied. See above, on Ps. civ. 27. *Exalted is his name*, as in Isai. xii. 4. *His glory* or *majesty*, a Hebrew word especially applied to royal dignity. See above, on Ps. xxi. 6 (5.) xlv. 4 (3.) xcvi. 6. civ. 1. cxi. 3. *Above earth and heaven*, i. e, superior to their mere material splendor, or *on earth and heaven*, i. e. placed upon them as a crown. See above, on Ps. viii. 2 (1.) lvii. 6 (5.)

14. *And he has raised up a horn for his people—praise for all his saints—for the children of Israel—a people near to him. Hallelujah!* While all the creatures before mentioned have abundant cause to praise God for his infinite perfection and his goodness to themselves, a peculiar obligation is incumbent on his people ; first, for his distinguishing favour through all periods of their history ; and then, for a special mercy recently experienced, namely, the restoration from captivity, now completed by the renewal of the temple and the reconstruction of the city walls. This restoration is described, by a favourite Davidic figure, as exalting or lifting up the horn of Israel. See above, on Ps. lxxv. 6, 7 (5, 6.) xcii. 11 (10.) The previous condition of the chosen people might be well represented by the opposite figure, used in Job xvi. 15. *Raised a horn for his people* seems to be only another way of saying *raised the horn of his people.* The

first form of expression may have been here used for the purpose of assimilating this clause to the next, where *praise* is still dependent on the verb at the beginning, and to *raise up praise for his people* is to give them fresh occasion of still higher praise than they had ever yet been called to utter. The ancient church is here described in a fourfold manner; first, simply as *his people;* then, as *his saints* or *gracious ones*, the objects of his mercy and the subjects of his grace; then, by their national title, as *the sons (or descendants) of Israel;* and lastly as the *people near him*, i. e. nearer to him than all others, sustaining a more intimate relation to him. The same expression which is elsewhere applied to the priests (Lev. x. 3. Ezek. xlii. 13) is here applied to Israel as "a kingdom of priests and a holy nation" (Ex. xix. 6.)

PSALM CXLIX.

This may be regarded as the special song of praise required of Israel at the close of the preceding psalm; first, on account of mercies already experienced by the chosen people, vs. 1—5, and then, in the hope of future triumphs over all heathen and hostile powers, vs. 6—9. Nothing could well be more appropriate to the state of things under Nehemiah, when the city and nation had again been put into a posture of defence and resistance.

1. *Hallelujah! Sing unto Jehovah a new song, his praise in the congregation of saints.* Compare Ps. xl. 4 (3.) xcvi. 1. cxi. 1. cxlviii. 14, to which last there is an obvious allusion, connecting the two psalms in the closest manner.

2. *Let Israel rejoice in his Maker! Let the sons of Zion triumph*

in their King! Not merely the creator of individuals, but of the church and nation as such, and that not only at first, but by a kind of new creation, in the restoration of the people from captivity. They are summoned to rejoice in him, not only as their founder and restorer but their sovereign. See above, on Ps. xcv. 6. c. 3. cxlv. 1, and compare Isai. xliii. 1. xliv. 2. xlv. 13.

3. *Let them praise his name in the dance; with timbrel and harp let them play* (or *make music*) *to him.* The usual modes of expressing joy are here combined. As to the dance, see above, on Ps. xxx. 12 (11.)

4. *For Jehovah is pleased with his people; he beautifies the humble with salvation.* The first clause suggests the idea of a previous alienation and of his having been appeased or reconciled. See above, on Ps. lxxxv. 2 (1.) The verb is one applied in the Law to God's acceptance of the sacrifices, and might therefore awaken here associations with atonement and forgiveness. See above, on Ps. xix. 15 (14.) li. 22 (20.) The verb occurs in its general sense of being pleased or satisfied, Ps. cxlvii. 10, 11. With the last clause compare Isai. lxi. 3.

5. *Let the saints exult in glory; let them sing (for joy) upon their beds.* The word translated *saints* is the same that occurs in Ps. cxlviii. 14, and is there explained. *In glory* (or *honour*), i. e. the glorious or honourable state into which Jehovah has now brought them. The glory is not that which belongs to God, Ps. xxix. 9. xcvi. 7, but that which he bestows, Ps. lxxxiv. 12 (11.) lxxxv. 10 (9.) The very phrase, *in honour*, occurs above, Ps. cxii. 9. *Sing* or *shout*, as audible expressions of strong feeling, and especially of joy. *On their beds*, where they have been accustomed to lament their previous degradation, or what Nehemiah calls their "affliction and reproach." See Neh. i. 3 iii. 36 (iv. 4.)

6. *Praises of God in their throat, and a two-edged sword in their hand.* A striking coincidence has been observed between this verse and Neh. iv. 11, 12 (17, 18.) As then they worked with one hand and brandished the sword with the other, so now they might be said at the same time to praise God and defy their enemies. This singular mixture of devotional and martial spirit is characteristic of the psalm and furnishes a valuable index to the date of composition. The conclusion thus reached is corroborated by the account of the military and religious pomp, with which the walls were dedicated, as described by Nehemiah (xii. 31—47.)

7. *To execute vengeance among the nations, punishments among the peoples.* Not their own vengeance, but that of God, to whom alone it appertains. See above, on Ps. xviii. 48 (47.) xciv. 1, and compare Deut. xxxii. 35. Rom. xii. 19. Heb. x. 30. This is really nothing more than a prediction, that God would use his people as his instruments in punishing the nations by whom they had themselves been persecuted and oppressed. This was partially fulfilled in the successes of the Maccabees, but under a new and unexpected form, in the spiritual triumphs of the true religion, and its actual or prospective subjugation of the world.

8. *To bind their kings with chains, their nobles with fetters of iron.* The word translated *nobles* is properly a participle, meaning *honoured (ones.)* The verse simply carries out the idea of the one before it, that of the subjugation of the gentiles by the true religion. The objection to this, as a spiritualizing explanation of the text, springs from a narrow and erroneous view of the very end for which Israel existed as a nation. Those promises to Israel, which are not still available for us, were but of temporary local value.

9. *To execute among them the judgment written. An honour is that for all his saints.* This last phrase occurs also at the close of

the preceding psalm (cxlviii. 14). As *written* may mean written in the book of God's decrees, there is no need of supposing a reference to any part of scripture. If there be such reference, however, it is no doubt to the threatening in Deut. xxxii. 41—43. To act as God's instruments in this great judicial process, so far from being a disgrace or hardship, is an honour reserved for all the objects of his mercy and subjects of his grace. The psalm ends as it began, with *Hallelujah!*

PSALM CL.

This is the closing Hallelujah or Doxology, which marks the conclusion of the last series or cycle (Ps. cxlvii—cl), of the Fifth Book (Ps. cvii—cl), and of the whole Psalter. In form and structure it is perfectly simple, merely reciting, in an animated manner, the place (v. 1), the theme (v. 2), the mode (vs. 3—5), and the extent (v. 6) of the praise due to Jehovah.

1. *Hallelujah! Praise God in his sanctuary! Praise him in the firmament of his power!* The essential meaning of the verse is, praise him both in earth and heaven. The particulars detailed in Ps. cxlviii are here condensed into a pregnant summary. The *sanctuary* is the earthly one, and as such stands opposed to the *firmament* or *heaven*, called the *firmament of his power*, as being one of the most glorious proofs and products of its exercise, and still the scene of its most striking exhibitions. The phrase is to be understood as comprehending the *hosts of heaven*, both inanimate and living, both material and spiritual. The parallelism is

rendered still more perfect by the correspondence between *power* in the last clause and (אֵל) the divine name in the first.

2. *Praise him for his mighty acts! Praise him according to his plenitude of greatness!* His *mighty acts*, literally, *his mights* or *powers*. See above, on Ps. cxlv. 4. *For*, literally, *in* them, i. e. praise him as exhibited and viewed in these. The corresponding particle means like, in accordance with, in proportion to, in a manner worthy of his greatness. The last phrase in Hebrew is peculiarly expressive, consisting of the two strongest terms denoting magnitude, the abstract forms of *much* and *great*, which might be rendered, if our usage suffered it, *muchness of greatness.*

3. *Praise him with blast of trumpet! Praise him with harp and lyre!* Here begins an enumeration of the instruments employed in public worship, and therefore necessarily associated with the idea of divine praise. The trumpet was used to assemble the people, and would therefore excite many of the same associations with our church-bells. The other instruments were used as actual accompaniments of the psalms performed in public worship.

4. *Praise him with timbrel and dance! Praise him with strings and pipe!* The three great classes of instruments are here distinctly mentioned, namely, wind, stringed, and pulsatile. The last, represented by the drum or timbrel, still called by a kindred name in Arabic, is here accompanied by its inseparable adjunct *dancing*, which might seem misplaced in a list of instruments, and those employed in sacred music, but for the peculiar usages and notions of the ancient Hebrews, with respect to this external sign of joy. See above, on Ps. xxx. 12 (11.) cxlix. 3. The common version of the last word *(organ)* is derived through the

Vulgate from the Septuagint, where it denotes a system or combination of pipes. The Hebrew word, according to the Jewish tradition, means a simple pipe, and is so rendered in the Prayer Book version. It here represents the whole class of wind-instruments. See above, on Ps. lxviii. 26 (25), and compare 2 Sam. vi. 5.

5. *Praise him with cymbals of loud sound! Praise him with cymbals of joyful noise!* The dominant idea, that of audibly expressed joy, is sustained to the last, where the cymbals are mentioned in both clauses, as an instrument peculiarly appropriated to occasions of unusual rejoicing. See 2 Sam. vi. 5. Ezr. iii. 10. Neh. xii. 27. The effect is still further heightened by the qualifying epithets, the first of which strictly denotes *hearing* or the thing heard, i. e. sound, and here by implication, loud sound. To this idea the parallel term adds that of joyful sound, to which it is constantly applied in usage. See above, on Ps. xxvii. 6. lxxxix. 16 (15), and compare Num. xxiii. 21. The distinction, here assumed by some interpreters, between cymbals of a larger and a smaller size, is wholly unnecessary.

6. *Let all breath praise Jah! Hallelujah!* The very ambiguity of *all breath* gives extraordinary richness of meaning to this closing sentence. From the simple idea of wind instruments, mentioned in the context, it leads us, by a beautiful transition, to that of vocal, articulate, intelligent praise, uttered by the breath of living men, as distinguished from mere lifeless instruments. See above, on Ps. lxviii. 26 (25.) Then lastly, by a natural association, we ascend to the idea expressed in the common version, *every thing that hath breath*, not merely all that lives, but all that has a voice to praise God. There is nothing in the Psalter more majestic or more beautiful than this brief but most significant *finale*, in which solemnity of tone predominates, without

however in the least disturbing the exhilaration which the close of the Psalter seems intended to produce, as if in emblematical allusion to the triumph which awaits the church and all its members, when through much tribulation they shall enter into rest.

THE END.

www.ingramcontent.com/pod-product-compliance
Lightning Source LLC
LaVergne TN
LVHW020230110826
845151LV00003B/884

* 9 7 8 1 4 2 5 5 3 1 5 6 0 *